Garcilaso Inca de la Vega

AN AMERICAN HUMANIST

A Tribute to José Durand

Edited by

JOSÉ ANADÓN

University of Notre Dame

Notre Dame, Indiana

Library of Congress Cataloging-in-Publication Data

Garcilaso Inca de la Vega : an American humanist : a tribute to José
Durand / José Anadón, editor.

p.   cm.

Includes bibliographical references and index.

ISBN 0-268-01182-6 (cloth : alk. paper)

ISBN 0-268-01037-4 (pbk. : alk. paper)

1. Vega, Garcilaso de la, 1539–1616. I. Durand, José

II. Anadón, José

F3444.G3G37   1998   97-21481

861'.3—dc21   CIP

Garcilaso Inca de la Vega

José Durand (1925~1990)

CONTENTS

v

Contents

JOSÉ ANADÓN

PREFACE

THE PRESENT VOLUME ASSEMBLES a series of essays presented at the colloquium on Garcilaso Inca de la Vega which was held at the University of Notre Dame from March 31 to April 2, 1996. Some articles were added from an earlier symposium on Garcilaso which took place in May 1995 at the Pontifical Catholic University of Perú. The event at Notre Dame was organized to honor the memory of José Durand, one of the leading "garcilacistas" of his time, and to commemorate the acquisition by Notre Dame of his impressive library of rare books and manuscripts, one of the finest private collections of this century.

Garcilaso Inca de la Vega (1539–1616), the first renowned mestizo humanist of Latin America, was born in Cuzco, Perú, the son of a Spanish conquistador and an Inca princess. When he was twenty years old he traveled to Spain, never to return to the land of his birth. His long sojourn in southern Spain, however, never obscured the memories of his Indian past. He kept abreast of events in Perú by corresponding with people there and talking frequently with travelers returning from the Americas. Nevertheless, Garcilaso's first book was *not* about the New World, but about the European Renaissance, namely a translation into Spanish (1590) of Leon Hebreo's *Dialoghi d'Amore*, an influential treatise of Neoplatonic thought derived from Marsilio Ficino.

His next three books decisively established Garcilaso as a major figure in the Renaissance and one of the foremost initiators of Latin American letters. His beautifully written *The Florida of the Inca* (1605) was a seminal work on the conquest of Florida and the southern regions of the United States. It was followed by his *Royal Commentaries*, published in two parts, the first (1609) dealing with the Inca world, and the second (1617) with the Spanish conquest and initial years of the Spaniards in Perú.

Garcilaso is a key figure for understanding the development of the mestizo culture of Latin America. His life and his works embody the fusion of two different cultures. In his writings—considered to be models of sixteenth-century Spanish prose—he endeavored to harmonize his Inca and his Spanish heritages. His life and times were, however, clouded by tragedies. Not only did he lose both of his parents relatively early in his life, but the two worlds he knew as a child and youth ceased to exist. The remnants of the Inca Empire were brutally destroyed, and the world of the first-generation conquistadors had disappeared forever. The goals and methods of the Spanish colonial machinery were ruthlessly implanted by Viceroy Francisco de Toledo. Garcilaso thus tried in his writings to recapture two utterly lost worlds: his mother's and his father's. Furthermore, as a humanist historian, he also advanced an interpretation of those events which even today influences our historical understanding of that period. Widely read, translated, and the cause of many a heated debate from his own time to the present, he has always been a source of inspiration and reflection. Significantly, he is the first writer to envision the future of Latin America as a multiethnic continent where many races could and would live together in harmony. This message has resounded clearly throughout the ages, and was the inspiration behind the rebellion of the Second Túpac Amaru against the Spaniards in the eighteenth century, an armed insurgency that took place forty years before Bolívar proclaimed the independence of Perú. Garcilaso's message also influenced the leaders of the Latin American wars of independence well into the nineteenth century. Even today his ideas reverberate in relation to the current efforts toward multiculturalism, integration, and coexistence of Hispanic and Anglo heritages. Garcilaso Inca is thus an important bridge between the Western and pre-Columbian cultures, a person who can only be understood as belonging to both worlds, and a visionary prophet concerning the future reality of the Americas.

With this publication we honor the memory of Professor José Durand (1925–1990), who visited Notre Dame on several occasions to lecture on Garcilaso Inca and other topics. In one of his last visits he was named the honorary president of an international forum organized at Notre Dame entitled "Present and Future of Hispanic Literatures," attended by twenty-two leading creative writers and a few literary critics from Spain and Latin America. The presentations were later published in a collective volume.

Durand dedicated most of his professional life to the study of Garcilaso Inca de la Vega and became one of his most renowned interpreters. He advanced views that renewed our understanding of this author's complex life and works. Durand's achievement was possible in part because he defined the direction of his research very early in his career and thereafter proceeded systematically in realizing his goals. This is demonstrated by two significant examples: (1) in 1948, Professor Durand described and assayed for the first time the library Garcilaso owned at the time of his death; and (2) in 1955, in a Congress in Lima whose proceedings were published the same year under the title *Nuevos Estudios sobre el Inca Garcilaso de la Vega*, he clearly identified the areas that needed to be pursued in order to advance Garcilaso scholarship. As experts unanimously recognize today, these two fundamental contributions shaped the direction of Garcilaso studies for himself and others. In books and articles he wrote from the fifties through the eighties, while living and teaching in Perú, México, France, and the United States, Durand pursued his task relentlessly, elucidating the sources mentioned in Garcilaso's works and, as a result, reinterpreting a wide variety of related themes concerning religious, historical, literary, linguistic, philosophical, theological, and scientific topics of the sixteenth and early seventeenth centuries. Durand also revealed the variety and breadth of Garcilaso's knowledge in areas such as architecture, military science, and music, which Durand then used to compare European and Inca culture. Not only did he demonstrate that Garcilaso possessed a solid Renaissance culture, but most interestingly, that he had reverted to his lost Inca world and then recaptured it in his historical works. In the process of illuminating these areas, Professor Durand revealed that he himself possessed an unparalleled knowledge of Hispanic culture, Renaissance humanism, and Spanish American historiography.

As evidenced in countless publications, he was regarded as an authority not only on Garcilaso but also on the chroniclers of the Indies and Latin American topics from the sixteenth to the early part of the nineteenth century. He was, in short, a specialist in the total experience of Colonial letters. In addition, he wrote knowledgeably about the post-independence and modern periods. It is also significant that Durand was a creative writer, primarily of short stories, and in this genre he is considered to be one of the best of his generation in all of Latin America. Durand's library is an enduring legacy of this broad range of interests and activities.

* * *

The artwork describing the symposium and reproduced on the cover of this book was created by the Peruvian Fernando de Szyszlo, one of Latin America's most important contemporary artists. He and Durand were classmates in a Jesuit school in Lima and remained close friends throughout their lives. They shared a love for the past and for Garcilaso Inca, and they collaborated in cultural projects in Perú. Szyszlo was delighted to lend his painting for the symposium and the book, and insisted on calling it his tribute to Durand and Garcilaso. In a recent conversation, Szyszlo expressed poignant ideas about the nature of art, Latin American culture, and this painting. Through the medium of abstract art, Szyszlo explained, he establishes symbolic connections between pre-Columbian traditions and the present. He repudiates the static veneration of the past. He rejects closing one's eyes to innovations introduced elsewhere, or, conversely, opening them only to what has been done elsewhere. His goal as a painter, he asserts, has always been to create a historical project that will move people and achieve a unifying experience that gives transcendence to his solitary efforts. If traditions, myths, and a common history do not become the lifeblood of the people, Szyszlo warns, then they are destined to be absorbed spiritually and physically by others.

Inca history is the source of inspiration for Szyszlo's painting, called *Punchao*. In the Quechua language, *punchao* means "resplandor" (radiance) and was the name of a god who represented the day. *Punchao* literally means the moment of daybreak, when the first rays of the sun break over the horizon—an instant of clear beauty in the unhazy air of the high Andes. There were various sun images in Cuzco, but the most important one was kept in Coricancha, the temple of the sun. It was a beautifully wrought disc of great size, made of gold and set with many precious stones. Szyszlo was especially struck by one episode of this tradition which has been described by many chroniclers. They write that in Cuzco, during an Inca religious procession, a mummified Inca was paraded through the throng of worshippers. A *punchao,* a medallion of gold lying on the mummy's chest, suddenly emitted a blinding radiance. Beneath that golden disc rested a box containing the dust of the hearts of the dead Inca rulers. Szyszlo's painting tries to recapture ("and this is the greatest challenge in all of my paintings") the state of mind, the original spiritual atmosphere, that so moved him on reading about the incident.

* * *

The symposium, as well as this book, was made possible by the generous financial support of three academic units at the University of Notre Dame: the Institute for Scholarship in the Liberal Arts, the Helen Kellogg Institute for International Studies, and the Office of the Provost. We wish to express our deep appreciation for the assistance received from their representatives, Professors Jennifer L. Warlick and Guillermo A. O'Donnell, and Rev. Timothy R. Scully, C.S.C., Vice President and Senior Associate Provost. Many persons have contributed generously with their firm support of these activities, especially Peter J. Lombardo, Jr., Rev. Wilson D. Miscamble, C.S.C., and Harold W. Attridge. In the organization of these activities we have appreciated the suggestions and collaboration of José A. Rodríguez Garrido and Paul P. Firbas. We thank Allyson Hardin for transcribing the first draft of Appendix A. We must especially thank Randolph J. Klawiter, whose gift for precision and language propriety helped shape the original manuscript into a linguistically consistent and highly readable text. At the Notre Dame Press we have appreciated Jeffrey L. Gainey's enthusiastic encouragement and cogent suggestions, and the incredibly lucid and attentive reading of the manuscript by Rebecca DeBoer, who also introduced us to the works of yet another garcilacista from the twentieth century, the Irish novelist Patrick O'Brian.

*   *   *

Throughout the book we have consistently used the best English translations of Garcilaso Inca's works available, with one slight modification in the case of our lead essayist, Sabine MacCormack. Although she chose to provide her own translations of Garcilaso's text, the references indicated correspond to the English editions used by the rest of the contributors. The translation of *Florida of the Inca* was made by John Grier Varner and Jeannette Johnson Varner in 1951, and that of the *Royal Commentaries of the Incas* by Harold V. Livermore, in two volumes, the first dedicated to the Incas and the second to the Conquest of Perú and the Civil Wars (the two parts are indicated as 1966/1 and 1966/2). Curiously, Livermore did not translate the preliminaries of Part II, an important source of information which is studied by several essayists in this book. Thus, the references to Garcilaso's dedication and prologue located in the preliminaries were translated from the excellent Spanish edition by Angel Rosenblat published in 1944.

AURELIO MIRÓ-QUESADA SOSA

IN REMEMBRANCE OF JOSÉ DURAND

THIS SYMPOSIUM REPRESENTS a double tribute which deeply gratifies me. It is first of all a homage to Garcilaso Inca, the founding father of Peruvian and Latin American letters, who not only spreads his mestizo blood and Indian emotions over the vast landscape of Western culture, but at the same time represents a living example of cultural harmony and cultural synthesis. He was the son of a Spanish captain of illustrious noble descent and an Inca *palla*. Garcilaso Inca has described his early years in his native Cuzco, Perú, where he grew up in the midst of "weapons and horses, gunpowder and harquebuses," things he knew much more about in his youth than literature. He has also described for us his later, peaceful existence in the village of Montilla in Córdoba, Spain, in the company of learned friends or engrossed in humanistic books, decisive activities in his intellectual formation.

Garcilaso wrote primarily historical books (except for the translation of Leon Hebreo's *Dialoghi d'Amore,* an important Neoplatonic work). He commenced his historical saga with the conquest of Florida, which, as expressed in a well-known romance, he knew only by "hearing about it but not seeing it." Garcilaso subsequently wrote two books which are fundamental for Latin American culture and for Perú in particular. In the first part of the *Royal Commentaries* he traces a picture, which has yet to be

xiii

surpassed, of the life, events, costumes, and mental construct of the Incas. In the second part, entitled *Historia General del Perú* by seventeenth-century editors, he recounts the dramatic events of the conquest by the Spaniards and the subsequent civil wars among the conquistadors, having as their background the emergence of a new world.

Garcilaso's narrative is lively and profusely descriptive. Most of the information that he provides has been corroborated by earlier chroniclers and by friends who wrote to him from the New World. He also followed guidelines he learned from Renaissance sources. To the reader, Garcilaso can be complex; for example, he often feels that it is not necessary to mention Salust, Suetonius, or his admired Petrarch, although he has thoroughly assimilated them in his own thoughts. In this and other instances, it is sometimes most important to understand the things Garcilaso does not reveal to the reader.

Although Garcilaso's major objectives were historical, we cannot disregard the literary qualities of his writing, such as precision of language and beauty of style. Historical accuracy is not always crucially important—although his histories present the best information available to him at the time—but rather the profound interpretation he gave to events in America, in many of which he had participated. The literary and the historical achievements of Garcilaso are, therefore, equally important. Certain expressions and phrases cannot be forgotten. He writes, for example: "It was a place never before trod by man, nor beast, nor even the bird of the air: inaccessible mountains covered with snow." Here he is depicting the Andes with an impressive image of upward movement, from the ground to the sky. He characterizes Gonzalo Pizarro as "a handsome and imposing man riding a double-saddled horse"; Martín de Don Benito was a "repulsive old man, withered and tough, with a hazelnut complection"; whereas Francisco Hernández Girón, biding his time before initiating his famous rebellion, looked "more pensive and brooding than Melancholy itself." When Garcilaso refers to himself, his words seem to acquire tremors of human flesh. When he addresses the Peruvian people, he calls for integration and harmony. The prologue to his last book is dedicated "to the Indians, Mestizos, and Creoles of Perú." That is to say, to those already physically rooted in an autonomous region, to the mestizos like himself, and to those who might or might not have Indian blood, but who had been born in Perú.

This symposium also honors the eminent Peruvian "garcilacista" José Durand, whose private library has been acquired by the University of Notre Dame. Durand was not exclusively a scholar on Garcilaso. Lucid, vivacious, universal in his interests, he could write an exemplary essay on Garcilaso or he could search and find "lost" issues of the earliest newspaper of the Americas from the eighteenth century. He could enjoy, to our amazement and also to our pleasure, beating the *cajón,* or drum box, a traditional instrument used in folkloric music, or he could interpret traditional songs, joyful or melancholic, from the rich repertoire of the blacks of Perú.

Those of us who knew Durand personally, as well as those who read his writings today, perceive in his work a sharp critical sense, an incredible knowledge of bibliographical materials, and the originality of his lines of inquiry. His scholarly work is an admirable combination of rigorous academic information and solid, incisive interpretation. With great pleasure I recall that when a group of friends generously published an affectionate book in commemoration of my eightieth birthday, one of the most brilliant contributors was José Durand, with an incomparable study on Blas Valera, the polemical author from Chachapoya, Perú, whose indisputable influence on Garcilaso has yet to be determined. And, insofar as Durand's in-depth interpretations are concerned, we can observe a common conceptual framework running throughout his entire corpus, from his university doctoral dissertation on the European Renaissance and Platonism in Garcilaso, to more recent and masterful essays such as his "Garcilaso, a Classic from the Americas," "Two notes on Garcilaso Inca," and "Garcilaso Inca, a Passionate Historian."

Through these cordial and sincere words, I extend my congratulations to the University of Notre Dame for organizing this important symposium, and I wish all of you great success.

Efraín Kristal explores the models which serve to represent the Indians in both Garcilaso and Ercilla, with parallels to other historical texts of the Spanish Renaissance. In those works, the Romans and the Goths are presented as preparing the way for the dissemination of Christianity, while the Turks and the Moors are depicted as a threat connected with the Devil, albeit one which could serve either to warn Christians or to punish them for their sins. Kristal goes so far as to suggest that the representation of the Turks in Pero Mexía's *Silva de varia lección* could have served as a direct source for Ercilla's characterization of the *araucanos*, as it did for Gómara's depiction of the Incas. Garcilaso, following Ercilla's example, accepts the paradigm of Moors and Turks in his references to the *araucanos*, whom he implicitly compares to the Indians living before the onset of the Inca Empire. At the same time, he appeals to the model of the Romans and Goths in order to validate the Inca experience with the Spanish conquistadors.

Rodolfo Cerrón-Palomino focuses on an aspect that is fundamental to understanding the notion of authority that Garcilaso attributes to himself as the authentic narrator of the Inca past, namely his expertise in Quechua. Cerrón analyzes the concept of "general language" as it was used subsequent to the conquest. In his opinion, this language originally corresponded to the *chinchaisuya* variant of Quechua, which was replaced by the one spoken in and around Cuzco after the Third Council of Lima. Garcilaso, on the other hand, assumed that the Cuzco variant was the general language. Nevertheless, he heightens the relative importance and aristocratic rank of this language by affirming that only the governing elite possessed a complete knowledge of it. Such a stance permits him to argue against the information gathered by other chroniclers and in defense of his own position, even at the expense of linguistic accuracy.

Eduardo Hopkins-Rodríguez's object of study is the *Florida of the Inca* and, more specifically, the construction of "exemplary discourse" in the text. Exemplarity, as evidenced by other contributions to this collection, constitutes a key element in Garcilaso de la Vega's concept of history, whereby the mestizo author validates the history of the Incas for his European readers. *Florida* is fundamental for understanding the formation of Garcilasian writing and needs further critical attention. Hopkins maps the text's exemplary dimension both in relation to the question of its designated reading public and in terms of the construction of the narrator himself. A particular focus is the didactic value which Garcilaso draws from the actions of historical characters, allowing him to posit the existence of a universal human dimension beyond the particularities of culture.

Miguel Maticorena Estrada's contribution is a description of an early manuscript of the *Florida*. According to Maticorena, this important document offers a version that is closer than the final manuscript to Garcilaso's interviews with his informant Gonzalo Silvestre, yet already includes the accounts of Juan de Coles and Alonso de Carmona. Although shorter than the final version published in 1605, it resembles the later edition both in structure and in content. In Maticorena's opinion, its date of composition would have been sometime around 1587. Most importantly, the appearance of this manuscript sheds considerable light on the relation between Garcilaso's work and Antonio de Herrera's *Décadas*. A comparison of the two texts seems to confirm that Herrera availed himself of a version of Garcilaso's work close to that which Maticorena discusses here. The future publication of this text is certain to foster substantial contributions to the understanding of the process of composition of Garcilaso's historical texts.

Lastly, José Anadón studies the important links between autobiography and history in the works of Garcilaso Inca. Although the presence of an autobiographical "I" is by no means infrequent in the chronicles of the Indies, Garcilaso's self-referentiality practically defines his literary production from the very beginning. Anadón discusses the role history and autobiography play in Garcilaso's writings. He then highlights the autobiographical elements in the preliminary texts of the *Diálogos de amor.* He indicates that *Florida,* at some level, is the autobiography of a friend, one to whom Garcilaso lent his voice and rhetorical abilities. He then turns to an analysis of Garcilaso's masterpiece,

of which autobiographical declarations constitute the main pil-
lar. Garcilaso thus draws even closer the ties between historical
past, as the object of his narration, and his own experiences:
"History and autobiography become equivalent in the depth of
his spirit."

One

SABINE MACCORMACK

The Incas and Rome

WHEN GARCILASO DE LA VEGA WROTE in the preface to the *Royal Commentaries* that his home was "the city of Cuzco, which was another Rome in that Empire,"[1] he was drawing on a tradition that was by then well established in historical writing about the Incas. Rome had been present in the minds of the very first invaders while they made their way south from Panama. It was the memory of the Roman conquest and government of Spain that made the Incas recognizable as rulers of an empire and as exponents of a culture that was, as the Spanish invaders came to perceive it, in every sense distinct from surrounding cultures. Even though it took some years before the Spanish were able to explain precisely how the Incas differed from their neighbors, the existence of such a difference was noted from the very beginning. Miguel de Estete, a member of Francisco Pizarro's invading force, wrote the following about his own first glimpse of the Incas at Tumbez:

> From this settlement begins the peaceful dominion of the lords of Cuzco and the good land. For although the lords further back and the lord of Tumbala, who was a man of note, were subject to the Inca, it was not as peaceful as from here onward. For those lords only recognized the Incas and offered a certain tribute, but no more; from here onward, however, they were all very obedient vassals. (Estete 1924, 20)

8

Soon after, Estete noticed that in many other settlements there were "governors and judicial officers who had been installed by that great lord" Atahualpa (21), and who received their orders from the center of the empire in Cuzco:

> This city of Cuzco was the head of all these kingdoms, where the rulers normally resided. Four roads converged there and formed a cross, coming from four subject kingdoms or provinces of considerable size, which were ruled by the Incas, and which were called Chinchasuyo, Collasuyo, Andisuyo and Condesuyo. These provinces rendered their tribute here in Cuzco, and in Cuzco was established the imperial seat. (48)

For sixteenth-century Europeans, the "imperial seat" *par excellence* was still Rome, the city which had ruled the world in classical antiquity. At the very time when the Spaniards in the Andes were learning about the roads of the Incas which all led to Cuzco, scholars in Europe were studying the roads that had once led to Rome. Printed editions of ancient itineraries helped to trace Roman roads on an imperial scale,[2] while in a more regional context, in Spain, Italy, France, and Germany, historians and antiquarians collected inscriptions from Roman milestones in order to understand the configuration of these lands at the time when they had been provinces of the Roman Empire. The very term "province" that Estete used to describe the four parts of the empire of the Incas had a Roman sound. As the lexicographer Sebastián de Covarrubias wrote in his dictionary of 1611,

> Province. It is an extended territory, and in antiquity, in the time of the Romans, [the provinces] were the conquered regions outside Italy, *provincia* in Latin, that is to say, conquered and distant. They sent governors to these provinces, and because nowadays we call this an office, *provincia* (in Latin) signified an office. (Covarrubias 1994)

Some years after Estete wrote his memoir of the Spanish invasion of Perú, Pedro Cieza de León, who devoted most of his adult life to studying the Incas and their empire, likewise used Rome as a paradigm by which to explain the Incas. But for Cieza the com-

9

parison went beyond visible phenomena such as roads, government officials, and the capital city of Cuzco, because he wanted to understand why the Inca government had worked so much better than the Spanish government in the Perú that he observed in his own day. The Incas, Cieza thought, had been extraordinarily efficient and absolutely incorruptible. Their wars were just in the same sense that Roman wars had been just, and the Inca administrative system invariably worked perfectly. The Inca storehouses, for example, were always filled with all manner of supplies for war and peace:

> When thus the Inca was lodged in his dwelling and the men of war had been accommodated, there was never lacking so much as one single item, however large or small, with which to supply them all. But if there occurred in the vicinity any kind of uproar or theft, the (offenders) were punished immediately and with great severity. In this matter, the Inca lords adhered so closely to justice that they would not have omitted exacting punishment, even if it had been upon their own sons. (Cieza de León 1986, 144)

The cultivated sixteenth-century reader would here remember stories about the heroic severity of Rome's founding fathers: how, according to the historians Sallust and Livy, military leaders would punish their sons for engaging the enemy contrary to orders, even if the engagement had been successful; and how, according to Livy and Rome's greatest poet, Vergil, the first consul Brutus had executed his sons for conspiring against the young Republic.[3] At issue in Cieza's view of the Incas was thus not merely Roman antecedents for Inca imperial road construction and urban architecture, an imperial iconography, as it were, but the moral fiber of the Inca state. Inca imperialism could be recognizable as a positive cultural, religious, and political force because it was explicable by reference to Roman antecedents. The central issue here was not whether the Romans were superior, for Cieza did not suggest this; for him, the crux of the matter was rather that empires were good, and therefore, the Inca Empire had been a good thing.

Not only Estete and Cieza, but also Francisco López de Gómara,

10

Bartolomé de Las Casas, Agustín de Zárate, and even Juan de Betanzos compared aspects of Inca government, culture, and religion to Roman equivalents. The Inca Chosen Women of the Sun were likened to Roman Vestal Virgins, and in more general terms, the Inca religion was in some sense thought to resemble the religions of the gentiles of antiquity, in particular that of the Romans. In addition, Domingo de Santo Tomás, author of the first Quechua lexicon and grammar, thought that the language of the Incas was like Latin, and thus explained the grammatical and syntactical structures of Quechua by reference to Latin equivalents as described in Antonio Nebrija's *Introductiones latinae.*[4] These and other comparisons continued to be drawn throughout the sixteenth and seventeenth centuries. Indeed, in 1575 the Augustinian friar Jerónimo Román published, in two heavy folio volumes, a treatise on the *Republics of the World*, the very title and arrangement of which articulate the thesis that cultures can be compared on the basis of their deities, sacrifices, temples, rites of marriage and burial, their methods of designating kings and nobles, their legal systems and manner of going to war, their pursuit of science and the liberal and mechanical arts, and finally, their calendars, mode of dress, and manner of celebrating festivals. Garcilaso cited Román's work, and he also knew the more famous comparative treatise on the republics of the world by Giovanni Botero.[5] At the same time, however, Garcilaso thought that "all comparisons are odious" (Garcilaso 1966/1, I, XIX, 51), since his primary interest was to write the history of the Incas and of the invasion and conquest of their empire by the Spanish. Yet, thoughts of Rome pervade his entire work.

As we know from the inventory of Garcilaso's library, which was published by José Durand (1948, 239–264; 1949a, 166–170), Garcilaso owned copies of all the major historians of classical antiquity, including the ones to whom Cieza alluded. But by the time Garcilaso wrote his *Royal Commentaries*, at the end of the sixteenth century and during the first years of the seventeenth, the situation in Perú was very different from what Cieza had observed. The activities of Spanish officials both at central and local levels, the progress of evangelization, and the policy of resettlement that had affected all but the most remote Andean communities, had conspired to create a society in which the Incas had become a memory rather than a reality that loomed into the present from a recent but still tangible past. The Incas had become, as Garcilaso so movingly expressed it, a "memoria del bien perdido," a memory of the good that has been lost (Garcilaso 1966/ 1, I, xv, 41). Perhaps it is true that in coining this memorable phrase, Garcilaso was grieving over his own lost childhood and over the life that he was not able to live in the land of his maternal forebears (Hernández 1993). What is not true—and this is what I hope to prove—is that Garcilaso wrote an imagined, fictionalized history of the Incas, a work in which the self-referential memory and imagination of the historian prevailed over the collective experience of a multitude of people.[6] What speaks against such a view, although it has been frequently expressed, is not merely the demonstrable care with which Garcilaso treated the writings of earlier historians of the Incas, the effort he expended on collecting his own documentation, and his interest in problems of translation from Quechua into Spanish,[7] but also his profound engagement with the historians of classical antiquity whose works crowded the shelves of his library (on Garcilaso's use of Livy, see Pailler 1992, 207–235).

The historians whose ideas and themes resonate in Garcilaso's writing—Polybius, Livy, Tacitus, Suetonius, Plutarch, and from the post-Roman period, Isidore of Seville—wrote to reveal, in Cicero's famous phrase, "the light of truth" (Cicero 1976, 2.9.36), where truth is inseparable from the moral dimensions that may be discerned in human action and in historical processes. When, for example, Polybius explained to his Greek readers the functioning of Roman military organization, his theme was not merely how one might organize an army, although this aspect of his work attracted a good deal of practically motivated interest from Garcilaso's contemporaries (Momigliano 1975, 79–98). He was rather explaining "how and thanks to what kind of constitution" Rome had arrived at world dominion (Walbank 1972, 130 ff.), and he repeatedly emphasized the connection be-

tween the moral sobriety and severity of the Romans and their
stunning success. Garcilaso pursued a similar theme. Thus, where
Polybius had commented on the speedy and efficacious quality
of Roman military justice, Garcilaso drew attention to these same
features in the judicial system of the Incas.[8] Simultaneously, he
described the dispensation of justice among the Incas as being
embedded in the very ordering of society. To drive home the
point, Garcilaso chose Roman terminology when explaining the
decimal organization of Inca society. According to Polybius and
others, the smallest unit in the Roman cavalry, a group of ten,
was headed by a decurion. The councillors of Roman municipali-
ties were likewise described as *decuriones,* as were the officials of
Roman professional and religious associations. This was therefore the term that Garcilaso chose in his description of the Inca
decimal organization: the head of each group of ten, who was
responsible for his group's material and moral well-being, and
who simultaneously acted as judge for them, was a "decurion."[9]

On several occasions, Garcilaso commented on the titles of
Inca rulers. Here also, he used Roman antecedents in order to
articulate Inca thought and government, while at the same time
discussing dimensions of Inca political culture that were not so
readily translatable. The third Inca ruler was Lloque Yupanqui.

> His proper name was Lloque, which is to say left-handed. The ne-
> glect of his tutors in raising him, which produced his left-handed-
> ness, led to this name. The name Yupanqui was given to him for
> his virtues and deeds. In order to show some of the ways of speaking
> which the Indians of Perú followed in their general language, it
> should be noted that this expression *yupanqui* is a verb, second per-
> son singular future perfect indicative, to wit "you shall have told."
> In this verb, thus simply stated, they enclose and express all the
> good things that can be told of a prince, as if to say, you shall tell
> his great deeds, his excellent virtues, clemency, piety and gentle-
> ness.[10]

As viewed by Garcilaso, the title Yupanqui, "you shall have told,"
enshrined a twofold content: on the one hand, it denoted the

deeds and virtues of an exemplary Inca ruler, while on the other it indicated the task of the *quipucamayos*, "remembrancers," and the *amautas*, "philosophers and wise men," who recounted these deeds and virtues in the form of "traditions" and "historical narratives" for all to learn and remember.[11] Garcilaso repeatedly commented on the economy and elegance of the Quechua language, which did not always lend itself to readily intelligible translations into Spanish, the title Yupanqui being one of his several examples.[12] By contrast, the royal title Capac, which had been borne by several Inca rulers, could be translated more straightforwardly because here Garcilaso was able to cite a directly applicable Roman antecedent:

> "Capac" means rich, not in possessions, but in all the virtues that a good king can have. The Indians did not speak in this way about anyone, however great a lord he might have been, but only about their kings, so as not to make common property of the dignity that they attributed to their Incas. For this they held to be sacrilege. It would seem that these names resemble the name of Augustus, which the Romans gave to Octavian Caesar for his virtues. For when such a name is given to an individual who is not an emperor or great king, it loses all the majesty contained in it.[13]

How Octavian Caesar came by the title Augustus is recounted by the imperial biographer Suetonius, whose works Garcilaso owned. Like Garcilaso, Suetonius had been interested in how a title enhanced the bearer's dignity, and in how it could do this only when it was appropriately bestowed:

> Some people thought that [Octavian] ought to be called Romulus, for being also a founder of the city, but the idea prevailed that he should rather be called Augustus, this being both a new and also a more noble title, because holy places and places in which something is consecrated by the ritual of the augurs are called "august," from the increase in dignity . . . as Ennius shows when he writes: "After glorious Rome was raised by august augury." (Suetonius 1989, 2.7.2)

An august place, or person or prophecy can be matched in Quechua by expressions such as the *kapac huaci* or "palace," a *kapac yahuarniyoc* or "person of royal blood," and by the verb *kapacchacuni*, "to make oneself different or noble" or "to raise someone as noble" (González Holguín 1952, 134–135; for *chacu*, p. 91). The name Caesar Augustus was thus a direct analogue to the name of the Inca ruler Manco Capac, the originator of the Inca lineage, whom Garcilaso and others described as the son of the Sun and founder of the city of Cuzco.[14]

Much thought had been given by the ancient historians, whose works Garcilaso owned, to the question of the origins of human society. Whereas the Bible, as well as the Greek poet Hesiod, had posited a golden age in the past, from which all subsequent human development was a falling away, historians often thought of an evolution in the opposite direction, from primitive savagery to civilization. Livy thus described how Romulus had founded Rome as a refuge for "an undifferentiated crowd of free men and slaves" (Livy 1988, 1.8.6) whom he invited to gather in his city, and how he then forged an ordered society from such unpromising beginnings. Cicero had a more idealized view of the origins of society, although in outline, the development from social disorder to civilization is similar. "There was a time when men wandered at large in the fields like animals," he wrote,

and they survived on wild plants. They did nothing by the reason of their minds, but acted mostly by strength of body. No order of religious worship or of human obligation was as yet observed, no one had seen legitimate matrimony, and no one had yet recognized his children as his own; nor had anyone understood the usefulness of an equitable law. . . . At this point, some great and wise man realized that a power and potential for noble deeds was latent in human souls, if only it could be drawn out and heightened by instruction. By some force of reason, this man gathered these humans, who were scattered and hidden in fields and wooded haunts, into one place and gave them a single and useful occupation. At first, since they were savages, they protested, but then they listened to his reason and his speech more carefully, and he transformed these wild and monstrous beings into kind and gentle humans. (Cicero 1976, 1.2)

More was at issue than a simple and schematized vision of the distant human past. The historian Tacitus described the activity of gathering uncultivated people who lived in scattered settlements and were always ready for war, into ordered towns with temples, fora, and houses, as fundamental to the governance of a recently conquered Roman province (Tacitus 1925, 21). Garcilaso remembered having been told in his boyhood by one of his maternal uncles that things had been no different in the Andes. "You should know," the uncle had said,

> that in the ancient times . . . people lived like beasts and brute animals, without religion or social order, without village or house, without cultivating and planting the earth, without clothing or covering their bodies, because they did not know how to work cotton and wool to make clothes. . . . Like animals, they ate herbs of the field and roots of trees. . . . In short, they lived like deer or game, and even with women they behaved like brutes, because they knew nothing of having separate wives. (Garcilaso 1966/1, I, XV, 42)

Then the Sun sent the Inca Manco Capac and his consort to "call together and attract these people and teach them" (Garcilaso 1966/1, I, XVI, 43). The first Inca couple thus "talked to people . . . and drew them out of the bestial life they were leading and showed them how to live like human beings." Clothing, house construction, the creation of settlements, the framing of laws and rules of worship, and the distribution of occupations followed (44), so that an ordered political society came into existence, just as it did when Cicero's orator and lawgiver persuaded primeval savages to come together in that very first dawn of human society, and when Romulus gathered people into his new city of Rome.[15]

Much effort was expended by Garcilaso's contemporaries in an attempt to determine when an ordered society began among people living in Spain. Some historians were still interested in one of the medieval answers to this question, and argued that the origins of Spain, and the Spanish language as well, should be looked for in the period after the universal Flood, when a direct descendant of Noah had settled in the Iberian peninsula.[16] This theory of origins was also a theory of sovereignty, according to which Spain had been ruled, from time immemorial, by a succession of rulers whose position derived, in the final analysis, from a divine mandate. Similar theories, which endeavoured to square the story of Noah with Andean and Inca legends of origin, were proposed to explain the earliest history of Perú. Garcilaso swept all such efforts aside by declaring, with his characteristic irony, that "I will not meddle in matters so profound, but will simply recount the historical fables that I heard from my people as a child" (Garcilaso 1966/1, I, XVIII, 49). In the words of his maternal uncle:

> Our first Incas and kings came in the earliest ages of the world, and from them descended the other kings whom we have had, and from them we are all descended. How many years might have passed since our Father the Sun sent his first children, I cannot tell you precisely, because they are so many years that memory has not been able to contain them. But we think that it is over four hundred years ago. (Garcilaso 1966/1, i, xvii, 46)

While the chronology that Garcilaso's uncle proposed was absolutely incompatible with speculations about the exploits of the descendants of Noah in the Andes,[17] it did converge with the more sober views of Pedro Cieza de León, Polo de Ondegardo, José de Acosta, and other respected authorities whom Garcilaso had consulted. Garcilaso's main interest, however, was not chronology, whether of oral traditions or of scientific historiography, possibly because he was aware that not much progress could be made in this direction, given the nature of Andean sources.[18] Legendary and historical narratives in themselves, on the other hand, interested Garcilaso profoundly. Here also, Roman historical writing, in particular Livy's history *From the Founding of the City* (*Ab urbe condita*), provided guidance and orientation. Livy began his story with the deeds of gods and founding heroes. Such an approach had its difficulties, as he explained in his preface:

I can neither confirm nor reject the glorious narratives from the time before the city had been founded or even thought of, narratives that have been handed down to us in poetic fables rather than in unimpeachable memorials of historical events. Antiquity is allowed this licence, that by mingling divine with human deeds it exalts the origins of cities. And if any people deserves the glory to exalt its origins and to transport its founders among the gods, then the Roman people has won this glory by warfare, since they praise Mars above all, he being both their own and their founder's father, and the nations of humanity ought to tolerate this Roman privilege with the same equanimity as they tolerate the Empire of Rome.[19]

Livy's work, known to sixteenth-century scholars as *Decades*, was famous in Spain. It was in the footsteps of Livy that Peter Martyr had written his Latin *Decades* about the New World, that Antonio Nebrija had transformed Pulgar's history into another Latin *Decades*, and that Garcilaso's contemporary Herrera published his *Decades* in Spanish about the conquest of America. Livy also figured prominently in Sebastián Fox Morcillo's small handbook about how to write history (1557). Little likelihood, therefore, that the voice of Livy would be overlooked in Garcilaso's description of his own historiographical program. Having recounted the foundation stories of Cuzco, which, like Livy's narrative about the origin of Rome, abounded in divine and legendary figures, Garcilaso stated:

> Now that we have placed the first stone, albeit a fabulous one, in our edifice of the origin of the Incas, kings of Perú, we should pass on with the conquest and settlement of the Indians, expanding the summary account which I heard from that Inca. (Garcilaso 1966/1, I, XIX, 49)

A little further on, he wrote:

> We will carefully recount the Inca's more historical doings, leaving aside many others as being irrelevant and prolix. And although some of what has been said, and of what will be said, may appear to be fabulous, I decided not to omit recording these matters, in order to avoid discounting the foundations on which the Indians

build to explain the greatest and best achievements of their Empire. For it is on these fabulous beginnings that the grandeur that today belongs to Spain was in effect founded. (50–51)

Like Livy, Garcilaso thus juxtaposed *fabulae* and the true "memorials of historical events." Both historians also contrasted the uncertain history of origins, where deeds of gods and heroes were interwoven with those of human beings, with the more reliable history of recent events. Finally, Livy and Garcilaso both brought the long distant past directly into the present, for it was the glory and grandeur of the present that warranted the study of legendary and shadowy origins. According to Livy, it was because of her present glory that Rome was entitled to exalt her legendary origins, while according to Garcilaso, Inca origins, fabulous though they were, deserved attention in his own day because Spain had become the beneficiary of Inca imperial power.

If, in one sense, legends were simply legends, then the historian's task was the relatively straightforward one of sorting legends from other, more accurate records, which was in effect what Livy and Garcilaso both did.[20] What remained to be understood was why anyone might actually have believed, for example, that Manco Capac really was a child of the Sun. Various etiological explanations had been attempted by earlier historians. According to one of them, Manco Capac, who wanted to be king, deceived the simple Indians by dressing in a golden tunic, wearing large golden ear spools, and proclaiming that he was a child of the Sun (Murúa 1946, I, 3). Viewed in this light, the story of Manco Capac showed how fiction became fact by means of simple fraud, and there were those who extended this method of interpretation to the Inca myth of origin in its entirety (Sarmiento de Gamboa 1965, VI, 206b ff.). Not surprisingly, Garcilaso found such a view of his mother's people unacceptable, but at this level of interpretation, the simple maneuver of separating *fabula* from history was not quite sufficient.[21] Here also, Garcilaso turned to Livy.

According to tradition, Romulus was a son of the god Mars, and was divinized at death, or rather, after performing many great deeds, he disappeared into a thunderstorm, leading his followers to believe that he had become divine. Livy recounted these matters with all possible brevity and concluded with one simple explanatory statement that enabled him to avoid expressing a personal opinion: "Such were the deeds performed at home and abroad while Romulus was king, and none were incompatible with the belief that he was of divine origin and was divinized after death" (Livy 1988, 1.15.6). Garcilaso evidently had this passage in mind when, in his summary of the career of Manco Capac, he wrote that

> the fable of his descent (from the Sun) gained credence thanks to the benefits and honors he bestowed on his vassals; hence, the Indians firmly believed that he was a son of the Sun who had come down from heaven, and they therefore offered him worship, just as the pagans of antiquity . . . had offered worship to others who conferred similar benefits on them. (Garcilaso 1966/1, I, I, xxv, 62)

There were thus many ways in which Cuzco was indeed "another Rome in that Empire." But Garcilaso did more than simply transpose Roman *fabulae* as recorded by Livy into Inca *fabulae* as recorded by himself, more also than merely explain the credibility of Inca *fabulae* in light of Roman antecedents. The point here is that, contrary to what Garcilaso's numerous critics have asserted, he did not create an Inca Utopia, but endeavored rather to portray the Inca Empire as a political society, with its lights as well as its shadows. In this sense also, Garcilaso's Incas resembled the Romans. Several authors of the late Republic and the Augustan period, whom Garcilaso had read, understood the Roman myth of origins as a paradigm of more recent Roman history. The ideals of joining together diverse peoples into one society and of fighting only just wars that were, according to Cicero and Livy, enunciated by Romulus, lived on in subsequent Roman experience; but so did the fratricidal passion for power, *regni cupido*, that led Romulus to kill his brother Remus (Livy 1988, 1.6.4). The power of *fabulae* that told of a remote and nebulous Roman past was thus all too real in the present, an issue that Garcilaso understood extremely well.

The Incas, Garcilaso wrote, had "fabulously declared that they were descended from the Sun" (Garcilaso 1966/1, I, xxv, 38b). The question was not whether the story as such was true or credible. "What I can conjecture," Garcilaso noted,

> about the origins of this ruler Manco Inca, whom his vassals called Manco Capac because of his greatness, is that he must have been some Indian of good understanding, prudence and judgment, who took account of the great simplicity of those nations and saw that they required teaching and instruction in order to live a natural life. To gain their esteem, he wisely and discerningly invented that fable and claimed that he and his consort were children of the sun and had come down from heaven and that his father had sent them to teach and do good to those peoples. And so as to be believed, he probably adopted the appearance and attire that he wore, especially the enlarged ears that the Incas had, which were truly incredible to whoever had not seen them. (Garcilaso 1966/1, I, xxv, 61–62)

That the Incas did good to everyone they encountered, whether in war or peace, is a theme that pervades Garcilaso's *Royal Commentaries* from beginning to end. In this sense, the story of Inca origins was infinitely replicated in Inca history. But just as the repetition of the Roman myth of origins in Roman history documented both the positive and the negative dimensions of that myth, so also with the Incas. The Incas made conquests, according to Garcilaso, in order to enhance their glory. Concurrently, they also did good to those whom they had conquered, although not everyone was a willing and grateful recipient of their beneficence.

To be conquered by the Incas, as Garcilaso described it, amounted to exchanging liberty for material benefits and for the numerous other advantages that the Incas bestowed on their vassals, above all peace and order.[22] Similar characteristics had been attributed to Inca governance by Cieza, while readers of Polybius and Livy would also recognize the theme as a familiar one (Walbank 1972, chapter 6; Momigliano 1975, chapter 2). For Garcilaso, however, this was not the whole story, as recorded in his account of the lord Hancohuallu, whom Inca Viracocha had taken prisoner during the Chanca assault on Cuzco and had then restored to his former status. But Hancohuallu's "proud and generous soul could not tolerate being an inferior and a vassal to someone else after he had been absolute lord of so many subjects, whom his fathers and grandfathers and forebears had conquered." He therefore "preferred to obtain his freedom, abandoning all he possessed, rather than enjoying yet greater honors but without freedom," and thus he fled far beyond the frontiers of the Inca Empire to the land of the Antis (Garcilaso 1966/1, V, XXVI, 300–302). Hancohuallo's prolonged inner conflict about choosing liberty in preference to honorable vassalage and his resolution of this conflict evoke the figure of the Stoic Roman hero Cato Uticensis, who in the face of an analogous choice committed suicide. Garcilaso noted that Hancohuallo's flight caused the Inca "much pain and sorrow," and he "would have liked to have prevented it" (Garcilaso 1966/1, V, XXVI, 300 and then V, XXVII, 302). Similarly, according to Plutarch, whose works Garcilaso had in his library,[23] the news of Cato's death elicited from Julius Caesar the remark: "Oh Cato, I envy your death, for you envied me sparing your life."[24] In the verdict of posterity, however, Caesar's well-known clemency was no substitute for freedom.[25] Inca Viracocha had no choice but to console himself over the flight of his unwilling subject, and

> the Indians, examining the event more closely, said that they were glad that he had gone away because the natural condition of lords is such that they do not easily tolerate vassals of such high spirit and valor, because such vassals constitute a danger to them. (Garcilaso 1966/1, V, XXVII, 302)

Far from describing an Inca Utopia, an ideal polity that had little foundation in reality, Garcilaso led his readers to understand that the Inca Empire had been a political society in which persuasion and benevolence inevitably went hand in hand with duress.[26] On the one hand, simple persuasion, the promise of a better, more peaceful way of life, was not convincing without the authority that the Incas claimed from their fabled, invented so-

lar ancestry. On the other hand, however, the exercise of that
authority, resulting in imperial expansion, which most of Garcilaso's contemporaries would regard as advantageous and laud-
able, entailed the negative dimension of preventing men of courage and high spirit from participating in political life. Such, at
any rate, were the lessons of Roman history. Conversely, therefore, the very existence of these tensions and contradictions
within the Inca polity gave the lie to those of Garcilaso's contemporaries who wished to assert that the Incas had run no more
than a tyranny of barbarians, a state that did not merit the attention of serious students of political institutions.[27]

Considerable effort was expended in the course of the sixteenth century on ascertaining who were the truly uncivilized
people, the real barbarians: were they Amerindians who for one
reason or another lacked some decisive characteristic of civilized
society? Or were they, as Las Casas would have it, the Spanish,
whose destructive advance throughout the Americas seemed to
know no limits?[28] Like his acquaintance, the linguist Bernardo
de Aldrete, Garcilaso had little interest in such questions of definition and instead viewed the issue historically.[29] The Greeks and
the Romans in their day, Garcilaso observed in the preface to his
General History, had described everyone other than themselves
as barbarians, and this included the Spanish (Garcilaso 1944,
"Prólogo," 10). Nonetheless, Spain did in due course produce her
own great men, including the conquerors of the Americas. These
men, who had destroyed the Inca Empire, were

> the joy and crown of Spain, mother of nobility and mistress of the
> power and the wealth of the world. Jointly with them she will be
> magnified and praised as mother and nurse of her noble, numerous
> and exalted sons, who were raised at her breast with the milk of
> faith and fortitude, better than Romulus and Remus. (Ibid., 12b)

This passage is in part a reformulation of the preface of Isidore
of Seville's *History of the Goths, Vandals and Suevi,* a copy of which
Garcilaso owned. Here, not long after the conversion of the Visigoths to Catholicism, Isidore praised the Goths as conquerors of

Rome and thus of the world, and Spain, which had formerly been conquered by the "valor of Romulus" but where the Goths now resided, as the mother of an empire:

> Holy and always blessed Spain, mother of princes and peoples, you are the most lovely of all the lands that extend from the West to India. Of right, you are now the queen of all the provinces, and not the setting merely, but also the rising sun never departs from you. You are the glory and ornament of the universe, the more favored part of the world, and the supreme delight of the glorious fertility of the Gothic nation, where they flourish abundantly. (Isidoro de Sevilla 1975, 168)

As viewed by Garcilaso, Spain had thus passed from being herself barbarian to being the nurse of the Goths and thence the nurse of the conquerors of the world. Perú, on the other hand, formerly ruled by her Incas, "Caesars in felicity and valor," had fallen victim to the "invincible Castilians, conquerors of both worlds" (Garcilaso 1944, "Prólogo," 11a). The two parts of the *Royal Commentaries* thus describe two grand cycles of development, juxtaposing and contrasting the histories of Perú and Spain. The theme is reminiscent of the theory of historical cycles or *anacyclosis* which Polybius, whose work Garcilaso owned, employed in order to contrast and juxtapose the Roman and Carthaginian constitutions, tracing the ascent of the former and the decline of the latter (Walbank 1972, 137 ff.). Like most of his Spanish contemporaries, Garcilaso took it for granted that the best constitution was monarchy; there was thus no room in his historiographical world for Polybius's view that the rise and decline of states is explained by the positive and negative transmutations of their constitutions. Nonetheless, the question as to why the Inca Empire fell was central to Garcilaso's work. In one sense, at least from his perspective, the Incas were overcome by Castilian valor. In another sense, however, Castilian valor proved irresistible because the larger force that transformed Perú from a "forest of paganism" into the "paradise of Christ" was also at work, while furthermore the war between the two brother kings Huascar and Atahuallpa brought with it the complete destruction of that Empire, because it facilitated the entry of the Spanish into the land so that they gained it as easily as they did. For this land is so rugged, mountainous and inaccessible that otherwise it could have been defended by a very small number of people.[30]

Garcilaso the historian recorded, and to a certain extent elucidated, the operation of this vast constellation of forces, while also commenting on the grief of his maternal kinsmen, the survivors of the catastrophe of conquest. Grief was entailed in the very telling of the story of this empire which "was destroyed sooner than it could be known" (Garcilaso 1966/1, I, XIX, 51). Indeed, such a story could only be told in tragic terms. As the aged Inca nobleman who first instructed the young Garcilaso about the history and institutions of the Inca Empire expressed it:

> I believe I have given you a detailed account of what you have asked of me, and have answered your questions. And in order not to make you weep, I have not told this history with tears of blood flowing from my eyes, even though I shed them in my heart because of the pain I feel from seeing our Incas dead and our Empire destroyed. (Garcilaso 1966/1, I, XVII, 46)

This personal, human dimension that pervades Garcilaso's writing endows his narrative with drama and immediacy. At the same time, Garcilaso did not invent this method of composing a work of history. Instead, the sorrow that his Incas felt when remembering their empire was an experience they shared with the survivors of other catastrophes that had been described by the historians of classical antiquity whom Garcilaso had read. Polybius, in particular, discussed repeatedly when, and to what extent, a historian could permit himself to write in dramatic and even in tragic terms. The destruction of the royal house of Macedonia, the fall of Carthage, and the disasters and misfortunes suffered by the Greeks, in calling for the human engagement and interest of the reader, provided the very substance of what was useful and instructive in the study of history.[31]

In declaring that Cuzco was "another Rome in that Empire," Garcilaso thus informed his readers not merely that the Inca Empire could in diverse respects be understood by reference to the Empire of the Romans, but also defined the Inca Empire as a political society whose destinies merited the attention of cultivated and thoughtful men.

NOTES

1. Editorial note: Although we have generally chosen to use the excellent extant English translations of works cited by the rest of the contributors, particularly those of Garcilaso Inca, the translations here are those of the author. Cf. the preface for information on the English versions used.

2. On the history and early editions of the Tabula Peutingeriana, a medieval copy of a Roman map of the empire, see Miller 1916. On the history and early editions of the map, see Bosio 1983.

3. Sallust, *Bellum Catilinae* 9.4; further references in Ramsay's introduction to Sallust 1984. On the consul Brutus, see Livy, *Ab urbe condita* 2.3–5; Vergil, *Aeneid* 6.820–823. Garcilaso owned a copy of Vergil, no. 186 in the inventory of his library (Durand 1948, 239–264).

4. See Domingo de Santo Tomás 1994a (*Grammatica*), the preface dedicated to Phillip II, where he mentions the third edition of Nebrija's Latin grammar. Moreover, according to Fray Domingo, anyone who studied the abundant Quechua vocabulary of courteous expressions and the elaborate Quechua terminology for kinship would understand that this was a civilized language of equal standing with Latin and Castilian; see Domingo de Santo Tomás 1994b (*Lexicon*), "Prologo del Auctor al pio Lector." For comparisons between Rome and the Incas, see MacCormack 1991, 106 ff.

5. On Botero (1598), see Garcilaso 1966/1, IX, XIII, 571 and Garcilaso 1966/2, I, VI, 647. In Garcilaso 1966/1, II, II, 71 and V, XVIII, 280, he mentions Román's work (1575), which was heavily censored by the Inquisition and appeared in a revised edition, Salamanca 1595. It is not clear which edition Garcilaso used. Neither of these two authors is mentioned in the inventory of Garcilaso's library, but since he cited them explicitly, it is clear that he had read them.

6. Jákfalvi-Leiva 1984, 4, discusses some earlier representatives of

this method of interpreting Garcilaso. For a more detailed discussion, see Zamora 1988, chapter 6. The personal component in Garcilaso's historical writing is stressed by Pupo-Walker 1982, 98: "His writings are something akin to a *recherche du temps perdu* which ensues from the proximity of his conflicting personal experiences ('vivencias'). Perhaps for that reason . . . he searches for the historical muse who renders possible the subtle displacement towards fiction."

7. For a helpful survey of the historians of Perú whose work was available to Garcilaso, see Brading 1991, 260 ff., and the fundamental study by Pease 1995, 378–389. Garcilaso himself mentioned his efforts to collect documentation. See, e.g., Garcilaso 1966/1, I, XIX, 49–52 and IX, XXXVIII, 619–622; Garcilaso/2, II, VII, 748–749. For Garcilaso's interest in Quechua and problems of translation and linguistic change, see Garcilaso 1966/1, "Notes on the General Language of the Indians of Perú," 5–6; V, XI, 262 (from Blas Valera), "they spoke like courtiers"; and VI, XXIX, 376 (the valley of Runahuanac).

8. The analogies between Inca and Roman justice and Inca and Roman social organization that Garcilaso describes here enshrine a further point, to wit, a latent criticism of the notorious delays of judicial procedure in colonial Perú. The Incas used to say, Garcilaso noted, "that delay in punishment encouraged crime" (Garcilaso 1966/1, II, XII, 95). Garcilaso was far from being alone in contrasting Inca and Spanish government in the Andes by way of criticizing the latter: on the *cause célèbre* of the *Brevísima relación* by Las Casas, see the introduction to that work by André Saint-Lu (1987). However, what endows Garcilaso's argument with new weight is the Roman context in which he presented it, given that Roman statecraft was universally admired in sixteenth-century Europe.

9. For Garcilaso on decurions in Inca society, see Garcilaso 1966/1, II, chapters XI, XII, and XIV; and also V, XIII, 268, quotation from Blas Valera, "The tribute which they paid was to work as decurions." Cf. also Polybius 1992, 6.25.1 ff. At 6.25.2, Polybius transliterated the Latin term *decurio* into Greek. See further, Varro 1964, 5.91; and Covarrubias 1994, s.v. "decurion." Other historians of the Incas also described Inca decimal organization, but without the Roman terminology; see Julien 1982, 119–151.

10. Garcilaso 1966/1, II, XVII, 106. For *lloque* meaning "left," see Domingo de Santo Tomás 1994b (*Lexicon*), I, 69r: "Yzquierda mano = llucque, o lluequi"; I, 7v: "alabar = yupaychani." For a very different meaning of *lloque*, see González Holguín 1952, 216, although the dimension of "left" is conveyed in various other expressions, such as, ibid., "Lloqueman qquessuani = torcer al revés." For "yupani = contar y hazer quentas," and related terms, see p. 371.

11. See Garcilaso 1966/1, VI, IX, 331–333, about traditions and historical narratives. The activities of Inca remembrancers and wise men, whose task it was to record and recount the deeds of Inca rulers, were mentioned by several Spanish historians of the Incas. One of the most detailed accounts is by Cieza de León 1986, chapters 12 (historical records) and 18 (tribute). But Garcilaso did not know this work, which was not published until the nineteenth century. A shorter account that he did have access to is by Acosta 1962, book 6, chapter 8. Note also Garcilaso 1966/1, V, XI, 261–264, which was transcribed from Blas Valera, contrasting the written laws of Numa, Solon, and Lycurgus to the unwritten but equally well-obeyed laws of the Incas. Some of the categories of Inca legislation that Valera distinguished, specifically "ley municipal," "ley agraria," and "ley sobre el gasto ordinario," are defined by reference to Roman antecedents. Cf. MacCormack, "History and Law in Sixteenth Century Perú," forthcoming.

12. Garcilaso 1966/1, II, XVII, 106. For further examples of Quechua brevity and elegance, see II, XXVII, 126.

13. Garcilaso, ibid. For an earlier discussion of Inca titles, see Garcilaso 1966/1, I, XXIV, 59–60; see further, V, XII, 266, "Capac Titu . . . god Augustus"; Garcilaso 1966/2, prologue, "Peruvian Incas Caesars in happiness and strength."

14. Cf. Garcilaso 1966/1, I, XIX, 50–51, where he expresses his awareness that the beginnings of Inca history were, in effect, legendary. That the Inca historical record as delivered to us in historical writings of the early Colonial period is open to much questioning has become generally accepted. In particular, the questions asked by Spaniards inevitably distorted the evidence; for an attempt to redress the balance, see the collection of essays edited by Murra, Wachtel, and Revel in 1986; see also the pioneering work in this direction by Rostworowski in 1993. In that the early historiography of Rome also came into existence, at least in part, in response to pressures exercised by a foreign culture, i.e., the Greeks, a comparative investigation suggests itself. For the Roman side of things, see Bremmer and Horsfall 1987 and Cornell 1995.

15. Garcilaso did not always forge such complete concordances between Inca and Roman history. Thus, for example, he reproduced a long quotation from Blas Valera in which Inca and Roman legislation are both compared for content, and then contrasted, because Roman law, as Valera viewed it, was a written law, whereas in the Andes, without recourse to writing, people still remembered laws that had been promulgated over six hundred years earlier "as though it had been today" (Garcilaso 1966/1, V, XI, 262). Valera then goes on to list, among other classes of legislation, an Inca municipal law and an agrarian law

which might be thought to have counterparts in Roman law; see Jolowicz 1952, 61 ff., 543–547, and then 309.

16. MacCormack 1992, 38–68; in addition to sources there cited, see the influential work of Mariana 1950, chapter 8, on the legendary Tubal, grandson of Noah.

17. A contemporary of Garcilaso's, whom he appears to have met (MacCormack 1991, 345), was Gregorio García, who published a book on just this topic (1607).

18. On *quipus* and the limitations of this kind of record, see Garcilaso 1966/2, "accounting (quipu)," index, 1489.

19. See Livy 1988, preface, 6–8. For Livy's use of the definition *fabula* in his narrative, see also 1988, 1.11.8, a fabula about Tarpeius and the Sabines; in 1988, 5.21.8, a fabula about the siege of Veii; but in 1988, 29.17.12, the term *fabula* means "tale."

20. Garcilaso used the term *fabula* in at least two different senses. On the one hand, there is *fabula* as the record of the distant past, as here discussed. See Cicero 1988, 2.2, "a fabulis ad facta veniamus"; in Garcilaso 1966/1, I, XVIII, he describes this kind of account as "fábula historial," which is a phrase that he coined himself. This is the sense of the term that is paralleled in Livy 1988, 1.11.8 and 5.221.8; but the *fabulae* of 29.17.12 are "tales." On the other hand, there is *fabula* as the account of the past that is taught to the young. See for example 1966/1, VI, IX, 332: "(historical narratives), no longer than fables, suitable for telling to children"; this is the kind of *fabula* that Garcilaso himself was told when young. See 1966/1, I, XIX, 49–50.

21. It is worth noting that even on the surface, Garcilaso's historical vision is very sophisticated. It is not merely a recounting of *fabulae,* even though he begins with the "fábulas historiales del origen de los Incas" (Garcilaso 1966/1, I, XVIII, 47). Accordingly, in VI, IX, 332 he described the historical fables that Andean young people learned from their wise men as *tradición,* thereby distinguishing oral historical narratives from the written texts that served as historical sources in Europe. Throughout his work, Garcilaso wrote history from an Inca point of view: for the Incas, history began with their own origin, and that is precisely where Garcilaso began. The larger issue was that every nation's historical vision begins and ends with itself. Hence, the beginning of the earliest memory that is shared within a given society amounts, in effect, to the beginning of time for that society. In this instance as well, the beginnings of Roman history as described by Sallust and Livy appear to have been helpful to Garcilaso.

22. See Garcilaso 1966/1, I, XXIV and XXVI on Inca royal titularity as an expression of the benefits bestowed by the Incas on their subjects.

The differentiations of origin and status that were mandated by the Incas as benefits are described in 1966/1, I, XXII and XXIII. On benefits granted by Inca Viracocha, see 1966/1, V, XIII, 267.

23. Durand 1948, no. 111 (*Bidas* de Plutarco); see also nos. 134 and 141. No. 67 is Lucan, in whose *Pharsalia* Cato plays a central role.

24. Plutarch 1989, 72.2; see also 55.2 where the possibility of living in exile, away from Caesar's tyranny, is contemplated. Note also that Hancohuallo arranged that some of his followers should secretly precede him to the land of the Antis (Garcilaso 1966/1, V, XXVI, 301); analogously, in 54.2 ff., Plutarch describes how some individuals gathered in Utica planned to leave and did indeed leave before Caesar's anticipated arrival. Only after these individuals were safe did Cato commit suicide (see 70.2).

25. The assassination of Caesar was condemned by Dante, *Inferno* 34.64–67; on the emergence of opposing views during subsequent generations, see Baron 1966.

26. For examples of successful conquests that resulted in the submission of opponents, see Garcilaso 1966/1, VI, XIV (the *curaca* Huamachuco); VI, XXIX (the lord Chuquimancu); VI, XXXI (the lord Cuismancu).

27. For a recent discussion of some of the relevant issues, see Pérez Fernández 1995; further, see the important essay by Karen Spalding, "¿Quiénes son los indios?" 1974, 147–193.

28. Of the voluminous literature on Las Casas, I cite only a recent major work, Gutiérrez 1993, which has a very comprehensive bibliography.

29. Aldrete 1972, argued that Spanish was a language derived from Latin, which in turn was imposed on the conquered peoples in the Iberian peninsula as a result of the Roman conquest, leaving little trace of the languages spoken before that time. Aldrete thus left little room for theories of aboriginal Spanish cultural and political continuity such as were favored by some of his contemporaries, for example, Juan de Mariana (above, n. l6). In III, 13, Aldrete mentions having consulted the *Royal Commentaries* before their publication, and reproduces Garcilaso's account of the origin of the name of Perú.

30. See Garcilaso 1944, "Prólogo," 10, and Garcilaso 1966/2, I, XL, 723. See also Garcilaso 1966/1, IX, XV, 578, where Garcilaso's Inca uncle rejects the accusation that the Incas had been cowards because they had defended themselves so poorly; rather, they had not fought against the Spaniards because the Inca Huayna Capac had foretold their coming, and had seen himself as the last of the twelve Inca rulers. On the much discussed issue of the providential design that underlay the Span-

ish conquest of Perú, here mentioned by Garcilaso, see most recently
Duviols 1994, 69–80. Garcilaso's "forest of gentility" is reminiscent of
"imaginum silva," the forest of misleading images, and "omnium visi-
bilium silva miraculorum," the forest of miracles proceeding from all
visible things that cannot give any true knowledge of God, mentioned
by Augustine, *Epistulae* 7.5 and 162.9, respectively. The expression possibly points to some patristic readings by Garcilaso that have so far not
been traced.

31. On "tragic history" in Polybius, see Walbank 1972, 34 ff. For the
fate of the royal house of Macedonia, see Polybius 1992, 10–11. Polybius'
account, which does not survive in its entirety, was used by Livy (1988,
40.3–59). For the fall of Carthage, see Polybius 1992, 38.1–2. For the
disasters which befell Greece, see Polybius 1992, 38.1–4, and for a discussion of Agathocles of Alexandria, which is material that does not call
for dramatic narration, see Polybius 1992, 15.34–36.

Two

FRANKLIN PEASE G. Y.

Garcilaso's Historical Approach to the Incas

IN ONE OF HIS LAST ARTICLES on Garcilaso Inca de la Vega, José Durand expressed a concern which, even today, is as profound as it is accurate:

> A simplistic idea is gaining ground, without the benefit of previously careful criticism, which asserts that the historical works of Inca Garcilaso have only literary value. Such generalizations, which are commonly heard today in American universities, constitute the beginning of several studies. . . . (Durand 1990)

This criticism extends to a wide range of literary studies. I subscribe to Durand's observation that Garcilaso is a conscientious historian. This, however, does not detract from the literary excellence of his work or his renowned prose style. Furthermore, it does not preclude analytical studies, because on the one hand, the study of history cannot be reduced to the examination of the *narrator,* and on the other, historians are not convinced that textual analysis resolves the problem of the quality of historical information. Garcilaso endorsed the manner in which history was written during his time, which differs considerably from our present method of meticulous verification of the data that constitute history.

In the sixteenth century, the role of historian was perceived in a far different light. The "academic quality" of a historian's work was measured in terms of his conformity to a *credible prove-nance/source,* a correspondence which facilitated the combination of various authoritative sources and an assessment of the variances among them. At the time Garcilaso was writing, the Bible was the only documentary form of ancient history that was accepted as true, since it alone provided "the one and only" true version of the origin of the world and man. It likewise attested that, after the destruction caused by the great Flood, the world was repopulated by the sons of Noah (Genesis 9:18) and, therefore, the conquistadors easily presumed that the peoples of the New World had appeared after the Flood and were, like themselves, also descendants of Noah.

During the Renaissance, the biblical version of history came into conflict with another almost equally respected authority, namely, classical tradition. Humanism tended to transform the new versions of Greek and Latin texts into "false histories" or rather, moralistic stories, as in the case of the "allegorization" of myths. Once myths were removed from their original context, they lost their sacred significance. Since people continued to look to ancient history as a source of inspiration, no one was particularly astonished by the "heroic" tale which portrayed Hercules as the first king of Spain. Toponymy was combined with mythological context. Another tale affirmed that Hespero, king of Spain, had conquered the Hesperides, which, according to the royal chronicler Gonzalo Fernández de Oviedo, were indeed "the Indies" (the Antilles). It could thus be established that the rule of the Spanish kings over America had originated in ancient times. Other texts on the history of Spain rendered the same basic information. In 1498, for example, Annio de Viterbo wrote that Tubal, a descendant of Noah via Jaffet, was the first king of Spain.[1] These biblical origins vested the Spanish monarchs with a special virtuous character which was legitimized by the continuity of the dynasty. Therefore, why not believe these affirmations since they were, after all, confirmed by the most "reliable" sources then known?

A third detailed source of information in the sixteenth century was found in the books of chivalry and in the literature of prodigious and wondrous events. This source was nurtured by the accounts of travelers who described mythical kingdoms (like that of Prester John), outrageous practices in the New World such as cannibalism, or polygamous "monks" in the land of the Khan as described by Marco Polo (Gil 1992, 61). These descriptions were also fueled by the Greek and Latin traditions as well as by numerous citations from popular lore.

There were seemingly no limits to people's imagination! Fauns, mermaids, amazons, "corismapos" (men without digestive systems), and monsters from far-away places were suddenly common fare. Accounts of astonishing deeds of fairies and magicians flourished, and, as long as these beliefs persisted, i.e., until the onset of the Age of Rationalism, they continued to exercise a powerful influence on the minds of scholars and the credulous alike. In his analysis of the credibility of the Hispanic-American chroniclers and the way they utilized these themes, Leonard (1953) determined that these historians did not *necessarily* believe that such tales were per se fiction, but rather that the existence of marvelous phenomena was a *remote* possibility.

The existence of these phenomena became more feasible in certain contexts, especially when they belonged to a distant time or far-away geographical area. The idea of the marvelous penetrated the rational minds of some chroniclers of European events, such as Marco Guazzo, who in 1552 wrote about a trip of Phillip II to Italy. In his description of the prince's entourage he stated: "The prince [Phillip] had brought with him three satyrs *just arrived from the Indies;* one was ten years old and the other was forty, and a female; also a *mermaid,* but dead" (Durand 1983, 109–111). In Greek mythology the satyrs were represented in different forms, but most of the time their lower extremities were partly horse or he-goat, including a tail. They were associated with an outrageous sexuality. Guazzo assumed that the satyrs had come from America. Similarly, many other monsters, giants, and fantastical beings appeared in the accounts of various chroniclers of the New World. The amazons and mermaids exercised a protracted effect: the former gave their name to the vast region extending east of the central Andes, whereas the latter reappeared consistently in Andean Colonial iconography (Gisbert 1980, 46 ff., passim). The images of wondrous lands where people lived effortlessly, or naked—then a proof of innocence— were also part of this total mind-set. Nostalgia for the Lost Paradise involved the belief in the Fountain of Eternal Youth and the lands where gold was bountiful (for example, the biblical Ophir, the islands of gold and silver), a conviction which of itself constituted "proof" of their existence.

Not only did the chroniclers of the Indies believe in these various historical-mythical contexts, but they also added one more, namely, the variously differing versions of the European royal dynasties. The European historians who wrote about America combined fictionalized origins—the fables mentioned by the chroniclers—and more concretely verifiable information. This situation ensued because at times the branches of some particular genealogical tree would encounter unexpected deviations far down the line, which rendered it incomprehensible. Although many a strange and even fabulous nexus was unearthed, the Chancellery scribes in Spain would record them literally when writing the official versions of their dynastic histories.

Garcilaso undoubtedly felt most comfortable within biblical and Greco-Roman contexts, especially the latter, since his *Royal Commentaries* were specifically patterned after classical histories. On several occasions his work was based almost entirely upon Roman historiographical models: the works of Titus Livy and especially of Julius Caesar, quotations from whose writings appear in the very first pages of the *Royal Commentaries* (Pailler 1993).

Garcilaso's sense for quality in historical writing dictated his preference for "reliable" sources. However, his personal library contained works by Marsilio Ficino and others versed in "arcane knowledge," a form of erudition that has been generally considered falsified since it was, in theory, based on spurious Egyptian manuscripts.[2] Although Garcilaso never expressly mentioned the "false Beroso" in his *Royal Commentaries,* he apparently also had it in his library. In the description of a particularly ambiguous item, Durand states the following: "No. 59: *Autor de barias antiguedades de España, Africa y otras provincias,* Córdoba, 1614 CF.

35

La Vinaza, *Biblioteca histórica de la filología,* Madrid, 1983, col. 59"
(Durand 1948, 249). Eugenio Asensio subsequently stated that
such a title could well be one of the later versions of Beroso. "It
is amazing," he said, "and anomalous in the list, that the copyist
twice writes *author* instead of so familiar a name to him as *Aldrete.*
I believe that it would be more natural to suppose that it refers
to *Antiquitatum variarum auctores,* Lugduni, 1552 or 1560, which
is the title indicating the *Antiquitates* by Beroso and his peers"
(Asensio 1953, 591 n). As Asensio notes, it is possible that one
of Garcilaso's friends, for example Ambrosio de Morales, alerted
him to such frauds as the "false Beroso." Asensio also notes that
Florián de Ocampo, the royal chronicler who preceded Morales,
had known the fake chronicle of Annio de Viterbo.[3] Garcilaso
himself refers to chroniclers of this type:

> Some Spanish scholars who have heard these legends think that the
> Indians heard of the story of Noah, his three sons, his wife, and
> daughters-in-law, and that the four men and women God spared
> from the deluge are the four in the fable and that the Indians
> mean the window of Noah's ark when they spoke of the window of
> Paucartampu; and the powerful man who, the first version says,
> appeared at Tiahuanaco and divided the world between the four
> men, they hold to have been God, who sent Noah and his three
> sons to people the earth. Other parts of this legend and the other
> seem to point to those of Holy Writ, which they are thought to re-
> semble. I do not venture on such profound matters: I simply repeat
> the fabulous accounts I used to hear my family tell in my childhood;
> let each take them as he wishes and apply whatever allegory he
> thinks most appropriate. (Garcilaso 1966/1, I, XVIII, 48–49)

This passage certainly far exceeds Asensio's basic premise dealing with fraudulent histories. This was not just a matter of rejecting the improper assimilation of Andean myths into Catholic beliefs, a matter on which Garcilaso was in total agreement with
Cieza de Leon. Insofar as Garcilaso treated myth as "historical fables," he diminished the credibility of the Incas. Yet he prudently
retained the historical information which the myths provided.
As he often complains, myths can contain a certain amount of

truth which is distorted by the poor quality or total absence of a written language.

While Garcilaso dealt prudently with such controversial matters as the retrieval of ancient information, his approach to certain themes clearly reflects the historical criteria prevalent in the sixteenth century. He was a careful reader and seems to have been notably influenced by contemporary historiography; by "commentaries and humanistic narratives that considered history as the lesser daughter of rhetoric and a relative of poetry"; and by "the chronicles of the Indies which combined ethnography and fragments of personal memories" (Asensio 1953, 588). Garcilaso's work, Asensio adds, "is also related to antiquarian literature, from which it receives orientations and methods." This antiquarian literature is associated with Ambrosio de Morales and Bernardo de Aldrete, both of whom Garcilaso knew well.[4] With the publication of his *Discurso de la lengua castellana,* Morales became well known for his interest in philological history. Garcilaso's concern for the language of the Incas has been amply demonstrated, both in his annotations to Gómara's *History* and by his observations in the *Royal Commentaries* (See Durand 1976, 125–130; Miró-Quesada 1977, 11–49). In the *Crónica . . . de España,* however, Morales sought to underscore the importance of institutions and toponymy rather than philology.

Garcilaso's historical vision has generally been delineated through his descriptions of the genealogy of the Incas, the Andean kings. Garcilaso was not the first to trace the development of the Inca dynasties (at most he introduced Viracocha as the victor over the Chancas). They had been clearly and completely described in the works of Cieza de León and Juan de Betanzos written in the 1550s. The information they provided was probably incorporated into the *Royal Commentaries,* since Cieza is one of Garcilaso's most quoted authors. However, it is unlikely that their works are the texts which most influenced Garcilaso. The information about the Incas which appears in Cieza and Betanzos constitutes the first appearance of what has been called the "Cuzqueño" version, which was continued by Pedro Sarmiento de Gamboa and then finally elaborated in the *Royal*

Commentaries. Sarmiento's work added a dimension of Renaissance culture which influenced Garcilaso. Furthermore, Garcilaso was also influenced by the antiquarian historiography and philological history practiced by Andalucian scholars and friends, and by his extensive study of Italian literature.

Garcilaso approached the Incas as an experimental field within his conception of history. Asensio noted the important parallels between the structure of Garcilaso's *Commentaries* and the Augustinian idea of the "three ages." The study of Garcilaso also made it possible to "bring to light the antiquities . . . which have been hidden up to our days" (Nebrija, quoted by Tate 1970, 186–187). And it has been well demonstrated that some Neoplatonic views which Garcilaso espoused came close to utopian thought (Durand 1963, 21). The Inca Empire, for Garcilaso, became a sort of political Utopia, where justice governed and hunger was eradicated.

The sources Garcilaso used are better known than those of most of the other historians of the Indies, and his constant communication with his childhood friends in Cuzco has been repeatedly stressed. He records that his fellow countrymen and relatives "talked to me at length about their laws and government, and compared the new rule of the Spaniards with that of the Incas" (Garcilaso 1966/1, I, XIX, 49–50). The confirmation of this correspondence with old acquaintances in Cuzco suggests illuminating contrasts between Garcilaso's statements made in Spain and the actual situation in the Andes prior to the writing of the *Royal Commentaries*. Garcilaso refers as follows to the information he received after 1590:

> As soon as I resolved to write this history, I wrote to my old schoolmates at my primary school and grammar school, and urged each of them to help me with accounts they might have of the particular conquests the Incas made in the provinces their mothers came from, for each province has its accounts and knots to record its annals and traditions. . . . [My schoolfellows] on hearing that an Indian, a son of their own country, intended to write its history,

brought from their archives the records they had of their histories and sent me them. (Garcilaso 1966/1, 1, xix, 50)

To this information he adds his own recollections which, in his words, were transmitted through his "mother's milk."

There are at least two other references to correspondence received after Garcilaso's arrival in Spain. First, the clergyman Diego de Alcobaza sent him the *Confessionario para curas de indios*, conceived during the Third Council of Lima (Garcilaso 1966/2, 1, xxiii, 683). Second, it is also known that he received a "Power of Attorney of said Ingas to Captain Garcilaso de la Vega Inga, a neighbor in the city of Badajoz, and to don Melchor Carlos Inga, a neighbor in the said city, and to don Alonso Fernández de Mesa, a neighbor in Toledo, and Alonso Márquez de Figueroa" (Vargas Ugarte 1938, 214–215). Several persons who had a particular interest in the Andes visited Garcilaso, for example friar Luis Jerónimo de Oré, from Huamanga, the author of several important religious and historical books. Although Oré's texts were not found in the inventory of Garcilaso's library, he was undoubtedly acquainted with them. Garcilaso wrote that during this visit he gave Oré copies of *Florida* and the *Royal Commentaries* (Garcilaso 1966/2, vii, xxx, 1410–1411). Another reference of note concerns the execution of Túpac Amaru of Vilcabamba. Garcilaso's account closely adheres to texts by Jesuit writers closer to the events than Garcilaso himself, and there are even similarities with the *Nueva Corónica* by Guamán Poma de Ayala, which he completed around 1615, particularly in the episode where the King of Spain condemns the actions of Viceroy Toledo (Garcilaso 1966/2, viii, xix, 1480–1482; and Vargas Ugarte 1938, 19–42).[5]

Previous chroniclers had created the stereotype of Atahualpa, the last Inca ruler, as illegitimate and a tyrant. Guamán Poma was in a good position to dispute this. Although Garcilaso probably had even better arguments at his disposal, it was not his intention to challenge the justice of the Spanish domination over America. Both Garcilaso and Guamán Poma, however, were in agreement concerning the necessity of respecting the ancient *natural lords*, not only the chieftains but also the descendants of the Incas.

History, for Garcilaso and other chroniclers of the times, was not only true insofar as it was verifiable, either by resorting to an authoritative source, to the testimony of informants, or to memory, which was particularly important to Garcilaso. The authoritative sources became part of the historical context itself. Truth was related to the moral and exemplary function of history, a characteristic which in that time and in certain authors rendered history close to a utopian mode of thought. History was not only to be found in an idealized past, as in Garcilaso, but also in the process of projecting teachings and examples to the rulers and governments of the present, in this case the sixteenth century. By their practice of instilling justice by example, the idealized Incas served as models for contemporary rulers. Therein can be found the political function of both the *Royal Commentaries* and the *Nueva Corónica*, as well as the works of Bartolomé de Las Casas. This moral function reflects an important distinction—already accepted in the academic world, although not sufficiently emphasized in general[6]—between the concept of history that was accepted in the sixteenth century and the concept of history today.

NOTES

1. As far as I know, Garcilaso Inca never cited Annio de Viterbo, whose work, however, circulated among authors close to him, e.g., Ambrosio de Morales. It is possible that at some point Garcilaso had this work in his library.

2. See Durand 1948, 247. On the translation of Hermes Trismegistus's work by Marsilio Ficino, see Yates 1983, 30 ff., passim. Garcilaso's predilection for occult philosophy has long been known. His translation of the *Dialogues* by León Hebreo was forbidden by the Inquisition due to his faithful rendering of cabalistic texts. As Garcilaso pointed out in the prologue to the *General History*, in the judgment of the Inquisition, his translation "was not for laymen."

3. Garcilaso wrote to the attorney Juan Fernández Franco: "I trust in His Divine Majesty that I will be able to serve Your Grace with it [*La*

Florida] all of next year and that Your Grace will approve of it, just as doctor Ambrosio de Morales approved the fourth part of it, together with my translation of [León] Hebreo, which His Grace was able to see before he died; for which approbation I rightly kissed his hands, and he then bestowed upon me the tremendous gift of adopting me as his son and accepting my works as if they were his own" (Asensio 1953, 586, translation mine).

4. Garcilaso and Aldrete were close friends, as witnessed in the note Aldrete wrote in his book *Del origen y principo de la lengua castellana* (1606): "this is the way Garcilaso refers to it in his *Commentaries,* which have not yet been published but which he has told me for my amusement."

5. Guamán Poma wrote: "How can (Viceroy Toledo) sentence to death the king, the prince, the duke, the count, the marquis, the gentleman, or one of his servants? Poor gentleman, it is called a revolt and to want to be more than the king"; and further on he added: "Viceroy don Francisco de Toledo, having completed his work in this kingdom of the Indies, went to Castille and when he attempted to kiss the hands of His Majesty . . . the Master of Chambers did not recognize him, nor allow him to enter; with this sorrow he went home, did not eat, sat on a chair, and while sitting he died without writing a will" (Guamán Poma 1993, II, 348, 355). On the other hand, Garcilaso wrote that the king of Spain "received the Viceroy, not with the applause he expected, but with much opposition. And in a few words he told him to go home, that His Majesty had not told him to go to Perú to kill kings, but to serve kings," and with this and other displeasures "he fell into such a deep sorrow and melancholy that he died a few days later" (Garcilaso 1966/2, VIII, XX, 1483).

6. In popular culture, it is difficult to differentiate between history as "master of life" and history as experience; similarly, the transformation of a specific moment in the past into a glorious occasion has been carried to an extreme, almost with the same enthusiasm with which rulers and peoples are glorified, as though by the voice of God.

Three

JUAN BAUTISTA AVALLE-ARCE

The Self-Baptism of Garcilaso Inca

DURING THE YEARS that Garcilaso lived in Spain, a notable event took place in his life which has been little addressed by the scholars of Colonial literature. Many critics still continue to react to slogans which originated during the times of Marcelino Menéndez y Pelayo, who spoke of the "semi-barbarous, semi-educated" mind of Garcilaso and of his "rich, yet always infantile, imagination." One of the positive results of gatherings such as this one will be to bury forever such inanities. The study of Garcilaso reveals a man who was as complex as he was learned, with numerous sides to his personality, as evoked by the phrase "a mestizo humanist from the Renaissance."

Garcilaso's name in Perú was Gómez Suárez de Figueroa. Under that name he traveled to Spain, settled there, and soldiered for Phillip II in the sad war of the Alpujarras against the Moors. Soon after, on a day documented as November 22, 1563, he signed his name as Garcilaso de la Vega (many years later he will add "Inca" to his name). Shortly before this extraordinary change of name, Garcilaso had been denied permission to return to the Indies. The destiny of the Peruvian mestizo was thus to be circumscribed within Spain and by whatever the new land had to offer him. The umbilical chord that had tied Garcilaso to the Inca state and furnished him with his primary physical and spiri-

tual support had been forcibly severed, against his will. Faced
with this new situation that he would have to endure for the
rest of his life, it was necessary for him to find a new sustenance.
His search began by re-identifying himself, since the old "I" had
died. The "new" man was confronted by the risk of spiritual mal-
nutrition and, therefore, contemplated evasive measures. His
next step was clearly to forge for himself a wholly new personality,
by means of which to encounter his new reality, a reality which
had become unavoidable from the moment he was forbidden to
return to the land of his birth.

In response to this anguished personal dilemma, Garcilaso
threw overboard the old name of Gómez Suárez de Figueroa and
in its stead adopted the new name, which, with the subsequent
addition of the word honoring his mother's lineage, became Inca
Garcilaso de la Vega, with its variant, Garcilaso Inca de la Vega.
To a certain extent, this act reproduces the sacrament of baptism.
The new name became the identifying label of the new man, in
the same manner in which a newborn receives the confirmation
of his identity at the baptismal font. We can likewise, and indeed
appropriately, compare this phenomenon with the vital experience of Saul of Tarsus, which occurred during the first years of
the Christian era. Saul, a Jew who actively persecuted the Christians, set out on a trip from Jerusalem to Damascus in his furi-
ous hunt for members of the new heretical sect. On the road to
Damascus he had a sudden and marvelous vision, which literally blinded him. A voice told him: "Ego sum Iesus, quem tu
persequeris" (Acts 9:5). In Damascus, after miraculously recover-
ing his sight, Saul was converted ("baptizatus est." Acts 20:18).
Thereafter the new Christian was a new man with a very different
vital horizon, and his identification with the old name of Saul
was no longer applicable. The new man would proclaim his
new identity in resounding terms, in numerous instances, such
as the text in the Epistle to the Galatians: "Paulus apostolus non
ab hominibus neque per hominem, sed per Iesum Christum et
Deum Patrem, qui suscitavit eum a mortuis" ("Paul, an apostle
not from men nor through man, but through Jesus Christ and

God the Father who raised him from the dead." Galatians 1:1).
The old man had died, and with him, his name. The new man
baptized himself with a new name.

Another comparison to the change of name from Gómez
Suárez de Figueroa to Garcilaso Inca de la Vega appears in the
case of that old nobleman who lived in an unnamed village of La
Mancha. He based his happiness on eating "a pot of something
containing more beef than lamb, stew most of the nights, duels
and afflictions on Saturdays, lentils on Fridays, and pigeons occasionally on Sundays," and wore "leather breeches to parties,
and slippers of the same material." While living this peaceful existence, the nobleman called himself Alonso Quijano and identified himself with that name. But a moment arrived when, after
a maddening vision, in a beautiful act of self-baptism, the nobleman transformed himself into the knight-errant Don Quijote de
la Mancha. In axiomatic fashion, the new man acquired a new
name.

The act of self-baptism contains a very deep element of human
truth, a kind of truth which an individual gains about himself
through intense individual effort, whether the person is Saul of
Tarsus–Paul, Alonso Quijano–Don Quijote de la Mancha, or
Gómez Suárez de Figueroa–Garcilaso Inca de la Vega. In these
self-baptisms the words of Saint Paul are pertinent, as pro-
nounced in the Epistle to the Romans: "Consepulti enim sumus
cum illo per baptismum in mortem ut quomodo Christiis surr-
exit a mortuis per gloriam Patris, ita et nos in novitate vitae am-
bulemus" ("We were buried therefore with Him by baptism into
death, so that as Christ was raised from the dead for the glory of
the Father, we too might walk in newness of life." Romans 6:4).
According to the apostle, the words "in novitate vitae ambule-
mus" ("let us walk into this new life") carry new self-definitions.
What is seen ahead in life has completely changed. In the case
of Garcilaso, the forced self-identification with Spain evoked a
deep reflection from which emerged the consciousness of being
a new man. The new vital horizon that Garcilaso perceived from
a distance can be surmised by the illustrious literary ancestry of
the name which he conferred on himself. It is not relevant that

the name had already been chosen by other members of his family. In Spain the new name was identified above all with the famous Castilian poet, and it therefore placed him directly within the strongest and most noble literary tradition of the Spanish Golden Age. In abandoning the involuntary baptismal name given to him by others, he had conferred upon himself a name which was consistent with the new possibilities now open to him, a name already deeply associated with letters.

Garcilaso, in my judgment, found his vocation at the moment when his links with the old man had been severed. "Old man— old name, new man—new name." On November 22, 1563, when Gómez Suárez de Figueroa died, Garcilaso Inca de la Vega made his profession of faith. It was a vital and vocational faith, which was to serve as encouragement and inspiration throughout those almost thirty years that would elapse until the publication of his first book. His road to Damascus, and his new vital goals, would remain forever inscribed with his new name: Garcilaso Inca de la Vega.

45

Four

PIERRE DUVIOLS

The Problematic Representation of Viracocha in the Royal Commentaries, and Why Garcilaso Bears and Deserves the Title of Inca

THE WAR BETWEEN the Incas and their neighbors, the Chancas, is certainly one of the most important events in the history of the Peruvian dynasty, and Garcilaso's account of this episode differs significantly from those of historiographers who preceded him. Critics have noted this discrepancy. I would like to offer an explanation and attempt to prove that it was necessary for him to assume the position he did in order to justify his self-proclaimed title of Inca.

According to historians known to Garcilaso, when Viracocha, the seventh Inca king of Cuzco, learned of an impending attack by the small neighboring kingdom of the Chancas, he became frightened and abandoned his capital. His youngest son, the prince Inca Yupanqui, announced that the supreme god Viracocha, creator of the world, had appeared to him, encouraged him to fight, and promised his support. Inca Yupanqui organized a resistance, and via a supernatural intervention which transformed stones into warriors (the so-called *purunruna* sent by the god), he crushed the enemy, thereby saving Cuzco and the empire. He was subsequently crowned Inca and chose Pachacuti as his name.

Garcilaso was also aware of another event which took place much later in Inca history. At the time of the Spanish conquest, the Inca Atahualpa held prisoner his brother and enemy Huáscar, who was the Inca ruler of Cuzco. The inhabitants of that city offered a bounteous sacrifice to the god Viracocha, requesting him to save their king. Shortly thereafter, the Spaniards imprisoned Atahualpa. The people, believing that the Spaniards had been sent by their god, began calling them Viracochas, and the name stuck.

Garcilaso alters the account of the war with the Chancas. According to him, the cowardly Inca king who had abandoned Cuzco was not Viracocha but Yawar Huacac (he who weeps blood), a name generally considered to be a bad omen. Since his son had proven to be of a rebellious nature, this Inca banished him to Chita, near Cuzco, to watch over the flocks destined to be sacrificed to the Sun. One day the prince returned to his father with an important message. A strange man—bearded, dressed in a long robe, and holding a strange animal on a leash—had appeared to him and addressed him as "nephew." He had told him that his name was Viracocha Inca and that he was the son of the Sun god and brother of the first Inca, Manco Capac, who had died previously. The Sun god had sent him to inform the Inca Yawar Huacac of an imminent uprising in the province of the Chancas, who were plotting to attack Cuzco. Finally, the ghost or "phantom," as Garcilaso calls him, offered his assistance to the prince. The Inca Yawar Huacac, however, ignored the warning. The Chancas did indeed attack and the king panicked and fled. The prince organized the resistance, and with the help of reinforcements, fought back and was victorious. He was subsequently crowned the new king and chose to be called Viracocha, in homage to the "phantom." The commemorative statue which he erected in Cacha bore a resemblance to Saint Bartholomew, who some believed had come earlier to Perú to evangelize the Indians.

The differences in these two accounts of the war with the Chancas do not present an ethno-historical problem. Nor is it necessary to consult other sources to verify the originality of Garcilaso's version. In order to understand why he introduced his modifications, we must follow the evolution of his critical and creative thought processes to clarify his primary motivation. We will see that he did examine the facts known to him and then adjusted, dismissed, or added to them according to his conception of what the historical reality must or should have been. One of the primary difficulties of interpretation is that he mentions three very different characters, an Inca king, a god, and a phantom, and to each of them he gives the same name, "Viracocha." The roles and actions of these three identities do not seem to be completely coherent.

Concerning the *Inca* Viracocha, Garcilaso completely altered the chronology of his reign by moving it back a generation. This adjustment was brought about by a desire for semantic coherence. It seemed to Garcilaso that a vanquished king should bear a fateful name in keeping with his destiny, and that the Spanish historians must have been mistaken in not attributing the defeat to Yawar Huacac, the "Inca-who-weeps-blood." This earlier Inca, therefore, not his son Inca Viracocha, assumes the role of a coward and deserter in the *Commentaries*.

The *god* Viracocha, on the other hand, is a more complex figure. Acosta depicted him as the supreme god of the Incas, the creator of the universe, thus prefiguring the role of the Christian God. If Garcilaso acknowledged that Inca monotheism existed alongside idolatrous practices, a fact that would eventually allow the Peruvians to accept more easily the Christian faith, then he could not allow a supreme god to be called Viracocha. Garcilaso had already constructed his religious system based on the theology of Pachacamac, who represented for him the creator god and whom he had chosen for semantic reasons. He said of *Viracocha*, "I do not know what this name could mean." In contrast, he explained that *Pachacamac* was composed of two concepts: *camac* (he who enlivens, he who creates) and *pacha* (world). Thus, the definition of this god coincided with the definition of the Christian God given by Luis de Granada. In the *Commentaries*, Pachacamac is eventually associated with the Trinity. Garcilaso referred to him as the "unknown god" of Perú, identical to the god described by Saint Paul to the Athenians (Acts 17). Garcilaso realized, however, that he could not realistically disregard a god called Viracocha, because he was associated with the victorious prince, a well-known historical figure. Garcilaso thus established his hierarchy of the gods as follows: (1) Pachacamac, the invisible and abstract god, who has no special cult; (2) the Sun, a concrete and visible god, whose worship constituted the main idolatry of the Indians; and (3) the *huacas,* or sacred objects of veneration. The first place had already been undisputably accorded to Pachacamac, and the phantom Viracocha could only be granted secondary or tertiary status. But Garcilaso's main innovation was that he identified the supernatural apparition of a god with that of a *man,* brother of the first Inca and therefore a dead ancestor, who bore the same name as the Inca as well as that of his father the Sun god. This manipulation established a *family tie* between the phantom of the uncle Viracocha, the Incas, and, as we shall see, the Spaniards. These relationships are essential in order to ascertain one of Garcilaso's central themes.

Having portrayed the phantom as an ancestor of the Incas, and by the same token a son of the Sun god, Garcilaso could now use him historically not only on a human level (by the blood relationship) but also on a divine level (due to his origin as a god). At the beginning of the book, he made it clear that the worship of the Incas by the Peruvians as "children of the Sun god" was fictitious and based on a tale which Manco Capac, the first Inca, told his subjects for political purposes. The phantom of the uncle was, therefore, worthy of veneration and even worship (Garcilaso passed progressively from the use of the term *dulia* to that of *latria*), not only because of his mythical, solar origin, but also because he has saved Cuzco. By means of this phantom, Inca Garcilaso could then construct an euhemeristic cult based on respect, admiration and gratitude, just as other famous civilizations had done before him. Garcilaso carefully defined the "veneration" and "adoration" towards Viracocha simply as "a vain belief," which enabled him to establish his final hierarchy: (1) Pachacamac, (2) the Sun god, (3) Viracocha, and (4) the *huacas.*

Garcilaso's other innovation was to provide his "god-man-ancestor" Viracocha with a long beard and a long robe, thus evoking the image of an early Christian apostle, namely Saint Bartholomew. It seems very likely that he appropriated this image (although he does not say so) from the *Crónica del Perú* by

Cieza de León, in which Cieza offers the following description of a statue in the temple of Cacha: "An idol of stone, the height of a man, clothed and with a crown or tiara on his head; and some said he had been made in the likeness of some apostle who had arrived in this land" (Cieza 1986, 98). Garcilaso imagined that, in gratitude, the Inca Viracocha had a statue made of his vision, which indeed resembled the apostle, and had installed it in the temple of Cacha.

Garcilaso can now explain the nickname "Viracochas" given to the Spaniards, emphasizing its importance. When the conquerors arrived in the Andes, the Peruvians were struck by the resemblance between the long-robed, bearded men and the statue of Viracocha. Using the concepts of relationship and similarity applied to his invention of the god Viracocha, Garcilaso is finally able to formulate and justify one of the main themes of his book, based on the following syllogism: after the Peruvians had noticed the similarity between the statue of the god and the conquistadors, they considered the latter to be the god's sons whom he had sent to them. It followed that the Incas (themselves descendants of the god-ancestor Viracocha and considered to be sons of the Sun god) and the Spaniards (also called sons of Viracocha, and therefore descendants of the Sun god) *were members of the same family*, at least on a mythological and symbolic level. These permutations, added to the historiographical tradition, are indispensable in order to justify the affirmation found at the end of Part I of the *Commentaries*: "The female line is, as we have said, ignored by the Incas, unless they are the sons of Spanish conquistadors who subjugated Perú, for these too are called Incas, in the belief that they are descendants of their god, the Sun" (Garcilaso 1966/1, IX, XL, 626). Garcilaso, son of a princess who was the niece of the Inca Túpac Yupanqui and of a captain of the conquistadors, could not inherit from his mother the title of Inca which he longed to claim, because the Inca rules of succession disallowed it. The creation of his historical *tour de force* was, therefore, necessary for him in order to claim the title of Inca through the intervention of a deified phantom! Sylvia Hilton was right when she wrote that Garcilaso "calls himself an Inca in memory of his mother, but also through the dynastic authority of his father" (Garcilaso 1986b, xc). Garcilaso considered this matter of such great importance that he continued to justify his explanations throughout the first two books of Part II of the *Commentaries*.

Several chapters of the first book of Part II are dedicated to the unsuccessful attempt to establish a pact of permanent peace and friendship between the Incas and the Spanish conquerors. The Spaniards would restore the empire to the legitimate Inca, provided the Incas would convert to Christianity. Historians have judged that such an agreement was improbable and have even considered Garcilaso's treatment of it naive. These chapters seem much more logical, however, when we note that Garcilaso closely associated this chivalrous pact with the symbolic family kinship between the two parties. It would have represented a real family covenant. The meetings between the ambassadors provided a venue to remind the reader of the common solar origin of the conquerors and the conquered. Obviously, Garcilaso sought to prove the authenticity of the titles invoked in this context, as well as their legitimacy. To obviate critical objections, he portrayed the king Manco Capac as conferring the title of Inca on certain vassals, thereby establishing a group of "Incas by privilege" and "adopted sons" (Garcilaso 1966/1, I, XXIII, 58). Garcilaso thus demonstrated that, according to Inca custom, it was the king alone who could grant titles and dignities.

These observations provide a better understanding of the meaning and importance of the famous encounters between Francisco Pizarro and Hernando de Soto with the ambassador of the unfortunate Inca Huáscar, and especially with the Inca Atahualpa. On receiving the two conquistadors the latter exclaimed: "Welcome to my realms, Capac Viracochas." The Inca was immediately impressed by their resemblance to the statue of Viracocha, and he told Pizarro that the god Viracocha was "both your father and ours." The Inca wished to place himself at the service of these "children of the Sun god," who were his brothers, and he was ready to sign a family pact (Garcilaso 1966/2, I, XIX, 672–673). Another Inca king, Manco II, later told the Spaniards that he saw in them "the true sons of the god Viracocha and brothers of the Incas," and "they [and him] were all of one lineage" (Garcilaso 1966/2, II, XII, 761).

Could Captain Garcilaso also have received honors similar to those which had been conferred upon Governor Pizarro and Hernando de Soto? His son reflects at length on this serious question. He wrote: "All the conquerors of Perú were called Viracocha Inca, including the first ones who entered the country with Pizarro and the second who came with Almagro and Alvarado; and all them were worshipped as gods" (Garcilaso 1966/2, I, XL, 725). In fact, we know that Captain Garcilaso came to Perú from Nicaragua with the second wave of conquistadors, under the orders of Alvarado. It seems, therefore, that Garcilaso could adopt the title. But could this title be passed on from father to son according to the Inca laws that Garcilaso acknowledged? At the beginning of the *Commentaries,* referring to vassals whom he had just honored, the Inca Manco Capac "ordered that they *and their descendants* would forever bear the title of Inca." Garcilaso has carefully thought out and explained everything.

According to Garcilaso, as we have already noted, those vassals to whom king Manco Capac had given the title of Inca could call themselves "Incas by privilege" or "adoptive sons." However, they deserved the title of Inca to a lesser degree than the Spanish "Viracochas," since the newcomers were adopted members of the family of the Inca king. They were like brothers as a result of the fabulous intervention of the Viracocha–St. Bartholomew phantom. Captain Garcilaso was, therefore, the adoptive brother of the Incas, which gives his son the right to use the title of Inca.

What did it exactly mean for Garcilaso to have the title of Inca? He himself clearly explained this: "The name of *Inca,* applied to the prince, means 'lord,' or 'king,' or 'emperor.' . . . To translate its real meaning, it is 'a man of the royal blood,' for the *curacas,* however great lords they were, were not called Incas" (Garcilaso 1966/1, I, XXIV, 60). Garcilaso could thus claim, as he did here, to be "a man of royal blood," both from his father's side and from his mother's as well.

*   *   *

In the previous discussion I have given special consideration to Garcilaso's self-designation of Inca. I now intend to analyze further the roles which he allotted to the three Viracochas in relation to the providentialist scheme which dominates his vision of the history of the Incas.

The Inca Viracocha, because he had been chosen by the phantom-god Viracocha, acquired the reputation of being an oracle. One day he announced that "after a certain number of [rulers] had reigned," strangers would arrive, take control of the empire, and change its religion (Garcilaso 1966/1, v, XXVIII, 305). The twelfth Inca, just before his death, confirmed the prophecy and added: "These new people will come and fulfill what our father the Sun has foretold, and will gain our Empire and become masters of it. I bid you obey them and serve them as men who will be completely victorious, for their law will be better than ours and their arms more powerful and invincible than ours" (Garcilaso 1966/1, IX, XV, 577).

These last wishes of the widely-respected Huayna Capac predetermined the voluntary paralysis of the Inca troops, which, as Garcilaso explained, was the reason why a small number of Spaniards were able to conquer Perú so quickly. These two "predictions," as the author calls them, also explain the divine appellation of the Spaniards as Viracochas:

> Because Inca Viracocha had uttered this prophecy and because it was fulfilled by the coming of the Spaniards to Perú and their conquest of it, with the overthrow of the Inca religion and the preaching of the Catholic Faith of our Holy Mother Church, the Indians applied the name Viracocha to the Spaniards. *This is the second reason for using the name for them,* the first being the belief that they were sons of the imaginary god Viracocha, sent by him, as we have said, to assist the Incas and punish the rebels [emphasis mine].
> (Garcilaso 1966/1, v, XXVIII, 306)

When the tyrant Atahualpa was accused of trying to seize control of Cuzco, the Spaniards executed him, and Cuzco was saved a second time. Acting as children of the god Viracocha, the Spaniards had saved the capital. Garcilaso's interpretation of this exploit, like that of the god and the prince, and the prophecies of Viracocha and Huayna Capac, follows a providentialist line. Garcilaso seems to have borrowed this view of history from St. Augustine as well as from Eusebius of Caesarea, who for a long time was the only historian who mentioned the legend of Constantine's vision of a cross.

Marcel Bataillon, addressing the banished prince's vision in Chite, notes: "We refer to the motto of the first Christian Emperor: *in hoc signo vinces*" (Garcilaso 1982, preface, 41–46). According to Eusebius, on the eve of the decisive battle near Rome against Maxentius, Emperor Constantine had the vision of a bright cross in the sky inscribed with these words: *in hoc signo vinces* (in this sign you will be victorious). After the victory, it was said that Christ commanded Constantine to make it his standard image. This was the famous *labarum*. In the *Commentaries,* the prince's vision of the phantom god Viracocha, now also identified with the apostle St. Bartholomew, corresponds to the vision of the cross, and the statue which the new king made in the image of the apostle corresponds to the *labarum.* Just as the victory of Constantine marked the advent of Christianity in Rome, the victory over the Chancas likewise marked an important step toward the future evangelization of Perú. Garcilaso believed that the same model of world history, under God's guidance, could be repeated in different places and at different times. God had already "allowed" Manco Capac, the first Inca, to bring civilization to the people of Cuzco, such as the idolatry of the Sun, a practice which was then superior to all other forms of idolatry and close, in some respects, to monotheism. The Peruvians had thus been "rendered more docile to receive the Catholic faith" at a future and appropriate time (Garcilaso 1966/1, I, XV, 40). Other Peruvian chroniclers follow a similar historical model.[1]

From a theological and mystical point of view, Garcilaso established in the *personae* of Viracocha the three levels of a providentialist plan: (1) Viracocha, both as the god-man and as the future Inca, saves Cuzco from the Chanca threat; (2) the Spanish

Viracochas save Cuzco from the "tyrant" Atahualpa; and (3) the Spaniards, besieged in Cuzco by the troops of Inca Manco II, are saved by the apparition of St. James (Santiago) holding a thunderbolt (*illapa*); the terrified Indians abandon the battlefield because they have seen "a Viracocha with an *illapa* in his hand" (Garcilaso 1966/2, II, XXIV, 802). At this point in the *Commentaries,* Garcilaso had already explained that the Peruvians also called the Spaniards Viracochas and thought that their firearms had been given to them by the Sun.

The figure of Viracocha as conceived by Garcilaso is a composite god drawn from two symbolic men: the Andean Inca and the Christian apostle. Both would engender the future ethnic "mestizaje." Culturally, however, the apostle would predominate because the future mestizo would adopt his religion. Garcilaso stated that around 1570 the mestizos from Cuzco had created a brotherhood (*cofradía*) which did not accept the Spaniards "and took the blessed apostle as their patron, declaring that as he was said to have preached in Perú, whether truly or falsely, they would have him as their advocate, though some malicious Spaniards, seeing the adornments they put on for the occasion, asserted that this was done for the Inca Viracocha, not for the apostle" (Garcilaso 1966/1, V, XXII, 291–292). The three apparitions of this apostle correspond to the following purposes: (1) to evangelize pre-Columbian Perú; (2) to save Cuzco from the Chancas and to facilitate the second stage of evangelization; and (3) to inspire the foundation of the brotherhood. These constitute the three stages of the providential path towards faith.

Finally, as I have tried to demonstrate, Garcilaso also established a personal claim through the figure of Viracocha. Without the assistance of the phantom Viracocha, Garcilaso would not have deserved the title of Inca.

In this essay, I have attempted to show that it is not necessary to rely on problematic external sources to understand the *how* and *why* of Garcilaso's close attention to the war against the Chancas. Our author thought that he must impose order and harmony ("orden y concierto") to the "confused" history written by the Spanish historians who were given false information by the Indi-

55

ans, often misunderstanding their use of flattery, information which they were unable to fully comprehend anyway because of their insufficient knowledge of Quechua. Garcilaso had to add order to the linguistic expressions and remove the linguistic confusions. Last but not least, through a providentialist vision, he intended to instill in the history of Perú a holy and divine order.

AFTERWORD

Three other analyses have appeared dealing with the version of the war between the Incas and the Chancas in the *Commentaries*. In 1910 José de la Riva Agüero defended Garcilaso's historical position against that of other historians. However, most of the supporting sources he quotes were published after the death of Garcilaso, and thus Garcilaso could not have known them (Cf. Riva Agüero 1952, 119 ff.). Only one ancient document, the *Informaciones de los quipucamayos a Vaca de Castro,* mentions the Inca Viracocha as the victor over the Chancas. Riva Agüero relies on this text, which seems to him to be an authentic source of Inca tradition. It contains information, as its title indicates, obtained from the *quipus* by the official historians of the Inca Empire. These historians "state that the victor of the Chancas was Viracocha and not Pachacuti, which is a strong argument in favor of Garcilaso. This information does not mention the often repeated tradition of the attack of the Chancas who reached Cuzco, nor the flight of the Inca" (Riva Agüero 1952, 121). Riva Agüero bases his argument on his confidence in the accuracy of this document, attributed to Inca informants. I hope that I have shown that in reality the *quipucamayoc* do not intervene in this text (Duviols 1979). In any case, I do not think that, as far as Garcilaso was concerned, it was a question of establishing the "historical truth" of this matter. This would have been impossible, and we will probably never know.

In 1953 María Rostworowski advanced an opposing view. She maintained that the other historians and not Garcilaso provide the truthful version: "After having analyzed the events which took place in Cuzco at that period, we can see that it is Garcilaso who is the origin of all this muddle" (Rostworowski 1953, 57).

She considers the *Commentaries* a utopian epic, and attributes the shifting of the reigns and other changes to the author's personal, family motives. His maternal family, the *panaca* of the Inca Túpac Yupanqui, was decimated by Atahualpa, himself descended from the Inca Pachacuti (alias Pachacutec). "It is filial piety and post-humous revenge that prompt Garcilaso to belittle the figure of this Inca Pachacuti, the traditional victor over the Chancas, by shifting his reign and thus assigning him to the forgotten pages of history books" (Rostworowski 1953, 57–68). Although this explanation is difficult to prove, it is interesting and completely plausible, and facilitates a better understanding of these passages in the book.

In 1982 Marcel Bataillon discussed the same question in his preface to an edition of the *Royal Commentaries,* comparing the *Commentaries* with the sources used by Garcilaso concerning the war (Garcilaso 1982, 43). These sources were limited to the histories of Diego Fernández "El Palentino," Jerónimo Román y Zamora, and José de Acosta. I would add to these the *Confesionario Para Curas de Indios* (Lima, 1585), with respect to the name and role of the god Viracocha. Bataillon's conclusions are as follows: (1) the aggression of the Chancas noted by historiographers becomes, in the view of Garcilaso, the rebellion of an already conquered province, a position which has the advantage of giving greater historical depth to the expansion of the empire, a depth which is further accentuated by moving back a reign; (2) the suggestion of Yawar Huacac as the vanquished king was primarily the result of philological and semantic explanations; (3) the figure of the statue is drawn from Cieza de León, although Garcilaso does not acknowledge this; and (4) The apparition of a deceased Inca spares Garcilaso the introduction of a miracle. For the same reason, he has removed the apparition of the *purunruna* and rationalized the event by postulating help supplied by neighboring provinces.

These deductions seem to me completely justified. By elucidating via semantic analysis the different meanings Garcilaso applied to the word *Viracocha,* I have also explained the role of the Inca Yawar Huacac. Bataillon, however, does not explore the re-

lationship between the apparition of the phantom and the justification of the title of Inca which Garcilaso applied to himself,
which has been the subject of this essay. I have, nevertheless, applied Bataillon's logic to this particular case, which, in my esti-
mation, seems to be the most effective approach. This logic also
led Bataillon to formulate his overall judgment concerning the
Commentaries. He considered it "the Peruvian book par excellence," and adds: "It has remained, like the books of Las Casas,
contentious in the question of its historical value. It is not at all
paradoxical to say that in order to give a fair judgment of its
historical value, we should first of all understand it as a work of
art instead of placing a superstitious confidence in its slightest
details, or accusing it of deceit" (Garcilaso 1982, 55). As he says,
"We then admire the natural way this Inca takes possession of
history . . . by revealing his character of historian and representative man" (24).

NOTE

1. For instance, Santa Cruz Pachacuti's *Relación*. The analogies between this text and the *Commentaries* are surprising, notably in relation to the providentialist plan. Was Pachacuti influenced by Garcilaso?
For a discussion of this point, see my study on the *Relación* (Santa Cruz
Pachacuti 1993, 92–93).

Five

CARMELA ZANELLI

The Virgin Mary and the Possibility of Conciliation of Distinctive Cultural Traditions in the General History of Perú

ONE OF THE CRITERIA of historical truth prevalent in the sixteenth century was the understanding of God's presence in historical processes. Thus, the sixteenth-century historians recognized the theological basis of every human act. Miraculous apparitions and prodigies prevailed in their providentialist historical accounts. This perspective, based on Saint Augustine, was renewed and enriched during the Counter-Reformation. Within this context, the Virgin Mary plays three fundamental roles in Garcilaso's *General History of Perú*. First of all, she is the addressee of the entire text, since it is dedicated to her and written in her honor. Secondly, the Virgin is a protagonist in the work, because during the siege of Cuzco she makes a miraculous appearance in order to assure the victory of the Spaniards for the benefit of the evangelization of the Incas. Her intervention is a crucial event in the consolidation of the Spanish conquest.[1] Finally, the Virgin is a fundamental concern of Gonzalo Pizarro during his uprising against the Spanish crown.

The *General History* contains conflicts and contradictions: Garcilaso would like to present the Inca civilization and Spanish ideals as ultimately compatible, yet there is rampant war and a sense of general chaos. Misunderstanding and strife, civil wars and fratricide, prevail not only between Indians and Spaniards but also within both groups.

59

Kenneth Burke has shown that symbols have the capacity to integrate and sometimes reconcile contradictory meanings. I will argue that the fundamental significance of the Virgin in the *General History* is symbolic in that sense. In the Virgin the conflicts and contradictions of the Andean world are transcended and resolved.[2] She occupies, therefore, a privileged vantage point from which to understand the conflicts and contradictions underscored by Garcilaso, who wishes to reconcile, either in this world or in the next, the predicaments of the Spanish and the Andean peoples.

First, I will discuss how the Indians embraced the cult of Mary as a result of the events of the siege of Cuzco, and how she establishes the groundwork for reconciling Spaniards and Indians. Secondly, I will describe Gonzalo Pizarro's devotion to Mary. For Garcilaso, Pizarro represents a paradigmatic and somewhat exemplary conquistador. Finally, the detailed analysis of the book's dedication—which is a privileged textual space—will provide a revealing synthesis of the Virgin's attributes in the text.[3]

In the aftermath of the siege of Cuzco, the Spaniards regained and consolidated their control over the administrative capital of the Inca Empire. Garcilaso's text is not the only source that recounts the dramatic events in which fewer than two hundred Spaniards not only resisted the ferocious assault of many thousands of Indians, but then also faced starvation for a year in the surrounded city. Garcilaso criticized the depictions of these episodes in Francisco López de Gómara's *General History* and Agustín de Zárate's *History of the Discovery and Conquest of Perú,* because of their extreme brevity. Neither of them mentioned miraculous events or the apparition of the Virgin, without which the Spaniards would have surely been defeated. In a despairing tone, Garcilaso asked himself why the conquistadors, eyewitnesses of the prodigies, had not properly described the facts, and suggested that these privileged eyewitnesses were deceitful. The conquistadors did not reveal elements of such import because they wanted to take full credit for the victory. Garcilaso is certain that the Spaniards could not have resisted the onslaught of the Indians or regained the control of the capital without divine intervention. He was relieved to verify that José de Acosta mentioned the miraculous apparition of the Virgin during the siege. He needed an authoritative source to corroborate his own data, although he noted that he had read Acosta's reference "many days after writing this chapter," thus confirming the originality of his own information (Garcilaso 1966/2, II, xxv, 807).

Francisco Pizarro and Diego de Almagro promised Manco Inca—the legitimate heir of the Inca throne—that they would restore his power once he had made a commitment to effect the evangelization of the Indians. The Incas, according to Garcilaso, were already prepared to receive the Christian revelation because of their achievements in the understanding of natural law, and as a result of the omens and prophecies that preceded the arrival of the conquistadors. The Spaniards should have provided exemplary models of Christian values, but they failed to do so. On the contrary, Francisco Pizarro—consumed by the sin of pride, according to Garcilaso—provoked the massive uprising of the Indians because he did not keep his promise to Manco Inca. The indoctrination was postponed as a result of the bitter confrontation that ensued. Garcilaso thus interpreted all the miracles witnessed during the siege, especially the apparition of the Virgin, as manifestations of God's mercy towards these gentiles: "[God] sent them His Gospel . . . this we shall see from the many miracles He performed on their behalf in the course of the conquest" (Garcilaso 1966/2, I, I, 634).

The apparent paradox of divine intervention *against* those wronged can be resolved. Pizarro had deceived Manco Inca, which explains the Incas' military response and perhaps even justifies it. On the other hand, the Spanish ultimate purpose of evangelization is a goal superior to the failings of the conquistadors. The Virgin intervenes for this reason. The defeat of the Indians by Spanish sinners is justified for the sake of the Indians' salvation. Similarly, when the Indians tried to burn down the palace in which the Spaniards lived, the fires were extinguished every time. Garcilaso explains that "this was one of the marvels performed by our Lord in that city to establish His holy Gospel there; and the city has proved this, for it is certainly one of the most religious and charitable in the New World today, among both Spaniards and Indians" (Garcilaso 1966/2, II, XXIV, 799).

According to Garcilaso's account of the battle at the siege of Cuzco, the apparition of the apostle St. James (Santiago) preceded that of the Virgin. The saint appeared on the battleground throwing thunderbolts against the Indians. Both the Spaniards and the Indians witnessed the prodigy: "The Indians were terrified at the sight of this new knight and asked one another: 'Who is the Viracocha with the *illapa* in his hand?' (meaning 'lightning, thunder, and thunderbolt')" (Garcilaso 1966/2, II, XXIV, 802). The Christians were encouraged by the apostle's intervention, while the Indians became discouraged and decided to wait until dawn to attack the Spaniards. When night fell, St. James disappeared and the stage was set for the apparition of the Virgin. She appeared with baby Jesus in her arms at the exact moment when the Indians were about to launch the final assault to annihilate the last survivors. According to Garcilaso, she paralyzed the Indians by the splendor and beauty of her figure cast against the sky. The infidels—as he calls the Indians in this passage—felt a soft white powder that blinded them and forced them to withdraw from the fight. The Indians were the only ones who saw the Virgin Mary, while the Spaniards never fully understood why they had escaped from total destruction.

According to Garcilaso, the memory of that episode is the main reason for the profound devotion the Indians subsequently professed to Mary. The Indians revered the Virgin by calling her *mamanchic*, "our Lady and mother," *coya*, "queen," and other epithets (Garcilaso 1966/2, II, XXV, 805). To bestow a name is to make something more one's own. The Indians embraced the cult of Mary and explained their final defeat in terms of the impossibility of fighting against the Virgin's supernatural power.

The importance Garcilaso gives to the proper interpretation of words in Quechua reappears in his detailed and lengthy enumeration of the Virgin's epithets expressed in the Inca language. As we have seen, some of them are direct translations from Christian words, but others appear to be more original, such as *yurac amáncay*, which he translates as "white lily," or *huacchacúyac*, "lover and benefactor of the poor" (Garcilaso 1966/2, II, XXV, 805). The latter epithet is also applied to the powerful Incas.

Rubén Vargas Ugarte, in his *Historia del culto de María en Iberoamérica,* has written extensively about the tremendous impact of the prodigious apparitions of the Virgin in the popular culture of Cuzco during Colonial times.[4] Indeed, Garcilaso himself remembers the celebrations in which he participated, and even the pictorial representations he saw in Cuzco commemorated the miracles as a living tradition in his community. The version he narrates came fom the oral accounts of both Spaniards and Indians. Garcilaso explains: "The Inca uprising was in 1535 and it ended in 1536; and I was born in 1539, so that I knew many Indians and Spaniards who had taken part in the war and seen the wonders I have mentioned, which I heard about from them" (Garcilaso 1966/2, II, XXV, 807). Garcilaso is thus describing the beginning of a new religious tradition in the Andes.

The next important episode in which the Virgin intervened was during the civil wars among the Spanish conquistadors. Garcilaso denounced the chaos and turmoil of war that had postponed and even prevented the Christianization of the Indians. Capital sins like greed and avarice drove the Spaniards into the civil wars. In his sympathetic account of Gonzalo Pizarro's rebellion against the Spanish crown, Garcilaso distinguishes him from the rest of the conquistadors. Pizarro was chosen by the first settlers (*vecinos*)[5] and marked by destiny to defend the hard-won rights of the first Spanish colonizers and their mestizo families in Perú against the New Legislation issued in Spain, which prohibited their ownership of land. Garcilaso viewed Pizarro's political enterprise as the last, and unfortunately lost, possibility to articulate a mestizo society with its own distinctive values. When he was writing several decades later in Spain, this episode reminded Garcilaso of the transitional society that had made possible his own existence and his childhood as the son of an important Spanish captain and an Inca noblewoman in his native Cuzco. The society that he had known early in life no longer existed when he was writing.

In his depiction of Pizarro, Garcilaso underscores his wise administration of justice while in power, his capacity for showing mercy, and his profound devotion to the Virgin Mary: "[Gonzalo Pizarro] was a good Christian, and was very devoted to Our Lady the Virgin Mary, the mother of God, and the president [Gasca] set this down in the letter he wrote. He was never asked for anything for the love of Our Lady that he refused, however great it was" (Garcilaso 1966/2, V, XLIII, 1219). During moments of profound joy and success, as well as those marked by profound sorrow and death, Gonzalo Pizarro's intense devotion to Mary always prevailed. After his astonishing victory in the battle of Huarina, the rebel went directly to venerate the image of the Virgin. Garcilaso also recalls that he himself participated in the spontaneous celebration during Gonzalo Pizarro's triumphant entrance into the city of Cuzco:

> [Pizarro] entered the church of the Mercedarians to worship the Blessed Sacrament and the image of his mother, our Lady the Virgin. . . . I entered the city with them, for the day before I had gone out as far as Quespicancha, three leagues from Cuzco, to receive my father . . . and I saw all I have described. (Garcilaso 1966/2, V, XXVII, 1163)

At his execution, Gonzalo Pizarro carried with him an image of the Virgin Mary and petitioned her to intercede for the salvation of his soul. Garcilaso describes Pizarro's final moments in a tone of deep apprehension:

> He carried in his hands an image of Our Lady, to whom he was most devoted. He begged her to intercede for his soul. After going half way, he asked for a crucifix. One of the ten or twelve priests who accompanied him happened to have one and gave it to him. Gonzalo took it, and gave the priest the image of Our Lady, kissing the hem of the image's robe with great devotion. (Garcilaso 1966/2, V, XLIII, 1216)

The Virgin is as fundamental for Gonzalo Pizarro as she was for the Incas. In this light, we can consider the full significance of Garcilaso's dedication of the *General History* to the Virgin. Before the *General History*, Garcilaso had preferred to dedicate his works to powerful individuals. He dedicated the translation of the *Dialogues of Love* to Phillip II, *Florida* to the Duke of Braganza, and the first part of the *Royal Commentaries* to Catherine of Portugal. Thus, the dedication to the Virgin is a significant change. Garcilaso is no longer looking for confirmation in the political circles of men. He opts rather for the spiritual realm. Aurelio Miró-Quesada (1994, 304) believes that the dedication is tantamount to an act of contrition, evidence of a deeper religious feeling at a time when Garcilaso is near his death. This may be so, but I also think that the text of the dedication is particularly revealing since, besides the expected homage to the addressee, it incorporates aspects more suitable for a prologue than a dedication. The prologue during the Golden Age serves not only as an introduction to the text, but also may become a sort of confession (Porqueras Mayo 1957, 43; 1968, 105). And, as we shall see, Garcilaso's dedication gives him the opportunity to express his most personal, intimate, and final thoughts.

A closer reading of the dedication clarifies Garcilaso's underlying motivations. The first one, as expected, refers to the absolute excellence of the Virgin. Garcilaso describes the Virgin with an explosion of hyperbolic epithets, in evident contrast to the modesty with which he presents himself. He states: "Dedication of the book and dedicatory from the author to the glorious Virgin, our Lady, daughter, mother and virginal wife of her creator, supreme princess of all creatures. From Inca Garcilaso de la Vega, her unworthy servant; in adoration of hyperdulia" (Garcilaso 1966/2, dedication, 7).

Garcilaso is an early subscriber to the not-yet-declared dogma of the Immaculate Conception of the Virgin, a lively topic in the Spanish intellectual circles during those times.[6] The Virgin is "the image of his devotion and of divine perfections, [she is] so perfect that God, from the very first line of her being, since her very inception, prevented her from original sin" (ibid., 8).

The superiority of the Virgin resides in her representation of the temporal power of the Catholic church. She clearly represents the embodiment of a military power when Garcilaso openly compares her not only to Athena but also to Bellona, the Roman goddess of war. In this regard, the Virgin is the appropriate addressee to receive the historical account of these military deeds. When Garcilaso mentions her "Celestial favor," he clearly refers to the Virgin's miraculous apparition during the siege of Cuzco. However, her characterization as Bellona and the emphasis given to the militant aspect of the Church contrast with her "pacific" intervention during the siege. It is important to point out that thanks to the religious conversion of the Indians, which was the direct result of the Virgin's actions in favor of the Spaniards, the Indians became "triumphant" in Garcilaso's eyes. They defeated the Devil and accepted the true God, a new faith, and baptism (ibid., 7). This episode marked the beginning of a new devotion toward Mary in the New World, as we previously indicated. The fundamental point is that Mary's intervention, as a consequence of her conciliatory stance, resolves the opposition between victors and vanquished. She becomes the ideal subject of adoration for the Indians, a caring mother, and even a "protector and lover of the poor." She reunites under her tutelage the subdued Indians and their dominators, the Spaniards. This idea of unity may be somewhat farfetched, however, because Garcilaso maintained throughout his text that the evangelization of the Indians had not been easily accomplished.[7]

The second reason for addressing the text to the Virgin was to emphasize the conversion of Garcilaso's mother, the Inca noblewoman Isabel Chimpu Ocllo. It was thanks to the holy waters of baptism rather than to her royal blood that she became more illustrious and noble (ibid., 7).[8] Although Chimpu Ocllo is addressed, like the Virgin, as mother and noble lady, she is absent from most of the story. She is mentioned a few times in passages concerning Gonzalo Pizarro's rebellion.[9] Since Garcilaso appears as a direct eyewitness of important events, it is particularly significant that he decided to suppress sorrowful episodes in his own life, such as his father's desertion of his mother and his subsequent marriage to a much younger Spanish woman.

Garcilaso does not directly criticize his father's behavior toward his mother; however, his deepest feelings surface when he unexpectedly describes a comic episode, a digression regarding the prearranged marriages between young Spanish ladies and the old Spanish conquistadors of Guatemala. One of the young brides reveals her true intentions regarding her future husband. She and others in the same predicament are willing to marry these old, ugly, and disabled men with the sole purpose of inheriting their *encomiendas,* expecting an early death of their husbands so as to remarry as soon as possible with very handsome young men. One of the grooms overhears the lady, alerts his companions, and decides to marry his Indian mistress instead. Garcilaso laments:

> Some in Perú have done the same and married Indian women, though not many. Most have given grounds for the words of the lady in the anecdote. Their children can testify to the wisdom of this course, for from the hospitals where they lie they can see the offspring of others enjoying what their fathers gained and their mothers and relatives helped to gain. (Garcilaso 1966/2, II, I, 734)

The whole episode contains theatrical and literary elements, with entanglements common in Golden Age comedies. But the moral conclusion drawn from the episode is a subtle, indirect, yet bitter reflection on the writer's own life and on the situation of his own mother.[10]

As a final motivation for his dedication, Garcilaso thanks the Virgin for honoring his paternal lineage. The genealogical perspective is overtly present throughout his writings.[11] As Garcilaso remarks in the dedication, the family name, de la Vega, was given to his great ancestor Garcilaso for fighting against the Moors at *la vega* (the fertile plains) of Toledo (Garcilaso 1966/2, dedication, 7). Garcilaso's proud ancestor is compared to the Cid, the Castilian hero who fought the Moors, and Bernardo del Carpio, the Spanish knight who defeated Roland. He was even proudly called the "Knight commander of the Hail Mary," which underscores the importance of Mary in Garcilaso's genealogical constructs. It is not gratuitous that Garcilaso emphasized his ancestor's name, which happened to coincide with his father's and his own. Garcilaso needed to restore his father's honor because Captain Garcilaso de la Vega was considered a traitor, due to his ambiguous participation during the rebellion of Gonzalo Pizarro. But, as Garcilaso states in the dedication, Captain Garcilaso, along with the vigorous first conquistadors, fought for the Spanish crown like a true Alcibiades or Christian Achilles in order to gain the most important and richest part of the New World.

The dedicatory piece is a privileged textual space because it provides important interpretative clues for the rest of the text. On the one hand, the Virgin as a powerful symbol of the Church becomes the needed emblem that helps to justify under her protective mantle the enterprise of the conquest of the New World. She projects the possibility of an ideal world in which the distinction between victors and vanquished is finally resolved. She legitimizes the spiritual crusade of evangelization and at the same time she masks the horrors of the destruction of the indigenous way of life. Also because of the Virgin, Garcilaso's own mother is mentioned in the dedication. Her conversion and devotion to Mary elevate her figure. Garcilaso's father is depicted as an exemplary authority in Cuzco and his death is accompanied with a long prayer. Both Garcilaso's maternal and paternal heritages are thus remembered in the dedication. What reunites them is their individual devotion to Mary. In the dedication, Garcilaso established a textual refuge, a place where he could redeem his parents from either oblivion or dishonor. They, with Mary, became the three protagonists of that privileged space.

NOTES

The present article is an extended and modified version of a paper first presented at a conference in Montilla, Spain, in November 1994. I would like to thank Efraín Kristal for his careful reading and suggestions.

1. The different and sometimes contradictory criteria of historical truth that coexisted during the sixteenth century are examined by Víctor Frankl (1963).

2. Kenneth Burke draws his views from Coleridge's symbiology. He

develops his ideas in various theoretical writings, starting with his *Counter-Statement* (1984).

3. The dedication, as well as the prologues, titles, subtitles, and illustrations are part of those verbal and non-verbal productions that identify any text. Gérard Genette has coined the terms *paratext* and *paratextual* to refer to them. Paratextual elements like the name of the author and the date of publication are merely informative, while prologues and dedications may reveal an authorial intention and provide clues to guide the interpretation of the whole text (Genette 1987, 7–8, 18–19).

4. This extraordinary event was known during Colonial times as "the descension of the Virgin at Sunturhuasi" (Vargas Ugarte 1956, 658).

5. The key concept of *vecino* (settler) is defined early in the *Commentaries*. It usually referred to the first conquistadors who received a piece of land and a group of Indians under their tutelage after the foundation of a new city (cf. *Advertencias*).

6. Cf. Mayberry 1991, 207–224, for a more detailed discussion of the evolution of the controversy over the Immaculate Conception of the Virgin during the sixteenth and seventeenth centuries in Spain and the rest of Europe.

7. Garcilaso identifies the culprit: "the Devil, the enemy of the human race, used all his strength and wiles to prevent this and impede the conversion of the Indians; and though he could not completely stop the conversion, at least he did so for many years with the loyal aid of his diligent ministers, the seven deadly sins. . . . The Devil stirred up all these wars one after another, over a period of twenty five years. . . . These were the obstacles that prevented the Gospel from being preached as it otherwise would have been, for *the faithful* could not preach the faith owing to the daily disturbances that took place, nor could *the infidels* receive it because during the whole of that period there was nothing but war and murder with fire and the sword" (Garcilaso 1966/2, II, VI, 746, emphasis mine). Even though the Indians are prepared to receive the Gospel, Garcilaso still places them within the categories of *gentiles* or *infidels,* revealing once more the need for their evangelization in order to surpass their achievements in natural law. Cf. Efraín Kristal's description in this volume of the different paradigms of historical representation of pagans and infidels during the sixteenth century.

8. Cf. José A. Rodríguez Garrido's discussion in this volume of the different kinds of nobility that apply to Garcilaso's mother.

9. Garcilaso mentions his mother in the episode when Gonzalo Pizarro's followers looted the houses of his father, Captain Garcilaso (Garcilaso 1966/2, IV, x, 982). He does so again when, acting on her behalf, he paid a visit to Diego Centeno in 1547 (Garcilaso 1966/2, v, x, 1115).

10. Julie Greer Johnson (1981, 47–51) analyzes this particular episode in greater detail.

11. The *Commentaries* as a whole can be understood as a long genealogical account of the Inca rulers, while his *Relación de la descendencia de Garcí Pérez de Vargas (1596)* is a first approximation of his patrilineal heritage, continued in the *General History*.

Six

JOSÉ A. RODRÍGUEZ GARRIDO

Garcilaso Inca and the Tradition of Viri Illustres *(Dedication and Prologue of the* Royal Commentaries, *Part II)*

THE PUBLICATION BY JOSÉ DURAND in 1948 of the inventory and the identification of the books in Garcilaso's library constituted one of the most substantial works of Garcilasian studies. Since then, specialists have counted on a reliable corpus through which to approach the works of a man who acquired his humanism not through the university but through dialogue and, more than anything, through books. Although the inventory does not reflect everything that Garcilaso read,[1] it contributes substantially to our understanding of the general thematic nuclei of his intellectual interests and occasions a guided reading of his works in relation to these pivotal themes.

Despite the significant contributions to the study of Garcilaso's sources and his position in the history of ideas, these topics have not yet been exhausted. On the contrary, much rewarding work is still to be done on Garcilaso's intertextual dialogues with various intellectual traditions. In this essay we will study a form of historical discourse on *viri illustres* to which Garcilaso explicitly alludes in one of his works and which comprises an important part of the *Royal Commentaries*. Works on *viri illustres* are closely related to another subgenre prevalent in the sixteenth and seventeenth centuries, i.e., treatises on nobility. Both types of texts confront a common problem (the roots of which extend back

71

into the fourteenth century), namely the polemic between line-age and deeds in determining the quality of the individual.

The intention here is not to exhaust all that could be said about Garcilaso's appropriation of these traditions in the *Royal Commentaries*. We will rather focus on two specific passages: the dedication of the second part of the *Royal Commentaries* to the Virgin Mary and the "Prologue to the Indians, Mestizos, and Creoles" of the same book. Given their character as pre-texts to the work that completes Garcilaso's intellectual production, these possess extraordinary importance. In them Garcilaso formulates his vision of Peruvian history, and his readings about nobility and *viri illustres* serve him for that purpose.

GARCILASO'S LIBRARY REVISITED: BOOKS OF *VIRI ILLUSTRES* AND TREATISES OF NOBILITY

According to the titles in Durand's inventory, we can advance the hypothesis that the model of *viri illustres* followed by Garcilaso is closest to that of Italian and Spanish letters. There are few classical sources, for example, the three entries for Plutarch, whose *Parallel Lives* was translated into Spanish as *Vidas de ilustres y excelentes varones griegos y romanos pareadas* (1551).[2]

The references in the inventory to Petrarch are unfortunately very imprecise; however, the very fact that the list includes three references to the Italian humanist is a clear indication that his ideas influenced Garcilaso.[3] It is quite possible that these scattered references come from *De viris illustribus* (first edition, posthumous, 1379), a work that recovered the discursive genre for humanism and inaugurated a structure for historical texts that is still present in the Spanish writings of the sixteenth century: a universal history shown as a sequence of biographies starting with Adam and then running through biblical history and ancient history, up to the Middle Ages. Petrarch revised his ambitious project several times, but it was left incomplete at the time of his death.

The "Proemio" of *De viris illustribus* was a contributing factor to the humanistic conception of history, and it probably also left

its mark on Garcilaso.[4] Petrarch reaffirms the moral and exemplary goal of historical discourse, in particular that which narrates the lives of illustrious men; his objective is to show the readers what is worthy of imitation (Petrarca 1955, 225). To a great
extent, *De viris illustribus* is notably oriented to Petrarch's contemporary world, although, unlike Garcilaso, the author does not
deal with men of his time because he does not find in them anything worthy of praise; on the contrary, he finds more to censure
(219). On the other hand, the humanistic method elaborated by
Petrarch for the delineation of history is close to Garcilaso's ways
of confronting written sources (221) and to his formal preoccu-
pation with the unity of the work (223).

Another work which may have influenced Garcilaso was
Giovanni Boccaccio's *De casibus virorum illustrium,* a Spanish
translation of which is listed in the inventory of the library (*Caída
de príncipes,* no. 72). It probably corresponds to the translation
published in 1495, 1511, and again in 1552.[5] Boccaccio's work is
less historical in nature, which permits him to narrate the biographies of a spectrum of mythological characters. In addition to
the similar structure of their biographical narrations, Petrarch
and Boccaccio are united by their common moral goal. In effect,
Boccaccio reinforces the exemplary intention of his text with digressions that serve as commentaries, as introduction, and as
moralizing synthesis.

Although Dante did not produce a text like Petrarch's or
Boccaccio's, one of his most important works, the *Convivio,* focuses on the nature of a nobleman (specially the fourth treatise,
chapters 7 and 10), a theme treated by the other two authors
when determining the characteristics of the "illustrious man."
Dante advocates a nobility earned by the individual as opposed
to one acquired by lineage, a matter which is also discussed by
Garcilaso. Again, the indetermination of the inventory prevents
us from knowing if he owned the *Convivio.* However, no. 107 cites
the "works of Dante," and since we know Garcilaso's major interests, it would seem obvious that the book was also included under
this generic heading.[6]

José A. Rodríguez Garrido

In the same field of Italian letters, we find a treatise on nobility by Alessandro Piccolomini (no. 128), *Della instituzione di tutta la vita de l'huomo nato nòbile* (first edition, Venice, 1542), translated and published in Spanish in Seville in 1577. The book is dedicated to the young Alessandro Colombini. Offered as a service to the formation of nobility, the text speaks about diverse subjects that men of noble birth ought to know.[7]

One of the most confusing entries of the inventory is the one related to Spanish letters. No. 65 refers to a generic "Varones ilustres de España" that Durand cited without further clarification. The possibilities considered were the works of Fernando del Pulgar (*Claros varones de Castilla*), Fernán Pérez de Guzmán (*Loores de claros varones de España*), Juan Sedeño (*Suma de varones ilustres*), and Juan Benito Guardiola (*Tratado de nobleza y de los títulos y ditados que oy día tienen los varones claros y grandes de España*). The four titles are works of a very different nature. Pérez de Guzmán's is an elegiac poem, not his more famous *Generaciones y semblanzas,* a work which, given the historiographic interest of its prologue, Garcilaso must have known. Both Guzmán's *Generaciones* and Pulgar's *Claros varones* were biographies of the authors' contemporaries. It is only of Pulgar's volume, however, that one can speak unreservedly of the application of the *viri illustres* model, since Guzmán's critical and pessimistic vision diverges from this paradigm. On the other hand, Sedeño's book is an ambitious dictionary of *viri illustres* from antiquity, classical mythology (which, according to the euhemeristic tradition, is explained in historical terms), the Bible, and European, Turkish, Arab, and Spanish history.[8] Guardiola's book, in contrast, is a compendium of the nature of the noble man and the foundation of the Spanish nobility.

Although the references in the inventory do not exhaust the lists of books of the period on the subject, they nonetheless offer a relevant basis for an analysis of Garcilaso's dedication and prologue of the second part of the *Commentaries*. The aim of the following discussion is to examine Garcilaso's use and transformation of this textual tradition.

THE DEDICATION AND PROLOGUE OF
PART II OF THE *ROYAL COMMENTARIES*

Although the two texts with which Garcilaso opens the second part of the *Commentaries* fulfill different rhetorical functions
and presuppose diverse readerships, both share identical ideas
and motives. In the dedication the author chooses a supernatural
addressee for the book. More than a display of Garcilaso's disillusionment at this point of his life, his choice is an intentional re-
inforcement of the providentialist vision of history which unites
the two phases of Peruvian history—that of the Incas and that
of the conquistadors—discussed respectively in the first and second parts of the *Royal Commentaries*. The importance of the figure of the Virgin in Garcilaso's historical narrative is first announced at the beginning of the first part of the *Commentaries*.
Here the Inca emphasizes the Virgin's efforts via her intervention "to draw so many great peoples out of the pit of idolatry
and bring them into the bosom of His Roman Catholic Church"
(Garcilaso 1966/1, "Preface to the Reader," 4). The Virgin is depicted as a synthesis of the two worlds that constitute the social
history as well as the personal beliefs of the author. On one
hand, she is presented as God's Mother, but also, at the end of
the dedication, she is presented with the characteristics of the
Immaculate Conception ("wearing the moon and clothed with
the sun").[9] Garcilaso does not utilize, however, all the elements
of Marian iconography (for example, the crown of stars, the
trampled serpent, and the representation of the litanies, which
are included in the engraving that illustrate the title page), but
only those involving the sun and the moon. Thus, the Virgin appears with characteristics that connect her with Inca divini-
ties: the Moon, Mama Quilla, associated with maternal traits in
the first part of the *Commentaries,* and the Sun, Inti (the origin
and father of the Incas).[10] Furthermore, the Virgin acquires the
qualities of a warrior goddess ("Bellona of the militant Church,
Minerva of the triumphant one") that convert her into an agent
of the Spanish conquest, as appears later in the narrative of

the siege of Cuzco by Manco Inca (Garcilaso 1966/2, II, XXV, 803–808).

From an autobiographical point of view, the Virgin is also the agent of his mother's conversion to Christianity, and at the same time, an object of paternal veneration. Here the conquest is moved exclusively to the spiritual sphere (the conversion), which makes possible the author's synthesis of the two dominions initially in conflict (Inca and Spanish). At this point, Garcilaso inserts an important gloss on the title of his work, the *Royal Commentaries*, "more royal because they are dedicated to the Queen of the Angels." This passage, which is usually overlooked when the title is explained, is not merely a play on words but rather the fundamental bridge uniting the title and the content of both parts of the work.[11] On the one hand, Garcilaso extends the meaning of the adjective "royal," attributing to it an eschatological sense by means of which the discourse is moved from the material to the spiritual realm. On the other hand, the Virgin's providential intervention establishes a continuity between the two phases of Peruvian history.

Garcilaso's synthesis presupposes the Incas' nobility, which becomes more evident when Garcilaso announces that his mother is "more illustrious and excellent by the waters of holy baptism than by the royal blood of so many Incas and Peruvian kings." This comparison between nobility by lineage and nobility by the spirit is based on the classification established by Bartolus and repeated later by various writers of treatises on nobility, among them Guardiola. According to the celebrated Bartolus, there were three types of nobility: theological nobility, corresponding to those in God's grace; natural nobility, in those whose virtues qualify them to be leaders; and civil nobility, which is legally established and permits a distinction between the noble and the plebeian.[12] Bartolus proposed a connection between these three types and thus justified the organization of nobility as a correspondence to the divine order. Nevertheless, the main point of his argument rests on an attempt to equate natural nobility with civil nobility, thus leaving aside any consideration of theological nobility in the discernment of man's character. In contrast, Garcilaso makes theological nobility the central element of his discourse. His mother's conversion is a personal symbol in a historical process that concludes with the acquisition of the state of grace which legitimizes and brings the previous state to perfection. Thus, in the dedication, Garcilaso's mother is presented as the union of the three forms of nobility: theological, natural, and civil. We suggest that the selection of Mary Immaculate as "queen of heaven and earth," preserved from the "stain of original sin," for the dedication was motivated by the correspondence between the divine figure of the Virgin, represented with attributes of civil and theological nobility (a queen without sin), and the historical figure of Garcilaso's mother, with like traits (Inca Princess in a state of grace). Similar reasons can explain the dedication of the first part of the *Commentaries* to another woman, the Princess Doña Catarina.

Garcilaso employed the same strategies in the first part of the *Commentaries* to justify the nobility of the Inca governors. To defend their legitimacy, Garcilaso used the principle of natural nobility (the inherent virtue of certain individuals) converted into civil nobility. He also used the principle of theological nobility to defend the Inca governors for preparing the way for the Gospel's reception in Perú. Lorenzo Ducci, in a passage of his *Trattato della nobiltà* (1603) regarding the Indies, advocated that one way by which a man could acquire nobility was the introduction of the Christian faith to the indigenous gentile population (Ducci 1974, 127–128).[13] Garcilaso expresses a similar idea in the beginning of book 2 of Part I, when he comments on the civil organization imposed by the first Incas (chapter 1), a theme developed further in another chapter in which he tries to show that "the Incas searched for the true God our Lord" (Garcilaso 1966/1, II, II, 70).

The dedication of Part I of the *Commentaries* "To the Most Serene Princess, The Lady Catarina of Portugal" is a very significant text that introduces the perspective of nobility acquired by the principle of theological nobility. Addressing the Portuguese princess, Garcilaso declares: "Your exalted station is known throughout the world" and "Your Highness' generosity is patent to all."

Despite its seemingly secular meaning, in this address there is an implied praise of the princess not only for her natural nobility but also for her theological nobility. Garcilaso affirms: "For when we behold the great grace with which our Lord God has enriched Your Highness' soul, we find that it exceeds those natural qualities of piety and virtue of which the whole world speaks with admiration" (7). It is surprising to find the affirmation of the same principle, years later, in the dedication of Part II.

The topic of nobility also appears with respect to the conquistadors' position within the hierarchical Spanish social system. The prologue of the second part announces that one of the book's objectives is "to celebrate . . . the greatness of the heroic Spaniards" (Garcilaso 1944, prologue, 11). To honor the Spanish heroes of the conquest, Garcilaso refers explicitly to the textual tradition of *viri illustres*. He had several reasons to insist upon the interpretation of Peruvian history from this perspective. The exhaustive work of Juan Sedeño (*Suma de varones ilustres*) omitted any reference to the Spanish heroic deeds in the Indies.[14] Ercilla's *Araucana* and Castellanos' *Elegías de varones ilustres de Indias* provided the application of the models to the American reality. However, in both Ercilla's and Castellano's works there are only scant references to the conquest of the Inca Empire. Furthermore, the poetic structures of both works would probably not satisfy Garcilaso's intention of applying the model in the form of a strictly historical discourse.[15] On the other hand, while Gómara's chronicle modeled its exaltation of Cortés on the tradition of the *viri illustres*, it also denigrated the Peruvian conquistadors. Likewise, Palentino's chronicle proposed a negative vision of them, including Garcilaso's father.

The tradition of *viri illustres* permitted Garcilaso to honor the conquistadors, because starting with Petrarch, the illustrious man was defined not by his wealth or power but by the works through which his individual virtues became manifest and from which he gained fame and glory.[16] Furthermore, Fernando del Pulgar's work included among his *viri illustres* several cases in which the individuals lacked noble lineage but achieved honor through virtuous deeds.[17]

While the subgenre of *viri illustres,* as established by Petrarch and Boccaccio and imitated by Sedeño in Spain, had its point of departure in heroes and historical figures from antiquity, Pulgar projected the model exclusively on contemporary history. He thereby introduced a different point of comparison between the heroes of the classical past and those of recent Spanish history. Instead of assuming that the classical heroes were prototypes repeated through history, Pulgar confronts them with Spanish men of virtue to demonstrate the moral superiority of the latter.[18] Garcilaso assumes Pulgar's perspective when he refers to his ancestor Garcilaso de la Vega, the conquistador from Córdoba, and to his "victory over the Moors in the fields of Toledo, greater than the Roman's and a more glorious trophy than Romulus' " (Garcilaso 1944, dedication, 8).[19] Similarly, he describes the conquistadors as "true Alcibiadeses and Christian Achilles' " (8), and he refers to the "Peruvian weapons, worthier of praise than those of the Greeks and the Trojans" (Garcilaso 1944, prologue, 10). Finally, when he alludes to the myth of the origin of Rome, he compares the Roman she-wolf with Spain, mother of sons raised "better than Romulus and Remus" (11).

We have observed that the figure of the Virgin and the concept of theological nobility permitted Garcilaso to unite two worlds in conflict. The election of the model of *viri illustres* fulfills a similar function, allowing Garcilaso to connect the Inca warriors, who had pacified Perú, with the later Spanish conquistadors. In fact, Garcilaso proclaims the former, as much as the latter, to be superior to the heroic warriors of antiquity. Thus, in the prologue of Part II, the author refers to the Inca conquest elaborated in Part I as "glorious enterprises . . . which can compete with those of the Dariuses of Persia, Ptolemies of Egypt, Alexanders of Greece, and Cypions of Rome" (10). It is significant that Garcilaso would omit this comparison in Part I and use it in the same pages in which he proposes the theme of the Spaniards' heroic deeds in Perú. By introducing this comparison in the prologue, Garcilaso creates a bridge identifying the heroic Incas with the heroic Spanish conquistadores in a single historical continuum. In Part I he compared the Inca civilization with classical antiquity, not in matters of war but in matters of religion, in order to demonstrate the importance of the Incas within a providential plan.[20]

The model of illustrious men had an important exemplary function. In the preface to *De viris illustribus,* Petrarch announced his intention to offer these examples of virtue as a way to reprimand vices (Petrarca 1955, 218) and to show his readers which actions should be imitated and which avoided (224). Garcilaso revives this principle and applies it primarily to the conquistadors' descendants and successors, whom he urges to follow in "the footsteps of their elders . . . so as not to deny their lineage and stature" (Garcilaso 1944, prologue, 11). Thus, the exemplary function remains linked to the theme of lineage, a controversial subject in the texts of the period and one associated with the concept of nobility. The model of the *vir illustris* is not necessarily identified with the nobleman; on the contrary, we have shown that Petrarch implicitly proposes a distinction between these two. The basis of the equivalence that Garcilaso proposes between the virtuous conquistadors and their descendants resided in the idea that noble blood inclines man to act virtuously. In Garcilaso's case, the matter is complex, as Durand already showed in his study of the concept of honor with reference to Garcilaso (Durand 1976). However, the prologue of Part II does not employ the notion of lineage—as it does later in the text when Garcilaso debates the origin of Almagro—as the basis of the "illustrious" Spaniards' action. Noble lineage serves, rather, as a useful example of action to be emulated in the present and in the future. In other words, the concept of the illustrious man supports the notion of a foundational nobility that bequeaths more than blood, namely a model of conduct to his successors.

Obviously, we cannot maintain that Garcilaso breaks with the principle of nobility by blood, since he himself employs this principle in his autobiographical references in his texts, referring repeatedly to his maternal and paternal lineage. When alluding to the *Relación de la descendencia de Garci Pérez de Vargas,* conceived initially as the preface-dedication of the *Florida,* Durand maintains that "the basic fact of writing genealogies reveals the author's appreciation of nobility itself" (Durand, 1976, 95). Nevertheless, in the same text Garcilaso tries to reconcile exemplary virtue and lineage when he affirms that to boast about illustrious ancestors without imitating them is "more vituperation than honor" (Garcilaso 1951, 232).[21]

Reference to the origin of the conquistadors is not completely absent in the prologue. In the passage where Garcilaso admonishes the descendants of the conquistadors to imitate his model and not to disgrace their lineage, he exhorts them to take forward "the good name of their lineage, *which seems to originate in heaven, towards which, as their own and true fatherland, they must direct their steps as they go through this exile and valley of tears*" (Garcilaso 1944, prologue, 11, emphasis mine). Given the intellectual and intertextual context of the prologue, we know that Garcilaso is not simply referring to a religious topic that was very common at the time. The mention of a "heavenly origin" associated with the lineage of the conquistadors can only be explained with reference to the providentialist vision through which Garcilaso ultimately perceived the conquest. If the model of illustrious men permitted Garcilaso to praise the characters of history on the basis of their virtuous actions, it was because these individuals were essentially guided by a providential plan, the origin of all virtue. Indeed, if on the mundane level the Incas and Spaniards are joined together as *viri illustres,* on the religious level they are united in a progressive vision of providentialist history.

This matter is even more complex, however, given that in the first part of the *Commentaries*—to which Garcilaso refers repeatedly in the second part—the author revealed that the Incas had believed themselves to be of divine origin (especially in Garcilaso 1966/1, I, xv, 40–43). Even if Garcilaso regarded this belief as a "fable," he recognized that in the eyes of the Indians, the virtuous actions of the Inca rulers confirmed their divinity. This complex framework of artful implications opens the text to many interpretations. In fact, comparing this passage to the one that declares the conquistadors' "origin from Heaven" and that we have explained as an allusion to the providentialist base of history, we can conclude that the "fable" of the Incas' divine origin was proposed to convey another essential truth: the providential-ist origin of the Incas' actions.

According to Garcilaso's exhortation to the conquistadors' de-scendants, "heaven" is not only the origin of the conquistadors but also their "own and true fatherland." The text obviously re-peats a commonplace of Christian doctrine. It is interesting to note, however, that it is framed in a context that serves to ex-plain Perú's history. From this perspective, it is easy to construct the circular chain of historical phases that the passage envisions: Heaven as origin, the Incas, the conquistadors, their descen-dants, Heaven as destination. This circular vision, elaborated on a providentialist basis, seems to suggest the incorporation of Andean myth into history, but at the same time it provides a per-fectly flawless meaning to the succession of events in Peruvian history. Neither the dedication nor the prologue makes any ref-erence to those acts of human passions and the Devil's ministry which led to the inevitable destruction of the Inca Empire, al-though the main body of the text discusses these aspects at length. On the contrary, both of these texts omit any reference whatsoever to the elements of human origin that would dis-tort the perfect plan of Providence. In this way, the dedication and the prologue form part of what we can designate the utopian textual spaces in the *Royal Commentaries,* that is to say, the micro-texts in which Garcilaso abandons the detailed narrative of mere events in favor of a disquisition on the essence of history. The overall intent is to fashion a coherent meaning out of the chaotic events that marked the disappearance of the old Inca Empire.

The beginning of the prologue announces three reasons for the writing of both parts of the *Royal Commentaries.* The first and second reasons are to honor both of the protagonists of Peruvian history, the Incas and the Spaniards; the third reason involves the objectives of the author himself:

The third reason for having undertaken this work has been to make profitable use of time in an *honorable* occupation, and not squander it on idleness, mother of vices, stepmother of *virtue,* root, source and origin of a thousand evils that may be avoided with the *honest* task of study, worthy occupation of witty and of *noble* souls; so that these might entertain themselves in a *genteel manner* [*ahidalgadamente*], as befitting their *quality*, and spend the days of their lives in *praiseworthy* activities, and so that those might graze their fine taste in the pastures of wit and increase their wealth in the excellence of knowledge, which yield and amount to more for the *soul* than either the rent of estates, or the right of perpetual ownership of the pearls of the Orient and the silver of our Potocsi. (Garcilaso 1944, prologue, 12, emphasis mine)

The writing of the *Commentaries* is now proposed as an exemplary act to readers. In a previous passage, the author called upon the Indians, Mestizos, and Creoles to follow the example of his ancestors and to train "in the army of Pallas and Mars and in the school of Mercury and Apollo" (11). Garcilaso presents himself at the end of the prologue as an example of this advice, and then he adds those dedications that he had written for his first book, the translation of Hebreo's *Dialogues* (1590). Garcilaso presents himself to King Phillip II of Spain and explains, on the one hand, his double lineage ("being of the family and blood of the Incas" and "son of Garcilaso de la Vega . . . conquistador and settler of the kingdoms and provinces of Perú" [13]), and, on the other hand, his activities during his youth "in the army . . . at the service of Your Sacred Majesty" (12), and also during his mature years "in the exercise of reading and translating" (12–13).

Garcilaso's recontextualization of his earlier dedication within the structure of the prologue of Part II of the *Commentaries* permits him to make evident his implicit meaning. Inserted after a text that ponders the foundation of authentic nobility in virtue and works and that proposes an interpretation of Peruvian history, these passages acquire an exemplary dimension. As has been noted on several occasions, Garcilaso represents himself as an expression of the synthesis of Peruvian history, but he does so by depicting himself as an active agent of this history, as an individual who takes the "virtuous" model from his ancestors and follows them "in the army of Pallas and Mars" as well as "in the school of Mercury and Apollo."

Rejecting the "dispute between arms and letters," Garcilaso makes the two mutually complementary and equivalent, not only by repeating the slogan "with pen and sword" from his relative Garcilaso the poet[22] but also by qualifying the act of translating the *Dialogues* as "the rashness of a soldier" (16). This permits him to project upon the exercise of writing the values associated with the exercise of arms. In the passage previously cited, explaining Garcilaso's third reason for writing the *Commentaries,* we see that the terms Garcilaso uses to refer to nobility are the same ones that he uses to refer to the act of writing: honorable, virtuous, honest, noble, a genteel exercise (*ahidalgadamente*), praiseworthy.

This passage, like many others, demonstrates Garcilaso's thoughtful readings of the treatises on nobility and the books of illustrious men. The work of Juan Benito Guardiola offers a good synthesis of the position in that period of the exercise of letters in relation to nobility. In his *Tratado de nobleza,* Guardiola devotes three chapters to this topic. Summarizing diverse authorities, he affirms that

> science illustrates greatly, as it not only ennobles internally but also externally. It ennobles reason by illuminating and clarifying it, and reason thus illuminated governs the body and rules it with good and virtuous customs. (1591, 23)

Similarly, Ducci dedicates a chapter to "nobility originated from men of letters" (1974, 131), where he maintains that letters produce nobility because of their usefulness to the Republic. In the same manner, books about *viri illustres* also included models of individuals who had acquired fame and honor through letters, for instance, the portraits of the Bishop of Coria in the work of Pulgar (1923, 141) and of Cicero in Sedeño (1590, 218). As the quotation of Guardiola indicates, the nobility of the practice of letters is, more than anything, a spiritual and internal nobility. Another passage from Guardiola's book (which refers explicitly to Erasmus) develops this concept with greater precision:

> Those who presume of their lineages and ancestors have the walls of their houses painted with the shields, pavises, and portraits of

their predecessors; but learned men have their soul decked and embellished with good disciplines and arts. As the nature of the soul is more excellent than the nature of the body, so are the embellishments and ornaments of wit finer and worthy of greater esteem than the insignias of external nobility. (1591, 23v)

This quotation clearly explains the final part of the passage about the third reason for writing the *Commentaries,* in which Garcilaso affirms the spiritual benefit that the exercise of letters provides him. Thus, Garcilaso inserts his own personal history into the cyclical structure that explains social history: Garcilaso, descendant of Incas and of conquistadors, of those who seem to "originate in heaven," cultivates through his own work the return to his "own and true fatherland."

The character of the prologue to the second part of the *Commentaries* as a "utopian text" allowed Garcilaso to make sense out of the history of Perú as a whole. Furthermore, it allowed him to explain his own personal history. That is probably why Garcilaso superimposes upon his circular vision of history a parallel circular structure of texts as a conclusion to his prologue. In effect, by including in this prologue the dedications to his translation of the *Dialogues,* Garcilaso returns to his textual origin and closes his last work with pages excerpted from his first one. The dedication to Phillip II was also the announcement of several future writing projects: the "primitiae" (12) of the translation of León Hebreo's *Dialogues,* the account of "the journey that Hernando de Soto made to Florida" (14), and lastly "the conquest of my land" with "its customs, rites and ceremonies" (14). The prologue of Part II of the *Royal Commentaries* is the exemplary demonstration of the fulfillment of these projects.

As we have seen, in the complex gallery of texts that made up Garcilaso's library, the treatises of nobility and the books of *viri illustres,* in conjunction with the providentialist thesis, were fundamental models for his explanation of Peruvian history. The comparison between this historical vision, as it is proposed in the prologue to Part II of the *Commentaries,* and the historical facts presented in the book affirms the utopian character of the former. However, through the theme of exemplarity, the prologue transcends the merely intellectual utopian dream by invoking a model of conduct for its readers: the Indians, Mestizos, and Creoles of Perú.

NOTES

1. Durand observed that the catalog we know indicates what the executors of Garcilaso's will found after his death in 1616, i.e., his library in Córdoba, which probably "was not the same he owned in Montilla in 1591" (Durand 1948, 240). Durand was able to compare the inventory to what (thanks to the quotations in Garcilaso's books) we know he read or possessed, and in doing so he found notable absences (Durand 1948, 261–264).

2. Garcilaso refers to Plutarch when he cites Agustín de Zárate's parallel between Pizarro and Almagro in book 3, chapter 7 of the *Royal Commentaries,* Part II.

3. Petrarch's works are mentioned in entry nos. 120, 127, and 136. Furthermore, no. 167 corresponds to *Sonetos y Canciones,* which Durand identifies as one of the Castilian translations (perhaps Enrique Garcés') of the *Canzoniere.* Hereafter, the numbers employed correspond to the entry numbers in the inventory published by Durand in 1948.

4. There are two versions of the "Proemio," a long one that corresponds to a stage of the work between 1351 and 1353, and a short one that corresponds to the state of the work between 1371 and 1374. A summary of the transformations of this book with English translations of the two versions can be found in the work of Benjamin G. Kohl (1974).

5. Durand attributes the Spanish translation to Pedro López de Ayala and to Alfonso García de Santa María (1948, 251) and mentions only the editions of 1495 and 1552. V. Zaccaria, from whom we take the information on the edition of 1511, considers it to be an anonymous translation ("Introduzione" to Boccaccio, lii n). Besides this book, the inventory of the library cites Boccaccio's *Filocolo* (no. 121), *Corbaccio* (under the Spanish title of *Labirinto de amor,* no. 162) and an imprecise "Juan Bocacio" (no. 117), which Durand believed to be part of a volume of the *Decameron,* a work referred to in passing in the *Commentaries.*

6. *Il Convivio* was published in Florence in 1490 and in Venice in 1521, 1529, and 1531. Although the generic title "works by Dante" can designate the celebrated *Comedy,* I personally believe that Garcilaso knew and used to good advantage the ideas expressed in *Il Convivio.*

7. Garcilaso's interest in Piccolomini's work is shown by two other volumes in his library: (1) *Della institutione morale* (Venice, 1560) (no.

86

132), which according to Durand amplifies *Il Convivio* and is cited in the dedication to Maximilian of Austria in the translation *Diálogos de amor;* and (2) a volume of his *Comedies* (no. 182). For a study of Garcilaso's exposition on the Neoplatonic theory of love, it is necessary to consider the book dedicated to this topic in *Della institutione di tutta la vita de l'huomo nato nòbile.*

8. A summary of the little information that we have about this writer can be found in Pedro M. Cátedra's preliminary study to his edition of Sedeño's *Coloquios de amor y bienaventuranza.* Besides these two works, Sedeño was the author of a versification of the Celestina (edited by M. Marciales, Mérida [Venezuela], 1971). He should not be confused with the captain Juan Sedeño, translator into Spanish of the *Arcadia* by Sannazaro and the *Gerusalemme liberata* by Tasso.

9. Although the engravings are different, this motif is the basis of the illustrations at the frontispiece of the first edition in the two printings dated 1616 and 1617.

10. Mazzotti (1995, 401) has noted that Garcilaso could have adopted and reinterpreted such Christian images as "Sol de justicia" (Sun of justice) and "Lucero del alva" (the morning star) from the Inca tradition. Perhaps the attributes selected to describe the Virgin Mary obeyed a similar intention.

11. It is vital to reinstate the unitary title of the two parts of this major work and to abandon the spurious *General History of Peru* imposed on it by the first editors. I have given some factual reasons for this argument in my 1995 article.

12. Bartolus's classification is commented on by Keen 1984, 199–200. For Guardiola (1591), cf. fols. 2v–3v.

13. Ducci's passage concludes by stating that the nobility of Columbus's descendants should be honored, since "he was the first who, with the discovery of those kingdoms, made possible the dissemination of the light of true faith" (Ducci 1974, 128).

14. It is surprising that in the long article dedicated to Ferdinand the Catholic, there is no mention of Columbus's voyages nor of the possession of the American territories claimed in the name of the Catholic Sovereigns.

15. Garcilaso praises both texts. However, he seems to be very conscious of the poetic nature of Ercilla's work because he refers to his "galanos versos" (elegant verses) (Garcilaso 1966/1, I, XXVI, 64). In addition, Garcilaso objects to the work of Castellanos because it is written in verse (he calls it an "authentic and elegant history, although written in verse," Garcilaso 1966/2, VIII, XIV, 1468).

16. "Besides, not every rich and powerful person is similarly distin-

guished; these are the result of good luck, while the illustrious ones are the product of glory and virtue. In any case, I have not promised to describe lucky men, but illustrious ones. . . . I have promised, I repeat, to describe those men whom we call illustrious and who are remembered the most by their magnificent and illustrious deeds, although in fact some of these men are relatively unknown" (Petrarch, quoted in Kohl 1974, 140–141).

17. Don Alfonso, bishop of Avila (Pulgar 1923, 142), and Don Tello, bishop of Córdoba (151), are "from the lineage of farmers." However, it is true that the ecclesiastical hierarchy appears in Pulgar's work as more flexible than the military.

18. Examples of this comparison can be seen in the portraits of Don Fadrique (Pulgar 1923, 26), the Duke of Haro (34), the Marqués de Santillana (45), and Juan de Sahavedra (111).

19. Pulgar writes about this Garcilaso de la Vega: "Praiseworthy indeed is Oracio Teocles, Roman, who fought against the Tuscans at the bridge of Suhicia, in the Tiber River, and detained them fighting while an arch of that bridge was torn down so that the Romans might be saved; yet no less estimable is the effort of this Garcilaso who, seeing that his people were at risk as they fled from the onslaught of the Moorish knights that pursued them, turned to his enemies with great courage, offering his own life in exchange for the health of his people, and holding down a pass, deterred their advance for such a time as to allow his people to save themselves" (Pulgar 1923, 110).

20. When referring to the "idolatry and the gods they worshipped before the Incas," he concludes: "we need not be surprised that such unlettered and untaught people should have fallen into these follies, for it is well known that the Greeks and Romans, who prided themselves so greatly on their learning, had thirty thousand gods when their empire was at its height" (Garcilaso 1966/1, I, VI, 31). And then, when explaining why the Indians made a cult of their Incas, he affirms: "they accordingly adored him, just as the pagans of antiquity, though less savage, gave worship to others who conferred similar benefits" (Garcilaso 1966/1, I, XXV, 62).

21. In this passage Garcilaso probably had in mind the following text from Dante's *Convivio:* "He who degenerates from his good father or ancestor and is wicked, is not only vile but vile in extreme, worthy of scorn and vituperation more than any villain" (150). Garcilaso later defends the idea (in a passage that was ultimately eliminated) that the unworthy successors, because of their "hated deeds and cruel greed" (Garcilaso 1951, 237) must be excluded from noble succession. Lorenzo

Ducci dedicates several chapters of his treatise to the causes of descent into infamy and thus the loss of nobility (Ducci 1974, especially 87–90).

22. In the *Relación de la descendencia,* when he refers to the poet (236), in a passage of the dedication of the *Dialogues* (Garcilaso 1944, prologue, 13), and in the coat of arms that he himself prepared (reproduced in Part I, III).

Seven

JOSÉ ANTONIO MAZZOTTI

Garcilaso and the Origins of Garcilacism:
The Role of the Royal Commentaries
in the Development of a Peruvian
National Imaginaire

AS IS COMMON KNOWLEDGE, the *oeuvre* and person of Garcilaso
Inca de la Vega have occasioned numerous interpretations, and
responses ranging from superlative praise to an increasing dis-
trust. Especially since the nineteenth century, Garcilaso has been
the cause of many ideological battles, whether fought by hispan-
ists, indigenists, or mestizists. Most of these debates range beyond
the field of literary criticism. Garcilaso's histories have been used
as a point of departure for imagining a cultural past and for con-
structing a no less imaginary future.

The subject of this essay is the study of some of the initial readings of Garcilaso, specifically of the *Royal Commentaries* after the
first edition of its two parts appeared in 1609 and 1617, respectively. These readings may not be the most rigorous or the most
well known, but they are useful for rethinking the role of the
Royal Commentaries in the formation of different ethnic-national
projects since the seventeenth century in Perú. At the same time,
our examination of the initial readings will lead us to our own
interpretation, in which we will consider two forms of reception:
a learned one and an aural one, according to the possible meanings that different social subjects might have used for their own
purposes.[1]

Before beginning an examination of early readings of the

Royal Commentaries, three historical and terminological points deserve attention. The first is that the Creole readings in the seventeenth and eighteenth centuries took place in a colonial and therefore a frontier and nonmetropolitan context. The second is that the term "Garcilacism" is used here in a broad sense, not limited to the field of literary criticism. The latter is a recent product of the specialization of labor, remote from the discursive conceptions and practice of the intellectuals of the period.[2] The third is that the concept of nation is used here in the sense it had acquired in the time of Garcilaso: a human group with ethnic, regional, cultural, and racial ties, quite distinct from the modern and enlightened idea of nation as egalitarian, as homogenizing and embracing different groups with distinctions merely of social class. The latter concept has emerged with the so-called modern nation-state, which tends to develop a single "national" and linguistic identity. However, Garcilaso and his immediate readers were familiar only with the first meaning. The present study assumes the theoretical framework that Anthony Smith, John Armstrong, and James Kellas, among others, have advanced for the better understanding of the ethnic origins of modern nations. Their stance counterbalances the more frequent approach to nationalism, conceived as a cultural artifact of modernity and thus as an instrument of resistance in postcolonial societies (see Kohn and Anderson, for example, for this latter definition).

With reference to the *Royal Commentaries,* another fundamental premise is the well-known and indisputable early authority of the work as a source of information about the Incas and the conquest of Perú. Even before its publication, historians such as Gregorio García mentioned it, and philologists such as Ambrosio de Morales praised it for its elegant style and rigorous analysis of the Quechua language (see Cerrón-Palomino). Despite Marcos Jiménez de la Espada's editions of Pedro de Cieza's second part of his *Crónica del Perú,* Pachacuti Yamqui's *Relación . . . ,* Betanzos' *Suma . . . ,* and other Andean sources at the end of the nineteenth century, and despite the discovery of Guamán Poma's *Nueva Coronica* in 1908 and Marcelino Menéndez y Pelayo's comments about the utopian character of the *Royal Commentaries,* Garcilaso's

José Antonio Mazzotti

work had attained a very well-established reputation for truth during the first two centuries of its existence. This was due to the aristocratic and bicultural origins of its author and to his ingenious use of rhetoric within the historical language of the Renaissance. The *Royal Commentaries* was an inevitable source of information for anyone who wished to write about the Incas and the origins of the Creole and mestizo population in Perú.

Our study of initial readings of the *Royal Commentaries* seeks to extract from these "origins of Garcilacism" the mechanism of ethnic identity they propose, as well as some of the consequences they have for contemporary Garcilacism. The subsequent analyses will not focus on Convent chroniclers of the Spanish conquest, or on polygraphers for their own sake, especially since they form part of a long list of Colonial authors already studied in other disciplines and even in different trends within literary criticism. Our interest lies rather in pointing out how their readings of the *Royal Commentaries* can be articulated in a larger context that allows us to understand the scope of the early authority of the work and the critical tradition which established that authority.

The first early interpretation considered here is a summary of the *Royal Commentaries* discovered by Jiménez de la Espada in a group of manuscripts which includes the *Relación* . . . by Pachacuti Yamqui, *Ritos y fábulas de los Incas* by Cristóbal de Molina, the important manuscript of Huarochirí, and other valuable documents, catalogued with the number 3169 in the National Library of Madrid. In many of these manuscripts it is possible to discern the handwriting of Francisco de Avila, a Cuzco extirpator of idolatries. Recently, Duviols (Santa Cruz Pachacuti 1993, 15–16) has insisted on the fact that this brief summary of the *Royal Commentaries* was also written in Avila's hand. Since it is dated June 1, 1613, it is plausible to assume that this summary constitutes the first explicit testimony of reception of the *Commentaries* in the New World.

The possible intertextuality between the *Royal Commentaries* and Pachacuti's *Relación,* as also suggested by Duviols (1993, 92–93) in his recent edition of the latter, lends credence to the position that the *Royal Commentaries*' providentialist scheme had been welcomed by the local Indian chiefs for the purpose of accommodating their own interests within the colonial hierarchy. In this sense, the *Royal Commentaries* may have had an important discursive authority from the first years of its existence, although Pachacuti Yamqui did not even mention Garcilaso's work nor did Avila ever publish his summary. The reading of the *Royal Commentaries* contained in the summary would only become public some years later in the work of a distinguished Lima Creole, Fray Buenaventura de Salinas y Córdova.

Salinas's *Memorial de historias del Nuevo Mundo Pirú* was published in Lima in 1630. There Salinas established himself as one of the first voices of defense and praise of the Creoles in his native city, Lima. His appellation of this city as "Cabeça destos Reynos" (Head of these Kingdoms) manifests an alternative perspective towards the well-known title of "Cabeza de los Reinos del Perú" (Head of the Kingdoms of Perú) that Cuzco had received during the first decades of the conquest, because of the importance of this Andean city in Incan history. The space of cultural identity called Perú, as John Rowe points out in 1954, was the space of the colonial organization on the bases of the ancient Tawantinsuyu or country of the Incas. In this way, the premises of an apparently natural continuity were already established in the very Creole conception of "Pirú" or Perú. However, the dominant position of the Spanish "nation" (peninsulars and Creoles) within the Peruvian context required cultural icons which would support their self-accorded prestige. For that reason, Salinas's *Memorial* was dedicated to Phillip IV, "Powerful King of Spain and the Indies . . . to incline him . . . to ask of the Pope the canonization of our Patron Francisco de Solano," as Salinas wrote on the inside cover of the book.

The obvious intention of Salinas's dedication was to exalt Lima and the Creoles as descendants of the conquerors so that the Creoles would achieve the declared goal of Solano's canonization. Despite the courageous denunciation of the Spaniard's exploitation of the indigenous population, especially in the Third Discourse, Salinas reveals an interesting strategy of Creole justification, whose arguments are based on a series of what we could call vertical typifications.[3] In the initial chapter of the First Discourse he traces "the origins of the first Indians who inhabited Perú." His declared sources are the *quipus* as instruments of the official indigenous history, as well as texts by Peter Martyr, Fernández de Oviedo, Pedro de Cieza, López de Gómara, "Garcilasso Inga," and others. In the overall context of historians of the New World, Salinas was not the only one to adopt such a selection and intertextual composition. It did, however, allow him to decide which versions and passages he would elaborate for the general argumentation of the work. If Salinas' declared intention was to achieve the canonization of Francisco de Solano, what better argument than references to sources which speak of the "barbarism and pagan politics of the Inca kings" (1630, unnumbered folio). Garcilaso would be used only for the arguments related to "the treasures and richness of the Incas" (First Discourse, chapter 3). Only in those aspects would Garcilaso appear as a historian "to whom we should give credit, for having experienced what he tells about this land" (unnumbered folio). Salinas's version of the origin of the Incas was based, therefore, not on the fable about Manco Capac and Mama Ocllo related in the *Royal Commentaries* (Garcilaso 1966/1, I, XV–XVII, 40–46) but on the marginal versions that Garcilaso briefly mentions in the next chapter (XVIII, 47–49). I refer here specifically to the "deception" that Manco Capac's mother perpetrates by affirming the solar origins of her son, and to Salinas's mention of Lake Titicaca as the point of origin of the Incas, without naming the two founding siblings.

In order to distance himself from Garcilaso's version, Salinas refers to four ages preceding the appearance of the Incas. He shares this approach with Guamán Poma de Ayala (or Waman Puma), and it has given rise to many speculations concerning Salinas's access to Waman Puma's then unpublished *Nueva Coronica*. It is, however, known (see Duviols 1983) that the source for both Salinas and Waman Puma might have been the lost manuscripts written by Francisco Fernández de Córdoba. In any case, what matters is that Salinas does not propose a common version of history which characterized the times before the Incas

94

as a general chaos. The Incas would appear as idolaters whose major merit was the construction of impressive buildings and the accumulation of immense treasures (indirect praise of the mineral resources of the Andean land).

On the other hand, Salinas's praise of Pizarro and other early conquerors of three or four generations ago establishes a prestigious lineage for Salinas's contemporary Creoles. Salinas's claim to have composed an epic poem in celebration of Pizarro's deeds would be attested one hundred years later by another prominent Creole, Pedro de Peralta, in his *Lima Fundada*. Salinas wrote,

> About Pizarro, who navigated among pearls of the Southern Sea and traversed thirsty deserts giving strength to his travails and encouragement to his hope, and courageously dared to seize from the forehead and hands of Atahuallpa the supreme kingdom of America, throwing it to the feet of the Crown and on the Catholic shoulders of Spain, [about Pizarro] barely is his name heard in Perú, barely are his great deeds recounted, nor are his courage and bravery praised. Who has known how to relate the singular and unbelievable deeds of these Conquistadores, whom the bad fortune of sea and land had made explorers of the fruits and richness of Perú? What Spanish Virgil has taken in charge this navigation, like the other one who chanted Aeneas' voyage through the Tyrrhenian Sea? What Valerius Flaco of the renowned University of the [City of] Kings has been willing to celebrate the golden tuft of wool found by so many Jasons, and the seas navigated by so many courageous Argonauts? (Salinas 1630, unnumbered folio)

And so, in a long exhortation to academicians and Creoles in general, Salinas claims the restitution of a prestige extremely pertinent for the kind of Creole identity he seeks to formulate. For this reason, a passage in the *Commentaries* glorifying Pizarro (Garcilaso 1966/2, I, I, 634) will be Salinas's principal source for some of the anecdotes in his own narration about the conquest. Another passage (Garcilaso 1966/2, I, XI–XII, 654–657), about the tiger and the lion that the Inca authorities of Tumbes send against Pedro de Candía, is slightly altered in Salinas's work (First

Discourse, chapter 5). Salinas does not represent the Inca governor as the one responsible for this attack, but claims rather that the female chief Capullana loosed the cats in order to test the valor of the Christians. At the same time, according to Salinas, she entertains and regales Pizarro and his soldiers with tales from the Greek and Roman classics, referring indirectly to the passage in the *Aeneid* about Aeneas and Dido in Carthage. Salinas's claim to be a "Spanish Virgil" was attested a century later by Peralta. The latter's contemporary and colleague, Pedro José Bermúdez de la Torre y Solier, wrote in his prologue to Peralta's *Lima Fundada* that Peralta was the awaited "Spanish Virgil" who fulfilled a general and public longing. Thus, a type of discourse was established by a Creole elite who utilized Garcilaso in their own interests, deriving general meaning from selected passages of the *Royal Commentaries,* and, in doing so, imposing a particular interpretation on Garcilaso's work.

Another example of early interpretations of Inca history, and of Garcilaso, is the Augustinian priest Antonio de la Calancha's *Cronica Moralizada* (1639), which praised the virtues and superiority of the Creoles not only over the Indian, mestizo, and black population but over even the Spanish peninsulars. Yet, besides establishing a historical and cultural prestige for the Creoles, as Salinas had done, Calancha's *Cronica Moralizada* defended Spanish interests against the constant threat of British and Dutch corsairs. Sir Walter Raleigh's prophecy about the restitution of the Incas with the help of the English crown, as narrated in his *A Voyage to the Discovery of Guyana,* was mocked by Calancha.[4] He writes:

> What Walter Raleigh says is ludicrous, and he then alleges Spanish witnesses who assert that in the Temple of the Sun in Cuzco a prediction was found which said that the Kings of England would restore to these Indians their kingdom, freeing them from servitude and returning them to their Empire; he must have dreamed this, or he projected his own desire; he must have used the figure of Anagram, which by splitting syllables and mixing concepts, concocts various meanings for a word; Ingalaterra [England], divided,

is purported to signify 'Inga' [Inca] and then 'la tierra' [the land], and on this he based his prediction, saying that the land of the Inga will be [beholden to] England; something so ridiculous makes a mockery of Walter. (Calancha 1639, fols. 115–116)

John Rowe (1976, 25–32) notes Raleigh's prediction in his article on Inca nationalism of the eighteenth century. However, Rowe does not mention Calancha's criticism, nor the fact that by 1600 there was already a Dutch translation of the above-quoted passage from Raleigh's work. Theodore de Bry probably derived the information for his own Latin treatise entitled *America* from this Dutch translation. The Spanish historian and editor González de Barcia also sought to refute Raleigh's prediction in 1723, quoting de Bry's Latin version of Raleigh's account in the second edition of Garcilaso's *Royal Commentaries*. According to the information offered by Suardo and Mugaburu in their respective *Diaries* of Lima, the British threat to Spanish power and their alliance with the surviving Incas in El Dorado or El Paititi was a current subject during the seventeenth century.[5] Thus, the legend of the British restoration of the land to the Incas preceded the second edition of the *Royal Commentaries*.

In some respects, Calancha used the *Royal Commentaries* as a source of information and a pattern of authority. For example, one of the most polemic themes in Garcilaso's work is the Inca religion. In this area, Calancha did not have any problem accepting some of the postulates of the *Royal Commentaries*, such as the superiority and invisibility of the god Pachacamac[6] or the five-hundred-year duration of the Inca Empire as a natural cycle.[7]

There are, however, some possible misreadings in Calancha, such as the interpretation of the word *wak'a* (a sacred place or object worthy of admiration), which Garcilaso differentiates from the verb *waq'ay* (to cry). Despite Garcilaso's persistent philologic endeavor, Calancha ignores the first etymology to follow López de Gómara in his translations.[8] Calancha also lends credence to the legend about the sojourn of Saint Thomas the Apostle in the Andes, despite Garcilaso's arguments against it. Thus, Calancha proposes an early and pre-Hispanic evangelization as a premise for the justification of the Spanish presence. The latter would represent a restoration of the original and ancient belief of the Indians, spread in the New World by Saint Thomas. With Calancha's pro-Creole manipulation of Inca history, Saint Thomas becomes the true Andean Wiraqucha.[9] For the same reason, like Salinas, Calancha does not adopt the fable of Manco Capac and Mama Ocllo as an explanation of the origin of the Incas. He uses instead a popular version mentioned by Garcilaso in which Manco Capac becomes the first Inca thanks to a deception of his mother, who lied about her son's solar origin. Calancha thus accommodates one among several versions within his own work, and by transtextualizing Garcilaso's book, transforms it into an indispensable support for certain of his arguments.

A relatively marginal case of the early assimilation of Garcilaso, this time not the work of a historian, is the *Arte de la lengua yunga,* or Mochica, published in 1644 by Fernando de la Carrera, a Creole priest from the coastal city of Trujillo. In his "Dedication to the King," de la Carrera attributes to himself the same role of intermediary between languages and cultures that Garcilaso had assumed before him, both as philologist and historian. De la Carrera even points out that he "decided to write a grammar of this very difficult language, having sucked and learned it in my childhood, although not recognizing any advantage to the Indians themselves" (quoted by Medina 1965, vol. 1, 342). In addition to the expression "to suck [the indigenous language] in one's mother milk," so frequent in Garcilaso, de la Carrera remembers another expression of the *Royal Commentaries,* "to cry tears of blood" (Garcilaso 1966/1, I, XVII, 46), which becomes "to cry drops from the heart's blood" in de la Carrera when he was moved by the Indians' incomprehension of the Christian faith. Thus, the author of the *Royal Commentaries* is recognized in de la Carrera's work as a unique authority on Peruvian themes.

De la Carrera's favorable reading of Garcilaso was overshadowed by that of the Franciscan friar Diego de Córdoba Salinas, brother of the aforementioned Buenaventura de Salinas. In 1651, Diego de Córdoba published his *Coronica de la Religiosissima*

Provincia de los Doze Apóstoles del Perú, known today as the *Crónica Franciscana de las Provincias del Perú* after its second edition of 1957. In this history of the Franciscan Order in Perú, Córdoba, like Salinas, quotes Garcilaso only to support specific aspects of his narration of indigenous history, and only as long as Garcilaso's arguments are compatible with the Franciscan version. For example, Córdoba (1957, 17) quotes Blas Valera in Garcilaso's version with respect to the five-hundred-year duration of the Inca Empire. Córdoba also affirms the superior and creator status of Pachacamac in the Cuzco pantheon (ibid.) and repeats Garcilaso's explanation about the name Huiracoha given to the first Spaniards (19). Most important, however, is the fact that Garcilaso becomes the quarantor for the veracity of José de Acosta's *Historia natural y moral de las Indias* (1590), which constitutes Córdoba's central hypotext (Genette 1982). Again like Buenaventura de Salinas, Córdoba (chapter 3) uses the *Royal Commentaries* as his main source only when speaking of the magnificence of the Inca palaces and buildings. Having completed his exposition of the indigenous past, Córdoba then attempts to demonstrate the Creoles' superior intelligence (in the third book of his work).

Thirty years later another friar from Lima, Juan Meléndez, includes Garcilaso among his sources in the initial section ("To the Reader") of his *Tesoros verdaderos de las Yndias* (1681), a long and very eulogistic account of the prominent people born in Perú. Meléndez devotes his work, however, primarily to the exaltation of the "clerical and saintly" men who have flourished in the Peruvian viceroyalty and who constitute, as the title of Meléndez's book says, the "true treasures" that Perú has to offer to Spain.

An important example of the assimilation of the *Royal Commentaries* into the formulation of a Creole *imaginaire* is the work of Pedro de Peralta y Barnuevo, who carried on the challenge expressed in 1630 by Buenaventura de Salinas. However, to better explain the assimilation of Garcilaso's work in Peralta's epic poem *Lima Fundada* (1732), we must first refer to a minor work in Peralta's *oeuvre:* the *Descripción de las Fiestas Reales* (1723), also known as *Júbilos de Lima,* a work in which Peralta demonstrates a much deeper knowledge of Garcilaso's book than he evinces in the *Lima Fundada*.[10]

It is possible that the second edition of the *Royal Commentaries* had already arrived in Lima when Peralta was engaged in writing his narration about the feasts held in the city for several months of the year to celebrate the royal weddings of Luis Fernando, Prince of Asturias (the Spanish equivalent of the Prince of Wales) with the Princess of Orleans, and that of the Spanish Princess María Ana Victoria with King Louis XV of France (Peralta 1723, unnumbered folio). Regardless of whether Peralta had consulted the first or the second edition of the *Royal Commentaries,* what matters most is the form in which Garcilaso's version became the authoritative reference for comments on one of the many homages paid by the population of Lima to the Spanish prince and princess. Among the many expressions of fidelity to the royal family, like religious processions, parades, fireworks, bull fighting, and *cañas* (harmless chivalric jousts), one was of a very special nature: the masque or parade organized by the "indigenous population . . . of this Kingdom" (ibid.). Peralta inserts his own version of the Inca past within his account of the indigenous parade, which represented a succession and genealogy of the Cuzco kings. For this reason, Peralta parenthetically introduces into his chronicle a "Compendium of the Origin and Series of the Incas," in which he describes a pre-Inca time (first mentioned by Salinas in 1630) constituted by four ages. Peralta attributes the origin of the Incas to a trick performed by Mama Huaco in order to convince the inhabitants of the valley of Cuzco that her son Manco Capac was indeed divine, a descendant of the sun god. Peralta thus follows Salinas and emphasizes the popular and skeptical version offered by Garcilaso in his *Royal Commentaries.* Nevertheless, Peralta also details the genealogy of the Cuzco kings and accepts without hesitation Garcilaso's sequence of the Incas, which includes a mysterious Inca Yupanqui as the tenth ruler of the Empire, between Pachacutec and Túpac Inca Yupanqui. By doing so, however, Peralta contradicts the indigenous version offered by the *curaca* Don Salvador Puycón in the Masque of 1722, in which presumably a local popular version or

perhaps other chroniclers served as the source for the information provided. Peralta affirms his preference of Garcilaso's sequence over the other, indigenous sequence,

> although following this mistake, the natives represented in the
> Feasts only twelve Kings up to Huascar, omitting Inca Yupanqui; we
> draw your attention to this fact, and that we only believe Garcilaso
> because, in addition to the reasons we have already mentioned, his
> clarity helps to vanquish the obscurity of this material. (Peralta
> 1723, unnumbered folio)

Garcilaso serves, then, as a model of expository clarity, and his
work is recognized as an authorized version supported by his own
indigenous and Cuzco origins. Peralta has determined the value
of the *Royal Commentaries* with respect to his own conception of
the local past. On the one hand, for Peralta the Incas were accepted as wise rulers, but on the other, their origin was still considered illegitimate. Furthermore, their intuitive knowledge of
the Christian god (cf. Garcilaso 1966/1, I, I, 11) did not preclude
their condemnation as "barbarians who, mixing delight and hor-
ror, carried garlands and worshipped lions" (Peralta 1723, unnumbered folio). Although Peralta sometimes praises the Incas,
he never evinces an unconditional admiration for them. Moreover, Peralta feminizes the Incas by stripping them of manly
virtues in those scenes of *Lima Fundada* in which Pizarro picks
different lovers from the Cuzco royal families, and they react
with weakness and timidity; this is despite the many characters
and arguments derived from the second part of the *Royal Commentaries* (see Mazzotti 1996, 64–72 for a further description of
Peralta's feminization of the Incas).[11]

More examples of the Creole appropiation of Garcilasian discourse could be enumerated, but at this juncture we will examine
and compare the mestizo and indigenous readings of Garcilaso's
work. This is a complex matter, since there are no written testimonies of an early indigenous reception of the *Royal Commentaries,* and therefore we can explore only *the possibility* of readings
which would include indigenous and mestizo perspectives. For
that purpose, we shall consider the meanings and discursive

José Antonio Mazzotti

strategies of the *Royal Commentaries* which correspond to the Andean tradition, and which are just as much present in the *Commentaries* as are the resonances of Renaissance and classical historiography.

This particular form of analysis, however, requires the acceptance of an elementary principle of literary criticism: the distinction between enunciative subject and historical person or, in other words, the distinction between what is usually understood as the narrator and the author. In this case the term "narrator" has to be replaced by either the term "writing subject" or "enunciative subject" (see Mazzotti 1993, 1–3 for further references). The writing subject is the entity inherent in the text on whom the references to Andean history are focalized. It is also the entity who exercises various discursive functions, of which historical narration is but one among many. The distinction between writing subject and biographical figure, contrary to Creole readings, does not base the authority of the *Royal Commentaries* only on the explicit declarations about the author's noble origins or on the access he could have had to the indigenous informants of Túpac Yupanqui's *panaka,* to whom Garcilaso's mother belonged. This approach permits us to distinguish in specific texts (especially in the first edition) some resonances of a hypothetical indigenous mode of narration and of some specific symbols of the Cuzco court. By means of this critical approach, which establishes the rhetorical duality of the *Royal Commentaries,* we will be able to expatiate upon both those aspects emphasized by the learned Creoles as well as those stressed by mestizo and indigenous receptors. Thus, we will contribute to a partial explanation of the two projects of sociopolitical hegemony conceived by the main social subjects of the viceroyalty, the Spanish nation and the Indian nation.

We have already mentioned the selective criteria of the learned Creoles, from Salinas to Peralta, in their interpretation of Garcilaso's work. Indeed, it would be easy to compare those criteria with their counterparts on the other side of the Atlantic Ocean. The latter were the criteria that, after all, canonized the *Royal*

Commentaries by paying attention to its undeniable European rhetoric. However, it is useful to remember that the Creoles lived within a frontier context, and therefore, it was necessary for them to interpret the work in its most Hispanic aspects.[12] Their emphasis was especially on the *encomenderos* and the exaltation of the Pizarro brothers according to an ancient heroic tradition which has an important background rooted in the historical discourse of the Indies, a background that the *Royal Commentaries* shares. The learned frontier Creoles conceived themselves as writing from a new center, Lima, constantly referred to as the Rome of the New Empire, Head of these Kingdoms and Queen of the New World, and in their discourses they were able to establish their own position within the social pyramid without leaning on foreign historians.

However, the authority of the *Royal Commentaries* is not based on its masterful use of Renaissance historiographical rhetoric. Although this is the most studied aspect of the work, some subtextual aspects are still unexamined. This "gap" in Garcilaso studies is evident especially if we consider that recent studies about the rhetorical and discursive authority of the *Royal Commentaries,* such as Zamora's and Pupo-Walker's, are based on modern editions of the work and not on the original text of the seventeenth century.

For this reason, it is more than just an expression of good will to underscore the urgency of a critical edition which would overcome the inconveniences of Rosenblat's excellent edition in 1943–1944. We might call attention to the fact that the abundant punctuation of some of the chapters concerning Inca expansionism in the *princeps* edition of the work has not been sufficiently evaluated. If we consider the premise that one of the roles performed by the writing subject is that of an Inca "historian," who imitates the voice and the style of the declared indigenous narrator, great-uncle Cusi Huallpa, we can accept that the punctuation of the *princeps* edition is not as arbitrary as it would seem. It is with reference precisely to this point that the twentieth-century editions by Rosenblat, Sáenz de Santa María, or Araníbar have modernized and therefore occidentalized the text in a way that should be scrutinized with more current philological criteria and the aid of the most interdisciplinary Colonial studies.

An abundance of commas, colons, and semi-colons was frequent in the printings of the Spanish Golden Age. Many texts of the period also include the corrections inserted by scribes or compositors in the process of transforming a manuscript into printing fonts. These well-known facts, however, can be deceiving in the case of the *Royal Commentaries*, especially if we consider that the passages about the origins of the Incas and their successive territorial expansions include sequences of syntactic / semantic parallelisms, like the couplets that characterize pre-Hispanic Quechua poetry (see Husson 1985 and 1993 for an analysis of the Quechua lyric texts in Waman Puma's *Nueva Coronica*). Durand (1955) noted that the political chapters of the *Royal Commentaries* were very probably written subsequent to the original plan of the work. The distribution of the prose in the chapters dealing with Inca wars, expressly marked by the punctuation, admits of a reading evocative of a system of recitation and formulaic organization which simulates the original style of the official reciters of the Inca court. These official story-tellers are mentioned from Cieza and Betanzos to Garcilaso himself (for a more detailed description of this argument, see Mazzotti 1995, 388–399).

Another aspect of the Andean subtextuality of the work is related to the symbols and metaphors used by Garcilaso to refer to Andean spiritual history (Garcilaso 1966/1, I, xv, 40) and to reconstruct the initial arrival of the conquerors (Garcilaso 1966/2, I, xi–xii, 654–657). As some specialists have noted, the images of Obscure Darkness, Morning Star, and Sun of Justice, which represent the three spiritual ages of the Andean world corresponding to the pre-Inca, the Inca, and the Christianized Indians, may be understood within the general topic of the *preparatio evangelica* or the world ages according to St. Augustine (see Duviols 1964, Ilgen 1974, and Zamora 1988, chapter 5). At the same time, those images might be read in a subtextual way as an evocation of specific elements of the Inca pantheon. Such an interpretation connotes a profound critique of the Colonial system, if the images are deconstructed as a succession that implies a return to the original chaos, according to the *imaginaire* of the so-called societies of mythical thought. I have further developed such readings of the subtext elsewhere (see Mazzotti 1995, 399–413 and 1996a). I have only briefly sketched them here in order to enable us to return to our initial point of departure, namely the Creole readings and the potential indigenous and mestizo readings or aural receptions.[13]

We must weigh carefully various specific features of the first edition of the *Royal Commentaries* and the ways in which it might have been read from the perspective of each one of the reading subjects during the viceroyalty. If we consider the Creole consensus concerning the *Royal Commentaries,* and also the self-interested use of some passages of Garcilaso's work by Creole authors who follow Gómara and Acosta when describing the indigenous population, it becomes evident that only one of the possible readings is favored, i.e., the reading which denotes the superiority of Christian values and the justification of the conquest. On the other hand, if we consider the appearance of a nationalistic pro-Inca consciousness, which flourished during the eighteenth century and was literally decapitated with the repression of Túpac Amaru II, we can easily imagine the authority the *Royal Commentaries* had among that hypothetical Andean public.[14] The "oral" features of some of the passages in the first editons, almost always retained in the second edition of 1723, might serve as a criterion for considering the work as a projection of an internal focalization of the indigenous and mestizo social subject. The exaltation of the conquerors, from Francisco Pizarro to his brother Gonzalo, the great rebel against the Crown, can be understood also as a part of the general strategy of the work to legitimize the mestizos as the true heirs of the great deeds of the conquerors and the wisdom of the Cuzco rulers. In this sense, the pro-Spanish zeal of the work was used by the Lima Creoles for their own purposes, but at the same time might have been used by the mestizo elite with quite a different end in view.

It would thus seem obvious that the origins of Garcilacism

have more to do with immediate political problems than with a professional reading of his works. The tension of interests in the reading of the *Commentaries* mirrors the social tension between the colonial "nations" which coexisted within the same territory, reflecting not only the identity of the various groups who read and interpreted the work, but also the ends sought by these individual groups. The question remains: How convenient is this approach for a rigorous evaluation of the work itself and for a general classification of Garcilacist studies within literary criticism? Although this question is still very broad, recognition of the different potential readings beyond the authority exclusively attributed to the work is an important step toward the realization of a critical edition. With the scholarship from Buenaventura de Salinas to Peralta and the enlightened writers of the *Mercurio Peruano* as a basis, we can begin to trace a tradition of readings that may help to define some of the readings in our century. At the same time, this basis might be useful in evaluating within their own context readings by Riva Agüero and Víctor Andrés Belaúnde, on the one hand, and by Luis E. Valcárcel, on the other, in order to analyze their specific interpretations and their conception of Peruvian nationality.

The present essay intends only to mark another guidepost on the long road toward a more comprehensive vision of the healthy diversity of Garcilacism.

NOTES

1. Pedro Guíbovich has already mentioned a double reception of the work: one a "creole erudite" reading and the other a "mestizo nationalist" reading (1993, 120). Guíbovich's work is our basic reference for some of the authors we do not examine, such as Anello Oliva, Diego Altamirano, Fernando de Montesinos, Bartolomé Arzáns de Orzúa y Vela, Diego de Esquivel y Navia, Juan de Velasco, and the enlightened writers of *El Mercurio Peruano* between 1791 and 1795.

2. There were, of course, treatises of rhetoric and poetics, such as the *Filosofía Antigua Poética* (1596) by Alonso López, "el Pinciano," or the *Tablas Poéticas* (1617) by Cascales, which actualized and discussed Aristotelian principles about epic poetry and other prestigious genres during the Renaissance. However, even considering bibliographic ac-

counts such as the *Epítome de la Biblioteca Occidental* (1629) by Antonio de León Pinelo, or the *Bibliotheca Hispana* (1672–1696) by Nicolás Antonio, all are works which express prescriptive conceptions about literature. The independence of criticism as a discipline is a phenomenon parallel to the emergence of the modern concept of literature at the end of the eighteenth century, and especially during the period of Romanticism. In this sense, to consider Garcilaso and other historians as a target of literary criticism is a twentieth-century phenomenon.

3. In this sense, we should not take this defense of the Indians as an anticolonial plea or a pre-independence declaration. Nothing would be more anachronistic, especially if we consider that denouncing injustices and calling upon the King for improvements of the administration was usual within the tradition of "letras arbitristas" or "judgment writings" (see Maravall 1975, book 1, and Almarza 1990) and was very frequent within the complex cultural context of the epoch.

4. Raleigh writes: "And I farther remember that Berreo confessed to me and others (which I protest before the Majesty of God to be true), that there was found among Prophecies in *Perú*, (at such time as the Empire was reduced to the *Spanish* Obedience) in their chiefestie Temples, amongst divers others which foreshewed the Loss of the said Empire, that from *Inglatierra* those Ingas should be again in Time to come restored, and delivered from the Servitude of the said Conquerors" (Raleigh [1596] 1751, vol. 1, p. 235).

5. For example, Suardo mentions that some news arrived in Lima from Cuzco in March 1631 about the recent capture of a *pichilingue* (a term used to designate Englishmen and corsairs in general). The Englishman was arrested for "having said that in certain occasions he expected his relatives and acquaintances in a very short while, and that they would come from Buenos Aires" (1935, 124). In that same month, Suardo refers to a mestizo rebellion in Chiloé (current Chile). The mestizos "had tried to rebel and surrender themselves to the Dutch enemy whenever they had a chance to do so" (121). For his part, Mugaburu records a later rebellion of the Indians due to the supposed presence of "the English enemy" (1917, vol. 2, 74) off the coasts of Chile. The news raised great alarm in Lima, and the authorities sent a vessel to the Straits of Magellan in order to track the corsairs. When the Spaniards found out about the deception, the rebels were captured and the informants executed. These incidents occurred between January 1675 and April 1676 (70–92). Calancha himself mentions the surviving Incas in El Dorado or El Paititi (which for him were one and the same) and says: "Fleeing from the war, one of the children of Guayna Capac, brother of Guascar and Atagualpa (as Walter Raleigh affirms in his *America*), left with thousands of Indian *Orejones* [big ears, Inca nobles],

who were the most courageous, and populated that part of the land, which lies between the great river of the Amazones and the Baracoan, which is also called Orinoco, between the Straits of Magellan, between the River Plate" (1639, fol. 115). Despite the fact that he refutes Raleigh a few pages later, Calancha takes this information from him and presents it as a part of the common knowledge of his time. Escandell Bonet records many cases of psychological and social repercussions of the English corsairs within the Peruvian viceroyalty during the sixteenth century.

6. Calancha writes, "the Indians only adored the god Pachacamac as an invisible god, and the Sun as a visible god; but Viracocha and other Guacas, Idols and temples, were [only] considered deities or things who had something distinguished or divine, but were not gods or creators, such as the Moon, stars, lightning bolt or thunder, the sea and other celestial bodies, having them as brothers and familiar to the Sun" (fol. 365).

7. About the Incan government, Calancha points out that "the Cycle [of the Incas] arrived, their term and harmonious number, because God's will arrived, and wanted to take away the dominion of these lands from the idolatry, and give the dominion to the Catholic Church, to whom the World should belong" (fol. 115).

8. "Huaca (as Gómara indicates) means 'cry and weep,' since in their temples or places of worship [the Indians] gathered together to cry and beg favor or forgiveness from their idols" (Calancha, fol. 237).

9. Calancha mentions (fol. 320) that "commanded by the Viceroy, Betanzos found out that it was Ticciyachachec [another name for Wiraqucha] who taught the world and was a teacher." Further on, Calancha affirms that "all the Quipus, memories and accounts transmitted from parents to their children, both in prose and in poems, coincide in saying that [Saint Thomas and his aide] were of a high disposition, one taller than the other one, both white and bearded, one blue-eyed, both with white robes down to their feet . . . with sandals and long hair" (fol. 321). Thus, the Apostle and his aide would seem to merge with Wiraqucha and Tunupa. By this artful reworking of the past, Calancha achieves a historical justification of the Spanish conquest as a true restoration of indigenous history.

10. For some instances of the presence of Garcilaso's *Royal Commentaries* in Peralta's *Lima Fundada,* see Guíbovich 1993, 118–119.

11. Guíbovich (1993, 118) mentions a later version, between December 1724 and January 1725, in celebration of the recent proclamation of Luis I, son of Phillip V, as the King of Spain. This parade was described by Castro y Bocángel in his *Eliseo Peruano.* Apparently, the in-

digenous masque this time followed the genealogy proposed by Garcilaso.

12. Brading (1991, 315–334) refers in partial terms to the appropriation of Garcilaso's work by Salinas and Calancha.

13. The oral diffusion of Golden Age texts in Spain has been addressed by Frenk (1982). There is still a need for a study of the reception of this literature in the Indies, a study which considers the cultural and linguistic background of the audience as well as the derived implications in the decodification of canonical discourses. For the diffusion of the *Royal Commentaries* among the indigenous elites during the eighteenth century, see Rowe, Burga, and Guíbovich. Durand (1971) has also examined the role of the *Royal Commentaries* in the insurrection led by Túpac Amaru II.

14. The "trail of Garcilaso," as it was called by Buntinx and Wuffarden, is visible in the pictorial representations of the Inca kings during the Colonial period. A broader study of the indigenous and mestizo reception of the *Royal Commentaries* should inevitably consider the iconographic material of the period.

Eight

EFRAÍN KRISTAL

Goths and Turks and the Representation of Pagans and Infidels in Garcilaso and Ercilla

FOR GARCILASO INCA DE LA VEGA, the Inca Empire was another Rome inasmuch as it providentially prepared the way for Christianity in the Andean region.[1] The idea, however, that a pagan empire could establish the groundwork for Christianity is by no means unique to Garcilaso, and it is at least as old as the fourth-century church historian Eusebius.[2]

Since the 1950s, the best critics of Garcilaso have understood the significance of providentialist notions in the *Royal Commentaries*. In one of his most illuminating essays, José Durand argued that the thesis about "the cultural mission of the Incas providentially preparing the arrival of the Gospel" (1963, 33) must be understood as but one possibility, among others, of divine interventions in human affairs as expounded in such Renaissance works as the *Royal Commentaries*. Another important notion of divine intervention with clear roots in biblical traditions is what Durand called "providentialist chastisements": "The providentialist notion of the Chastisement of God was widespread in that age. . . . It was regarded as a tacitly accepted fact which needed no reasoning or philosophical support" (1963, 34). Durand argued that a common theme in Renaissance works was that God chastised the good in order to break their pride: "The Augustinian Zárate, an adviser of the Inca, wrote a treatise in which chastisements and calamities have a hidden meaning; they are hardships imposed by the Almighty in order to make men more modest" (1963, 35). I would like to broaden Durand's notion of providential chastisement to include all hardships and calamities as divine punishment of sins, including sacrilege and blasphemy as well as pride.

Providentialist notions were invariably used by medieval and Renaissance Spanish historians to explain the rise of an evangelical empire such as Rome or Cuzco; but they were also used to explain the fall of empires in terms of divine intervention. In the *Historia de los hechos de España,* a book that Juan Fernández Valverde has called the most representative historical work of medieval Spain before the *Primera Crónica General,* Rodrigo Jiménez de Rada underscored the point that "the fall of the Romans was not due to the strength of their enemies, but to the will of God" (1989, 93).

Providentialist notions were, however, not only at play in the history of pagans. They were also at play, as Juan Bautista Avalle-Arce has emphasized, in Spanish conceptions of history in the sixteenth century, where it was generally assumed that "God has designated Spain as the instrument of His Providence, and His intervention in Spanish history is direct" (1964, 16).

Divine assistance as well as chastisement are crucial notions in understanding Spanish medieval and Renaissance historical works in which empires rise and fall, and pagans, infidels, and Christians interact. Providential intervention, therefore, should also be a crucial notion in understanding sixteenth- and seventeenth-century Spanish works that explore the relationship between the indigenous populations and the Spaniards in America.

A clear and emblematic formulation of the providential notion in the Spanish sixteenth century can be found in Julián del Castillo's *Historia de los Reyes Godos,* a work that characteristically begins with the universal deluge and ends with the reigns of Charles V and Phillip II. Castillo made it clear that human affairs are guided by divine providence rather than by fate or fortune: "Everything touched upon in this history has been guided by Divine Providence, that is, by the will of God" (1582, fol. 4 [9, 121]). He likewise demonstrated that the Romans prepared the groundwork for the Christian evangelization of Europe and that the Goths produced the royal lineage that was to spread Christianity through both the Old and the New worlds. In Castillo's history of the Goths, pagan empires prepared the way for evangelization, pagan fables contained Christian insights, and pagan lawgivers had access to Christian truths, even before the advent of Christ. Julián del Castillo drew on many Renaissance and medieval sources including the *Coronica general del hombre,* where Valdés de la Plata insists that pagans were able to attain Christian truths by the intervention of the Holy Spirit:

> there were such men who foresaw the arrival of Jesus Christ, and all that befell our Redeemer, and many things that happened before His coming, and all that was to take place until the writing of the Sacred Scriptures. They did not learn these things in school but were made aware of them by the Holy Spirit. (1548, R, 58/[3/11])

Providentialist notions are abundant in Pedro Mexía's *Silva de varia lección,* a work that circulated widely in Europe. The success of the *Silva* earned Mexía the opportunity to become an official chronicler for Emperor Charles V and to write a history of the Romans, the *Historia Imperial y Cesárea* (1545), in which the providentialist paradigm is reiterated. The works of Mexía, as we know from Durand (1948) and Miró-Quesada (1971, 242–247), were among the volumes in the library of Garcilaso de la Vega. Mexía affirmed that ancient peoples such as the Egyptians had worshipped the cross in ways compatible with Christian revelation:

> A long time before Christ, our Redeemer, was crucified, the Egyptians and the Arabians honored the cross and held it in esteem. By the cross, the Egyptians signified the hope for the salvation that was to come, others say they meant the life that was to come. It all seems a prophecy and annunciation of the universal salvation that came to us through the Cross. (1989, I, 3)

In Spanish medieval and Renaissance accounts, the Goths appear as pagan and idolatrous peoples who nevertheless were predisposed to Christianity. In Rodrigo Jiménez de Rada's *Historia* (1989), Goths and other pagans are presented as peoples who had intuitions about the true God: "they sense the sweetness of God as a light in the fog."

In sixteenth-century historical works, the Spanish royalty is portrayed as descending from the Goths, a pagan and idolatrous people who had converted to Christianity. The connections to Garcilaso de la Vega's conception of the Incas should be obvious to any careful reader of the *Royal Commentaries*. I do not think it is coincidental that in Castillo's history of the Goths, the Goths are presented as an idolatrous people who worshipped celestial bodies, in particular the Sun: "they adored the sun, the moon, and the stars; as they had blindly forgotten our God, the creator of all things" (1582, fol. 9 [C2 39]). Castillo points out that the Goths may have been idolatrous, but they were predisposed to Christian truths and they had a sound political order (fol. 6 [C2 38]). In Castillo, as in medieval sources such as Jiménez de Rada, it is clear that the Goths' conversion to Christianity presented basically no difficulties, once they were exposed to it, because they had been predisposed to accept the true religion (see Jiménez de Rada 1989, 87–88). Once again, the connection between this account of the providentialist role of the Goths and that of the Incas in Garcilaso is more than obvious.

Divine assistance is but one aspect of the Spanish historical paradigm regarding the Goths. An equally vital perspective is the notion of divine chastisement, by means of which the fall of the Goths in the eighth century was readily explained. In most accounts, Witzia, the last of the Goths to have ruled over the whole kingdom in peace and prosperity, committed sexual and other kinds of sins. Upon his death, his empire was inherited by his two sons Sisberto and Eba, who were unable to reign. The famous don Rodrigo filled the power gap, but he also committed a grave sin when he forced himself upon "la Cava," the daughter of count Julian of Gibraltar. The count allied himself with the Moors, thus spelling the downfall of the Goths and initiating the *reconquista* period of Spanish history.[3]

Jiménez de Rada explained the fall of the Goths in precisely these terms of divine chastisement. The causes of the fall were the sexual sins of the last kings of the Goths, and the fact that illegitimate rulers were more than willing to commit fratricide or parricide in order to gain power:

> The wrath of God erupted on account of the sins of Witizia and Rodrigo and the sins of other kings before them who did not respect the established order of succession (some took power by means of incantation, others by means of fratricide or parricide). God no longer tolerated the Goths and He took away their glory. (1989, 152)

Julián del Castillo understood that the fall of the Goths was governed by the same principle that predestined the fall of other peoples and empires, namely the sins of their peoples and especially their leaders (1582, fol. 3 [1, 59]). Just as the Roman Empire fell to the Goths by divine intervention, so too the Goths would fall by divine intervention. The instrument of God's wrath was the invasion of the infidels: "because of their sins, the Goths, who had triumphed over Rome and over the world, were to be subjected to the Moors" (fol. 2 [12]). We are now in a position to explore the representations of infidels in Spanish historical works in which evil men were allowed, by divine intervention, to defeat either pagan or Christian realms when their respective leaders had sinned.

In the *Silva de varia lección*, Pedro Mexía summarized a commonplace in sixteenth-century Spanish historical works: through divine providence, God sometimes allows evil men and infidels to inflict punishments on other evil men, to punish sinners, or to test and perfect the good. (1989, I, XXXV, 477)

The paradigmatic cases for Spanish history are the intervention of the Moors to punish the Goths in the eighth century, and the intervention of the Turks to punish the Christians in the sixteenth century. Mexía branded Moors and Turks, the people of Mohammed, as infidels, "diabolical people," and "enemies of Jesus Christ" (1989, I, XII, 275). According to Mexía, the reason why Mohammed was revered in most of the known world, and the reason why his diabolical infidel followers had triumphed over Christian peoples in battles and wars—this is a crucial point for my argument—was because of divine intervention, i.e., the disciples of Mohammed are God's instrument for divine chastisement:

> After the death of Mohammed, the kingdom and the power went to one named Caliph, and from Caliph to another named Ali. These widened their power and their diabolical sect, and the creed of Mohammed. It was because of the sins and the cowardness of the Christian emperors that this pestilence came into being and spread throughout the world until we find ourselves in our present state. (I, XIII, 285–286)

The rise and the power of the Ottoman Empire were, therefore, instances of divine chastisement of sins committed by Christians:

> As it is right to believe, this has taken place with God's permission in order to punish and reform the Christian people. Because of our sins, God has allowed this to happen. For the same reason, He allows the Turkish Empire to expand. God has allowed this as punishment for our neglect. (I, XIV, 293)

One of the prime sins that explains the victories of the Turks was the sin of greed (I, XV, 309).

Originally the Ottomans were groups of roaming peoples who lived in "empty fields" (1989, I, XIV, 294). They were "barbarians without faith who received the evil sect of Mohammed" (295–296). In the beginning "they did not have a captain or a leader. They roamed in wild bunches and gangs" (296). In time, however, they acquired a leader, Ottoman:

> Ottoman began to gain a reputation among them because he was a man of great determination and will, and because his corporal strength was great, and he was rather clever. He took advantage of the discord amongst those people, and he was able to gain many supporters among the Turks. He then began to conquer and to become the lord of cities and provinces. (298)

Even though Mexía considered the Turks to be a diabolical sect, he recognized many admirable qualities in them. He referred to their leaders as "excellent captains," "excellent gentlemen," and "valorous and strong-willed." Mexía depicted their leaders as lovers of their freedom who "removed their nation and people from servitude" (1989, II, XXVII, 699–701). These are some of the exact epithets Ercilla would use to praise the admirable qualities of the Araucanian heroes.

Mexía also argued that the tides of war between Christians and Turks were changing, once again because of divine providence operating through the Emperor Charles V:

> By the grace of God, through the diligence and care of the undefeated Charles V, the king of Spain, and our Lord we have been saved from the danger of servitude and captivity that Soliman meant for all Christianity. (1989, I, XIII, 286; see also I, XV, 324)

Mexía expressed the hope that Charles V "with the favor and grace of Jesus Christ . . . would defeat and destroy the Ottoman empire" (I, XV, 327).

The views that Francisco de Gómara expressed about the Inca Empire were explicitly taken from accounts like Pedro Mexía's representation of the Moors and Turks. Garcilaso de la Vega was well aware of the Moor/Turk/Infidel paradigm as Gómara used it. In the *General History* Garcilaso quoted a passage from Gómara's *Historia General de las Indias* in which Francisco Pizarro told his soldiers that their mission was identical to the mission of the Goths during the *reconquista:*

> Pizarro placated them saying that they had deserved their rewards by their efforts and qualities, and indeed deserved all the rights and privileges won by those who helped King Pelayo and the other kings to wrest Spain from the Moors. (Garcilaso 1966/2, II, XXII, 794)

In the same passage quoted by Garcilaso, Gómara insisted that "the gold [was intended] for the Emperor, who was much reduced by the expenses of his coronation, and the affairs of the Turk and Vienna and Tunis" (Garcilaso 1966/2, II, XXII, 794).

Gómara makes the explicit claim that the conquest of America was part of a divine plan that included the conquest of the Moors: "The conquest of the Indies began after the conquest of the

Moors was accomplished so that Spain would always wage war against infidels" (Gómara 1993, dedication, p. i). Gómara's portrayal of the Incas is very similar to Mexía's account of the Turks. The Incas are devil worshippers who are enemies of the Christian religion. They may have been warriors who conquered vast regions, but they are "liars and robbers. They are cruel and ungrateful. They lack honor, shame, charity, and virtue. They have stuck to their idolatry and abominable vices. The converts renounce the Christian religion, some because it was convenient to do so, others because they were persuaded by the devil" (1993, 196). Their converts to Christianity are prone to renege on the true religion and are more inspired by their priests who conjure up the devil to offer advice to their leaders (122). If the Incas were able to defeat the Spaniards, if Spanish victory was not achieved as swiftly as it should have been—and this is a point that Garcilaso would take up in his own way—it was because of divine intervention in punishing the sins of the Spaniards, in particular those of greed and avarice. In a telling passage of his *Historia General de las Indias,* Gómara hoped that God would intercede to eradicate the greed and avarice of the conquistadors so that true evangelization might flourish:

> Civil conflicts increased because of avarice and that led to great anger, envy, and cruelty. We can but pray to God these conflicts will not last as long as those of the Guelphs and Ghibellines in Italy.[4] (86)

In the light of Gómara's use of the Moor/Turk/Infidel paradigm to represent the indigenous populations of the New World, let us now reexamine Ercilla's epic poem, *La Araucana*. A close reading of the description of the Araucanians, the Chilean Indians who resisted the Spanish invaders, reveals great similarities with Mexía's views of the Turks. In fact, the Araucanians are presented precisely as Mexía described the early Turks before their transformation into an empire of warriors united under Ottoman. Caupolicano in *La Araucana* plays a role equivalent to Ottoman in Mexía's account (notice the similarity in Spanish be-

117

tween Otomano and Caupolicano). One of the most interesting
anecdotes in Mexía's history of the Turks is the story of Lázaro
Hebreljanovic, a Christian prince from Serbia, who "was killed
by the treachery of one of his own [Turkish] slaves who cut him
to pieces with a dagger" (1989, I, XIV, 301). Lautaro, one of the
central figures of the poem, is equivalent to the Turkish servant
who turned against his master, the prince of Serbia.

As in Mexía's account of the Turks, the Araucanians wage in-
cessant battles with each other when they do not unite to wage
war against the Christians. Mexía's description of the Turks in
the time of Ottoman, but preceding the first Suleiman, corresponds to Ercilla's depiction of the Araucanians as "arrogant, gal-
lant and bellicose / who have never been ruled by a king" (Ercilla
1979, I, I, 6, 129).[5] The words Ercilla uses to describe the religion
of the Araucanians are identical to those of Mexía's account of
the Turks' religion, and compatible with Gómara's views of the
indigenous populations of the new world. They are of the false
sect (*la falsa seta*) of devil worshippers who consult with the devil
before undertaking any military action:

> These are people with no God and with no law.
> They respect the one who fell from heaven as a
> powerful and great prophet and they always
> celebrate him in their songs. In their false sect,
> they call upon his wrath and invoke him in
> everything they do. They accept as true whatever
> he says about what will take place, whether it be
> good or bad. (I, I, 40, 138)

Valdivia conquered the Araucanians, but instead of evangelizing
them, he and the other conquistadors fell prey to the sins of avarice and greed which engendered discord among the conquistadors: "The malice and conflicting interests grew out of unbridled
greed which caused harm to others" (I, I, 68, 146). The greed of
Valdivia and the other conquistadors fueled the propensity of the
converted infidels to apostatize, as was the case with Lautaro.

As in the Turkish paradigm, God intervened directly and allowed the infidel Araucanian Indians to punish the Spaniards for their sins:

> Thus the ungrateful Spanish people
> sought the vain attempt to gain
> personal fortunes.
> God allowed the same people who
> had been subdued by the Spaniards
> to become their executioners. (I, I, 69, 146)

Repeated defeat of the Spaniards as a result of divine intervention is a dominant motif throughout the poem:

> It was God's just punishment,
> given the Spaniards' great excesses,
> to allow the barbarous enemy
> who had once been subjected and oppressed
> to throw them out of their lands
> and cast doubt on their honor. (I, VIII, 4, 272)

The military aim of the Araucanians was not simply the defeat of the Spaniards in the New World. Like the Turks in Mexía's account, they sought to challenge the kings of Christendom. As Caupolicano, the Araucanian captain said:

> I plan to make an easy entrance into Spain
> and to subject the unconquered Charles
> to the domination of the Araucanians. (I, VIII, 16, 275)

It is no coincidence that in *La Araucana* Ercilla made direct references to the Turks, and that the description of the Turks in his poem appears often identical with his description of the Araucanians. The Turks in Ercilla are explicitly depicted as devil worshippers who have gained power by divine intervention because of Christian sins (II, XVIII, 57, 64).

Ercilla rendered Mexía's prose into verse when he said that, through divine intervention, Charles V and Phillip II were even then subduing the Turks:

But the Lord who is merciful
will also thwart the arrogance
of the ambitious barbarian.[6] (II, XVIII, 57, 64)

From this perspective, the San Quintín and Lepanto episodes in *La Araucana* are far from decorative (which seems to be the consensus of most Ercilla scholars). In order to offer a model the Spanish conquistadors in Chile should follow in their behavior towards each other and in their battles against the Araucanians (even though most of them were too greedy to do so), Ercilla made several explicit references to the roles Charles V and Phillip II were playing in the wars among Christians and in the wars against the Turks. If Ercilla presented himself as superior to Valdivia and other Spaniards in America, it was because his own intentions were compatible with the honorable aims of the Catholic kings: to punish Christian sinners and rebels, to wage war against infidels, and to show clemency to those who mend their ways, especially to those who convert or reconvert to the true religion (II, XVI, 18–19, 29–30).

From this perspective, one of the most important moments in Ercilla's epic occurred when Captain Caupolicano converted to Christianity and offered to help in the conversion of all the other Araucanians as well. Caupolicano's conversion took place, as is by now to be expected, through divine intervention: "God changed him / . . . and he wished to become a Christian" (III, XXXIV, 18, 352). In keeping with his desire to convert, Caupolicano offered to establish Christianity among the Araucanian Indians (III, XXXIV, 14, 351). The Spaniards, however, executed Caupolicano and thus lost a great opportunity. This is Ercilla's strongest criticism of García Hurtado de Mendoza, who was responsible for the execution: "had I been present / I would have stopped the execution." (III, XXXIV, 31, 356)

In his recapitulation of the consensus of Garcilaso research, Alfredo Alejandro Bernal (1982, 549–562) has emphasized that Garcilaso utilized *La Araucana* as one of his sources for Araucanian history. In the *Royal Commentaries* Garcilaso stated that Inca Yupanqui decided that it would be more prudent to leave the Araucanian Indians alone because they were too brutal to be part of the more gentle Inca empire:

> The Incas considered that it was more in keeping with the policy of their past and present rulers to give free rein to the bestial fury of their enemy rather than to destroy them by calling up reinforcements which could have been summoned within a short time. . . . With these instructions the Incas ceased to continue their conquests in Chile. (Garcilaso 1966/1, VII, VII, 450)

Garcilaso also conceded that the Araucanians may have been as brutal as described by Ercilla. He was, therefore, willing to admit with Gómara that there were Indians who fit the Moor/Turkish/ infidel paradigm; and he was also willing to concede, as Pierre Duviols has shown, that charges of demonic immorality and bestiality could also apply to the Andean world before the advent of the Incas. Garcilaso had no problem in arguing that the early Andeans "would have chosen their gods and cults according to the errors of the imagination, or by the inspiration of demons, and not by reason" (Duviols 1988, 189). The Incas, however, were much different. Through divine intervention they had achieved a state akin to Christian morality and revelation. Duviols has pointed out that, according to Garcilaso, the Incas "had caught a glimpse of the true God in their Pachacamac" (ibid.). There is a significant chapter in the *Royal Commentaries* in which Garcilaso seems to paraphrase Pedro Mexía's account of the Egyptians and the Cross. The chapter has the heading: "The Incas kept a Cross in a sacred place" (Garcilaso 1966/1, II, III, 73). Garcilaso lamented that the Spaniards had not exhibited the cross when they conquered Cuzco:

> It would thus have disposed the Indians toward our holy faith, for they would have been able to compare its objects with those of their own, such as this cross, and with other points in their laws and ordinances that closely approach the natural law and could be compared with the commandments in our holy law and the works of mercy. These, as we shall see, had close parallels in their gentile faith. (Ibid.)

With the example of the cross we have come full circle: depending on the intentions of the different authors who wrote about the New World (and this is not the place to discuss these intentions or motivations), the indigenous peoples could be portrayed within a Moor/Turk paradigm, or a Roman/Goth paradigm. The Roman/Goth paradigm involves divine intervention in preparing a pagan people for Christian revelation as well as divine punishment in the form of the fall of an empire or a lineage for the sins of their leaders. The Moor/Turk paradigm involves the use of barbarian infidels as people who should be defeated in war or as the instrument of God's chastisement for either sins and transgressions, or, as Durand has argued, for the subjugation of men's pride. Gómara chose to portray the Incas in terms of the Turkish paradigm, as did Ercilla in the case of the Araucanians. Garcilaso was likewise willing to apply the Moor/Turk/infidel paradigm to the Araucanians or to the Indians of the Andean region before the arrival of the Incas. He approved and extensively quoted Gómara in condemning the Spanish conquistadors and even the viceroys in their failure to evangelize the Indians, or worse, in failing to understand the Inca as a lineage—like the Goths—which had prepared the way for the evangelization of many idolatrous people. The failure to perceive this was in part a result of the sins and cruelty of conquistadors and viceroys, but it also involved the responsibility of the Incas themselves.

Let us recall the end of the Goths: Witzia, the last king of the full empire, commits various sins. His empire is divided in two. Don Rodrigo, who also commits sexual sins, tries to reunite the empire. On account of crimes of greed, fratricide, and improper transfer of power, God then directly intervenes to destroy the Goths.

The last of the Incas, Huayna Capac, also commits a sexual sin by fornicating with a whore in Quito. Instead of offering the empire to his legitimate successor, Huáscar, Huayna Capac divides it between Huáscar and Atahualpa, the son of the woman from Quito (although Garcilaso believed that she had conceived him by some other man). The pattern of the fall of the Inca Empire, like the fall of Rome after the division of Arcadio and Honorio, or the Goths, is identical: God chastised the pagan empires which had achieved Christian revelation on account of the sins of their leaders.

The tragedy, in the case of the Incas, involved the fact that the Spanish conquistadors and viceroys were unable to appreciate the evangelical work of the Incas. By failing to see the Incas as latter-day Goths, but rather interpreting their culture and history within the Gómara paradigm of the Turks, the Spanish delayed the ultimate evangelization of the Andean region and thus relegated to the realm of silence the work of an empire that, like the Goths, had once surpassed Rome.

NOTES

1. The Roman paradigm, as Aurelio Miró-Quesada has shown, is significant in the representation of both the Incas and the Spanish conquistadors. For the purpose of discussing providentialist notions in the history of pagan empires, we will concentrate on the former. For broader suggestions about the Roman paradigm, see Miró-Quesada 1971, 451–475, especially 470–472. For a useful review of the literature on Garcilaso from the perspective of Renaissance interpretations of the Greco-Roman world, see Hampe Martínez 1994, 69–94.

2. "Garcilaso endorsed Acosta's thesis, taken from Eusebius of Caesarea, that in the same way that the Roman unification of the Mediterranean world was assisted by Divine providence so as to prepare the way for the preaching of the gospel, so also the expansion of the Inca empire across the Andes equally served a providential purpose, smoothing the way for the entrance of Christianity" (Brading 1986, 21). I prefer Brading's formulation in the article quoted to the version in his monumental *The First America,* where he edits the reference to Acosta and suggests a more direct connection with Eusebius (1991, 162).

For important insights regarding the connections between Acosta and Garcilaso, see Pino Díaz 1992, 74. Pino Díaz suggests that the providentialist thesis in Garcilaso comes from Acosta, who in turn derived it from the fifth-century *Historia adversus Paganos,* written by the Spanish priest and disciple of St. Augustine, Orosius.

3. For the purposes of my argument it does not matter whether this account is actually historical or legendary. What matters is that it was taken as historical in the sixteenth century. Menéndez Pidal (1906) shows that a good part of the story of don Rodrigo is legend, and more

recently Caro Baroja (1992) wrote an illuminating account of historical falsifications in Spain where he also mentions the don Rodrigo incident (see, for example, 181). For the implications of Caro Baroja's general ideas on historical falsification as it applied to Garcilaso, see Pease's illuminating essay, 1994, especially 136–140.

4. In Mexía (1989, II, XLV, 834–837) the conflicts between Guelfos and Gebelinos are seen as another example of fratricidal warfare in which a political realm is divided. This paradigm is reminiscent of the fratricidal wars that precede—in sixteenth-century Spanish historical accounts—the fall of empires such as the Roman, Goth, and Inca.

5. The quotations from *La Araucana* indicate the book, chapter, stanza, and page number. The translations are mine.

6. See also Ercilla 1979, II, XXIII, 15, 162.

Nine

RODOLFO CERRÓN-PALOMINO

The Concept of General
Language in Garcilaso Inca

The processes of conquest, occupation, and colonialization of the Amerindian populations were, in effect, a mere recapitulation and amplification of those that had taken place for many centuries on the "cultural borderline" shared by the Muslim-Hispanic peoples of the Iberian peninsula (Solano 1991). The novelty in the American case, aside from the various groups involved and the violence with which they were subdued, has to do with the landscape and, for the point of our concern, with the language.

The earliest Spanish conquistadors encountered an amazingly Babelic situation in the Americas. Once acquainted with the great indigenous empires, however, the conquerors faced a new reality: the existence of many individual languages used within the immense territories of those regions. A sort of "Indian Latin" was used not only by the privileged members of the Indian ruling class but also by a considerable portion of the rest of the population, and this without the benefit of the "teacher's industry," as Garcilaso himself would later state. This particular vehicle was designated the "general language." In all probability, the one who coined the expression in an attempt to characterize the Quechua language was Friar Domingo de Santo Tomás, the first grammarian of that language (Triana y Antorveza 1987, 162).

Rodolfo Cerrón-Palomino

THE "GENERAL LANGUAGE"

According to the accepted definition, a general language has the following characteristics: (1) extensive diffusion within vast territories; (2) general use on the part of the ruling elite; (3) not necessarily spoken by the whole population; and, consequently, (4) practicable use as a second language. In this sense, it was opposed to the so-called "maternal," "natural," or even "particular" tongue, designated in the case of Perú as the *hahua simi*, "language other than the general" (Monzón [1586] 1965). Such characterizations, as will be seen, are both explicitly and implicitly contained in the passages we will cite in the following sections (for the functional-idiomatic hierarchization, see Tovar 1963 and Cerrón-Palomino 1995, chapter 9, section 9.3).

Friar Domingo de Santo Tomás, commenting on Quechua, states in his *Grammatica* that it

> is a language in which communication was held and was and is being used in all the realm of that great lord called Guaynacapa, that extends for a space of more than a thousand leagues long, and more than a hundred wide. In such a huge territory it was generally used by all lords and local principals, and a great part of the common population. ([1560] 1994a, "Address to the King")

In his *Lexicon* he stresses again that the language is "general and extended throughout the land, and largely used by the lords and important people, and by a very great portion of the rest of the Indians" ([1560] 1994b, foreword). Cieza de León, on his part, characterized Quechua as a language that "was known and used in more than a thousand and two hundred leagues; and although the language was generally used, everyone spoke their own, which are so many, that if I wrote about them, no one would believe it" (Cieza de León [1550] 1986, XXIV, 72). Finally, Father Acosta stressed the vast diffusion of the Quechua language, emphasizing that "in a space of three thousand miles and more, it is still used today," although admittedly he adds that "even though all the principals among the Indians commonly understand it, the populace of women and children and those called *atunrunas*, a genre of wild men, barely know it" (Acosta [1588] 1954, IV, VIII, 517).

Given such characteristics and attributes, communication was assured not only among the diverse nations that formed the vast Inca Empire, but also among the Spaniards and their new vassals. This was recognized explicitly by both the "historian soldier" and the "accountant chronicler," among others. In fact, Cieza acknowledged thankfully and yet at the same time with some concern "that the fact that this language existed was a great advantage for the Spaniards, because they could transmit it throughout all the regions, in some of which this language is being displaced" (Cieza de León [1550] 1986, XXIV, 73). Zárate stated pragmatically that "a Spaniard who knows the Cuzco language can travel throughout all Perú, along the plains as well as in the highlands, understanding and being understood by the local officials" (Zárate [1555] 1995, I, VI, 252). The use by chroniclers such as Zárate of the alternative and particularizing expressions "Cuzco's language" or "Inca's language," with reference to the general language, resembles the designations with which the populations more recently incorporated into the empire—especially those from the border regions—named the language. They either visualized it on a geopolitical basis (the kingdom's capital city) or associated it with the major sovereign's name (Inca).

Despite the variations in terminology, it is obvious that we are dealing with what is currently referred to as a "vehicular language," that is, a language used "for the intercommunication among geographically neighboring linguistic communities which do not speak the same language" (Calvet 1981, 23), and whose function rather than form plays the major role. However both Cieza ([1550] 1986, XXIV, 72) and Acosta ([1588] 1954, IV, VIII, 519) also praised its hegemonizing property and the advantageous ease with which it could be mastered ("as if one were playing," as was said by one of those who had quickly learned the language).

THE REFERENT OF THE GENERAL LANGUAGE

If Quechua formerly constituted (as it does today) a large family of languages, one might ask to which of its many variants the cited authors were referring when they spoke of the excellencies of the general language. It is certainly not hard to realize that not all of them had the same dialect in mind. This became even more evident after the standardization of the language by the Third Council of Lima (1582–1583), which was chaired by José de Acosta himself.

Basing our analysis on strictly linguistic data (see Cerrón-Palomino 1987), we can postulate that the specific referent of the general language, as evidenced by the first recorded testimonies of the early chroniclers, but even more so by the grammatical and lexical works of Santo Tomás, was probably the dialect called *Chinchaisuyo* and not the Cuzco variety, although, as we have seen, some still referred to it as "Cuzco's language." What is more, chroniclers such as Betanzos and Cieza provide us with "samples" of "general Quechua," highly distorted to be sure, but which, on closer inspection, belong not to the Cuzco variety but rather to the so-called Chinchaisuyo.

CHANGE OF REFERENT

With the selection and standardization of the Quechua variety which was to be used as the vehicle for evangelization, the translators and grammarians who took part in the Third Council of Lima not only changed the referent of the "general language" but assigned to it a new and indeed aulic attribute, thus making it more closely resemble the Cuzco variety. This new, refashioned, and courtly "general language" was thereafter considered the correct and paradigmatic speech, while the Chinchaisuyo dialect, like any other dialect distant from the new archetype, was soon designated as corrupt speech or even jargon. Jerónimo de Oré, the eminent Quechuanist born in Huamanga, described the new linguistic situation in these terms:

> for the Quechua language, general to all this reign, the city of Cuzco is like Athens, because there it is spoken with all the correctness and elegance one can imagine; like Ionic in Athens, Latin in Rome, Castilian in Toledo, so is the Quechua language in Cuzco, but in all the rest of the provinces, the more distant they are from

the city, the more corruption and the less elegance there is in the guttural pronunciation and periphrasis proper to this language, which is not too well-known by some who boast that they can speak it. (Oré [1598] 1992, fol. 33v)

Thus, Chinchaisuyo will henceforth be classified within the category of corrupt speech, at least from a phonological point of view, i.e., because of its pronunciation and "gutturalization," in spite of the fact that it was the very first dialect celebrated and studied by Friar Domingo de Santo Tomás. The codification of the language instituted by the Third Council of Lima was no longer based on the Chinchaisuyo dialect but rather on that from Cuzco (Anónimo 1586). Furthermore, within the first decade of the seventeenth century, González Holguín actually identified the general language with the dialect of Cuzco, which he described in the title of his *Vocabulario* ([1608] 1989) as the "general language of all Perú called the Quechua (language) of the Inca." However, the "general language" advocated by the Third Council of Lima had a written rather than an oral usage, and it would not be too far amiss to assume that the Chinchaisuyo dialect probably continued to function as the recognized vehicular language.

GARCILASO'S DISTORTION

The mestizo chronicler Garcilaso Inca assumed as his own the redefinition of the general language made by the Quechuanists at the Third Council of Lima, among whom his "compatriot" and "fellow-countryman" Blas Valera—a mestizo like him, though of Chinchaisuyan extraction—excelled. As Garcilaso writes, the Chachapoyan Jesuit Valera continually emphasized the advantages of the general language, pointing out that

> although it is true that each province has its own particular language which differs from the rest, what is called the language of Cuzco is uniform and general and in the time of the Inca kings was used from Quito to the kingdom of Chile and even as far as the kingdom of Tucma. Now it is used by *caciques* and the Indians whom

the Spaniards have in their service and as officials in their affairs.
(Garcilaso 1966/1, VII, III, 406)

Garcilaso would go even further, restricting the scope of the general language to refer, in a far more exclusive manner, to the Cuzcoan variety.

In fact, according to our mestizo historian, not only the general concepts pertained exclusively to the Cuzco dialect, but the language's correct usage, as Oré had believed, was likewise a specific attribute of the city dwellers of Cuzco. Garcilaso demonstrates "how far astray those who have not been suckled in the city of Cuzco itself may go (even if they are Indians) in interpreting the Peruvian language," for "those who are not natives of Cuzco are just as rustic and strange in the language as the Castilians" (Garcilaso 1966/1, V, XXI, 288). The disdain with which he refers to the Quechua language spoken by Felipillo should then come as no surprise, for the unfortunate interpreter "had in fact learned the language of the Incas, not in Cuzco, but in Túmbez, from Indians who speak as barbarously and corruptly as foreigners . . . [because] to all the Indians but the natives of Cuzco this is a foreign language" (Garcilaso 1966/2, I, XXIII, 681–682). But Garcilaso Inca was not content merely to endow the general language with a Cuzcoan territorial exclusivity. He sought to ascribe to it an imperial usage, thus restricting it even more. He asserts as much when he states that

> this language having been the idiom of the court, and the Incas having been the chief courtiers, they speak it most excellently and better than all others; and I, as the son of an Inca princess and the nephew of Inca princes, know how to speak it as well if not better and more eloquently than those Indians who are not Incas. (Garcilaso 1951b, II, Part 1, VI, 80)

Thus, the notion of a general language, as characterized in the beginning by the authors cited above, was completely "resemantized" by being circumscribed, in "diatopical" and "diastratical" terms, within a specific territory and ascribed to a particular "socio-elect." Garcilaso's reductionism is obvious, not only in view of the selective criteria that guided the Quechuanists at the Third Council of Lima who strove to standardize the general language. Concerned as they were to gain a major audience among the different "nations" of the old empire, they had tried to regularize the Cuzco dialect, stripping it of its "exquisite" and "obscure" attributes, since such qualities "went beyond the possibilites of that language, called appropriately Quechua, by introducing old terms which were not presently used, having borrowed them from those employed by the Incas and lords, or taking them from other nations they deal with" (Tercer Concilio Limense [1584] 1985, "Annotaciones," fol. [74]). From the perspective of the intercomprehension among the Quechua dialects, it also became evident that the Cuzco dialect was not the best one to guarantee a major audience. In fact, Pedro Pizarro, an observer who was familiar with the "general language" of a Chinchaisuyan origin, could rightly say that the language "of the lords and 'orexones' [Cuzco noblemen] was the most awkward of all" (Pizarro [1571] 1978, XIII, 75).

REVINDICATION OF THE CHINCHAISUYO DIALECT AS THE GENERAL LANGUAGE

To attempt to identify the approximate referent of what the early colonial recordings designated as the general language, it is necessary, as we have already suggested (Cerrón-Palomino 1987), to analyze the scattered corpus offered by the early documentation as well as that provided by the first "reduction in art" and the systematization of the Quechua grammar and lexicon, respectively. In comparing such a corpus with the one we have from the Cuzco dialect, one should seriously reconsider the tradition examined by Murúa, according to which Huayna Capac, the last Inca emperor,

> ordered that the language of Chinchay Suyo should be spoken throughout all the land, the language which is commonly now referred to as general Quechua, or Cuzco's Quechua, for his mother had been Yunga, a native of Chincha. It is, however, more probable that his mother was Mama Ocllo, wife of Tupa Inga Yupanqui, his

father, who commanded that the language of Chinchay Suyo should be spoken by everyone, in honor of his much beloved wife, a native of Chincha. (Murúa [1613] 1987, I, XXXVII, 136)

Garcilaso's distortions concerning the Cuzco-centric and aristocratic character that he attributed to the general language were more than successful, for they were dominant not only during the Colonial period but they persist even today. They are among the most "graceful fallacies" for those who oppose the Cuzco Quechua dialect and prefer instead other Quechua dialects, still often considered mere "corruptions" or "bastardizations" of the Cuzco variety (Cerrón-Palomino 1991, 1993). Despite the heated discussions on the supposedly original character of the Cuzco dialect and its orthographic standardization, many of Garcilaso's countrymen today (members of Academy of the Quechua Language) have denied Garcilaso's authentic "Cuzconicity," and have asserted that due to the fact of his early expatriation, the later historian had forgotten most of his mother tongue.

Ten

EDUARDO HOPKINS-RODRÍGUEZ

The Discourse on Exemplarity in Garcilaso de la Vega's La Florida del Inca

THE DISCOURSE ON EXEMPLARITY is an intrinsic component of Garcilaso de la Vega's *La Florida del Ynca* (1605). Such a discourse is not merely a set of sententious pronouncements expressed in a vague ethical or moral sense, nor is it employed for strictly ornamental purposes. On the contrary, exemplarity is one of the main constituents of the historical discourse of *La Florida*.

The theme of exemplarity recurs in other works by Garcilaso. In the prologue to Part II of the *Royal Commentaries,* he explains: "Great deeds of men, distinguished in peace and letters or in arms and wars, are perpetuated in writing for three reasons: to bestow perpetual fame on their merits; in order to honor the country, whose noble reputation comes from so illustrious citizens and neigbors; and to serve as models worthy of imitation by posterity" (Garcilaso 1944, prologue, 11).

In *Florida,* on the other hand, exemplarity is directly related to specific objectives the writer wants to achieve in the text. José Durand (1976, 144) insists that Garcilaso's ideas "follow a definite ethical orientation" and stresses the fact that Garcilaso was a highly ideological writer whose works contain a great amount of conceptual material in relation to the theme of the exemplar. It is our purpose here to provide an interpretation of this material in the *Florida.*

The concept of the exemplar prevalent in the European culture of the sixteenth and seventeenth centuries already had a long tradition which began during classical antiquity. In the Christian world it became a norm, especially when applied for didactic purposes in the fields of art, literature, and history. The rhetorical principle of persuasion thus commanded an exceptional role, because its basic purpose was to influence the spirit of the receptors—the intended readers—and guide them through life.

The receptors in *Florida* are the Spanish king, noblemen, lords, the Spaniards in general, and the people of the New World. Just as the receptors are complex, so is Garcilaso's ideological message. His position becomes clearer, however, due to the fact that Garcilaso advocates the universality of human nature. Juan Bautista Avalle-Arce has indicated that there is

> one supposition that is inherent in all of Garcilaso's works, which refers to the fundamental psychological uniformity of the human race, that in spite of differences in climate, race, time, etc., all people always react essentially in a similar way. In *Florida*, this position is evidenced through a series of parallelisms and comparisons between the Indians from Florida, people from classical antiquity, Indians from México and Perú, and the Spaniards as well. (1964, 120)

The narrator of *Florida* declares that "the desire for immortality through the preservation of one's fame is a natural instinct among men of all nations no matter how barbarous they may be" (Garcilaso 1951b, II, Part 1, XIX, 129). When chief Guachoya sneezes, his vassals make ceremonial salutes, and the governor "amazed at this, said to the cavaliers and captains who were with him: 'Do you not see how the whole world is one?' " The Spaniards were greatly impressed that among barbaric people "the same or greater ceremonies are used when sneezing as are observed by those who are considered to be most civil" (Garcilaso 1951b, V, Part 1, V, 491). A warrior says on another occasion: "If we possessed such large canoes as yours (he means to say ships), we would follow you to your own land and conquer it, for we too are men like yourselves" (Garcilaso 1951b, VI, X, 595). It is important to note that for Garcilaso it is not sufficient merely to suppose that human nature is universal. Rather, he insists on demonstrating this idea by providing concrete examples followed by explicit and implicit propositions. If we recall the European prejudices of the time against the culture, spirit, and intelligence of the New World inhabitants, it is easier to comprehend Garcilaso's efforts to include himself and his countrymen within the universal paradigm of human nature.

Social and ethnic differences are accidental or, in Garcilaso's words, they constitute a "particularity" within the universal. He believes that above social hierarchies and ethnic differences reigns the universal man. This thesis of Garcilaso, in which he insightfully readjusts and refines Eurocentric anthropological concepts of his time, allows the recognition of similarities within spatial and temporal diversity. Geography and history produce and display diversity, and yet with some degree of wisdom it is possible to grasp what is alike or similar. When that moment of insight is reached, the discourse on exemplarity intervenes and plays an essential role.

For Garcilaso, written history must be persuasive, whether it admonishes or provides a model. Historical facts reveal their meaningfulness after they are interpreted or explained through exemplary discourse, an interpretation achieved by exercising wisdom, precodified by tradition, common sense, religion, and history. The issues are then connected to concepts of universal value. Such concepts establish the relationship between the universal and the particular. In other words, when the particular coincides with a universal ethical and moral scheme, it implicitly becomes integrated into the universal. According to Garcilaso's argument, the inhabitants of the New World cannot be alienated from universal moral values.

In *Florida,* Garcilaso proposes the theme of equality between the Europeans and the Incas. This objective is just since the Incas deserve equal recognition. Although many differences exist between the Europeans and the people of the New World, they must be overcome for the sake of equality.

Florida tells the history of a frustrated conquest, and Garcilaso describes it as a peregrination which became more and more erratic. Peregrination is not an accidental term used in this book, as suggested by the author's comments on one of his sources: "Alonso de Carmona in his *Peregrinación* has the following to say" (Garcilaso 1951b, I, VIII, 28). Carmona had participated in Hernando de Soto's expedition to Florida. When this peregrination is interpreted as a metaphor of existence, it projects universal values concerning human behavior and destiny. *Florida* can be appreciated as an initiation episode: the reader feels he is witnessing a distant ritual that illustrates the transit of blinded men through life. After witnessing the collapse of the Spanish expedition in North America, the reader experiences a kind of catharsis, which elicits an insight into the meaning of his or her own life. Upon reflecting on the narrated events, the receptor is progressively enlightened. All moral example requires a mimesis, through which the lesson can be realized pragmatically in the reader. The use of the exemplar provides a model to be emulated. In the discourse on the exemplar, wisdom gives it authority. The projection of this exemplar on the image of a wise person or a wise author is the culmination of this process. The moral concepts contained in the text allow the narrator to introduce himself to the reader (Bajtin 1991, 164) and to reinforce the heroic character of his position in the world.

The exemplar implies an "ought to be"; it establishes an imperative, which concerns especially chiefs or leaders rather than the masses. For Garcilaso, all persons are subject to the same ethical and moral standards, but their obligations differ in accordance with their station in society. In *Florida,* a basic concept inherent in the exemplar is that it must be merited. This implies the notion of evaluation and justice, resulting in reward or punishment. Recognition or oblivion also play a prominent part. At times fortune and destiny break the continuity of the pattern and can, therefore, be judged as unjust. People can also be blind in their evaluation of themselves and others. The correct judgment of situations within our own sphere, as well as in that of others, is a central axis which establishes adequate conduct in the world. Thus the exemplar can be understood as the principle of universality of the human race, and also as the criterion which determines the relationships among people. In the New World, such relationship entailed accepting the fact that its inhabitants were just like anybody else. Therefore, for Garcilaso, the exemplar was not an abstract or neutral concept, but was related rather to concrete historical, cultural, and personal situations.

According to a universal morality, communication with the indigenous people ought to be conducted with respect, as the Europeans labored toward superior ends—expansion of the Spanish power and the evangelization of the natives. Their ethic of political action would be held accountable to their superiors, history, and divine powers. Irving Leonard has explained the importance of moral issues in the political discussions during the sixteenth century and their influence on Garcilaso (Leonard 1990, 62–63). Garcilaso, for example, held that the success of the Spanish conquest would prevent the natives from falling under the influence of non-Catholic governments, as long as the Spanish sovereignty were guided by the concept of the exemplar.

The discourse on the exemplar in *Florida* is markedly influenced by prudence. In this work, prudence encompasses all the other moral dictates. Garcilaso harshly criticizes the lack of prudence in the actions of powerful people. In these men, the absence of discretion (judgment) and the dominance of arrogance becomes one of his first concerns:

> But who is to control a wild beast? Or who is to counsel the free and powerful, confident of themselves and persuaded that wisdom accompanies material wealth, and confident that he who enjoys an advantage of riches over one who has gained nothing, enjoys the same advantage in wisdom and discretion, things that are not learned? Such a person does not seek advice, does not want to receive it, and cannot abide those who are willing to give it. (Garcilaso 1951b, II, Part 1, XII, 101)

Garcilaso argues that if someone has offended a powerful tyrant, that he would have to renounce his own pride in order to try to regain the tyrant's favor. The prudent way to proceed is to keep one's distance:

137

When tyrannous princes and powerful men feel, with or without reason, that they have been offended, they are seldom or never wont to grant the favor of reconciliation and pardon that generous spirits deserve. On the contrary it would seem that the more such a person insists on his virtues, the more he offends. Therefore, it appears to me in my poor judgment that he who sees himself in such a predicament should go, for the love of God, and beg his food wherever he may find it rather than persist in the service of this kind of master, for regardless of what miracles he may succeed in performing, they will not be sufficient to restore him to the grace of the one he has angered. (Garcilaso 1951b, II, Part 1, XIV, 113)

Garcilaso shows skepticism towards the conduct of tyrants: "Hence Casquin had remained passive and had contented himself with guarding his boundaries, neither going beyond them nor affording his enemy [Cacique Capaha] an occasion to attack, since it suffices not to give tyrants an excuse" (Garcilaso 1951, IV, VII, 435).

The imprudent tyrant will eventually bring about his own destruction:

The rashness and arrogance of Vitacucho, born of a spirit more ferocious than prudent and spawned in excessive presumption and lack of counsel, thus terminated in his having brought about without any purpose his own death as well as that of a thousand and three hundred of his vassals, who were the best and noblest of his state—and all because he had not taken counsel with some of his own people as he did with those strangers who later proved to be his enemies. (Garcilaso 1951b, II, Part 1, XXIX, 168)

Garcilaso's personal enmity towards Inca Atahualpa is well-known. In *Florida* he presents Atahualpa as a model of an imprudent tyrant who destroys himself and his people:

. . . that bastard son who stole the Inca throne from its legitimate heir and was the last of his race to rule the empire. Because of the tyrannies and cruelties of this man, the severest of which he used upon his own flesh and blood, the kingdom of the Incas was lost, or at least because of the division and discord which his rebellions and atrocities produced among the natives, the Spaniards found it possible to conquer his realm with the ease that they did, as with divine favor I shall reveal elsewhere. (Garcilaso 1951b, I, I, 3–4)

From the universal perspective of the human race, Garcilaso proposes that an example of a ruler worthy of emulation by all European princes is a leader from Florida, Chief Mucozo:

It suffices to represent the magnanimity of an infidel so that princes of the Faith may make efforts to imitate and if possible surpass him—not in infidelity, as some do who are undeserving of the title of Christian, but in virtue and similar excellences; for being of a more lofty estate, they are under greater obligations. (Garcilaso 1951b, II, Part 1, IV, 74)

Garcilaso paints an endearing portrait of Mucozo:

He was born with a most generous and heroic spirit and did not deserve to have come into the world and lived in the barbarous paganism of Florida. But God and human nature many times produce such souls in sterile and uncultivated deserts to the greater confusion and shame of people who are born and reared in lands that are fertile and abundant in all good doctrines and sciences, as well as the Christian religion. (Ibid.)

Hernando de Soto, leader of the expedition to Florida, is the subject of a long peroration by Garcilaso concerning the virtues and defects of his leadership. Garcilaso points out particularly his imprudent behavior, which he finds unfortunate and "the source and the principal cause" (Garcilaso 1951b, III, XXXIII, 387) of his failure. He believes that de Soto should have handled the insurrections forcefully instead of being paralyzed by indecisiveness:

In such a grave situation, it would have been wise for the Governor to have sought and accepted advice from those of his friends whom he could trust in order to have done prudently and harmoniously what would have been to the best advantage of all. Thus he could have prevented an insurrection by punishing its leaders and permitting the rest of the league, who were few, to take warning from the experience. In that way he would not have ruined himself and damaged all of his people by keeping secret the angry opinion which resulted in his own destruction. For although he was as circumspect as we have seen him to be in his own affairs, still, when enraged he could not maintain the clarity and liberal judgment that serious matters require. But let him who flees from seeking and accepting advice not hope to succeed. (Garcilaso 1951b, III, XXXIII, 388)

In accordance with what we have proposed above, the theme of exemplarity is a basic component of the ideological plane of *Florida* and should occupy a central role in the discussions about the persuasive intentions of Garcilaso's discourse.

Eleven

MIGUEL MATICORENA ESTRADA

A New and Unpublished Manuscript of Garcilaso's Florida

AN EARLY AND STILL UNPUBLISHED MANUSCRIPT of Garcilaso's *La Florida del Ynca* (*The Florida of the Inca*) has opened up new areas of inquiry.[1] The basic structure of this manuscript is similar to that of the first edition, published in 1605 in Lisbon, Portugal, but it varies in the order in which the themes are introduced. Whole paragraphs in the manuscript are exactly the same as those in the published edition. Other topics, however, are discussed in only a few lines, whereas they fill several pages in the 1605 edition. Although some of the information in this essay has appeared previously (Maticorena 1967, 1989), we here offer additional information, rectify some previous mistakes, and wish to affirm with certitude that this manuscript was written by Garcilaso Inca.

The manuscript is entitled *Historia de los Sucesos de la Florida del Adelantado Hernando de Soto*. It is comprised of forty folios, divided into ninety-six unnumbered sections. It narrates events from 1539 to 1543, ending shortly after the death of Hernando de Soto. It is a much shorter version than the book published in 1605, which contains 179 chapters. The features of the handwriting correspond to those of the late sixteenth century. Although the uniformity indicates that the text was written by one person, there are several marginal notes written by other hands. The years are written on the margins. The annotations at the end were not written by Garcilaso, since he is mentioned in them as being the author of the text. Furthermore, we believe that the anonymous annotator was reading another and still unknown copy of the same manuscript, since in fol. 18v an addition in brackets appears with the explanation, "this appears above"; and the added text appears in exactly the same place in the 1605 edition, although it is absent in Antonio de Herrera's *Historia de los Hechos de los Castellanos* (1601, 1615), also known as the *Décadas* (*Decades*), which is discussed below. The absence is significant, since Herrera had an early manuscript of *Florida*, although he does not identify Garcilaso as being the author.

On the first page, under the title, is written, "It cost me my own money and does not belong to the King." Whoever wrote this warning seemed to be interested in historical matters and had access to official or palace papers, as well as the clout and money to acquire them. In the manuscript the word "Pirú" consistently appears instead of "Perú". This is significant in dating the manuscript, as has been demonstrated by Durand (1949b, 278–290), because Garcilaso used the word "Perú" in his *Diálogos de Amor de León Hebreo* (1590), and from then on he preferred this designation. However, the manuscript coincides with the 1605 edition in certain orthographic preferences, i.e., both use "Avana" for "Habana," "Hamo" for "Amo," "hyzquierda" for "izquierda," and "Spínola" for "Espíndola."

The existence of this manuscript poses obvious hermeneutical as well as other very specific problems. First, an internal criticism of the manuscript clearly indicates that it is one of the first written accounts of the oral version Garcilaso received from Gonzalo Silvestre, his principal informant (Durand 1966). Yet the contents of this manuscript are duplicated almost entirely in Antonio de Herrera's *Decades*. There is written evidence that Herrera had in his possession one of Garcilaso's manuscripts of *Florida*. Garcilaso himself complained that his work had been plagiarized by an unnamed chronicler, and expressed his deep concern in a letter he wrote in 1609: "I now fear that some historian may have stolen [information] . . . because that book [*Florida*], due to my obligations, had to be dispatched away in order to receive the necessary approvals, and I know it was handled by several people" (Asensio 1953). It should also be remembered that Garcilaso had encountered resistance, indeed opposition, to the publication of his book, and he complained that due to "tyrannical" reasons he had to publish it in Lisbon rather than in Spain.

Another strong indication that the manuscript was written by Garcilaso and not Herrera has to do with the different ideological positions in both texts. The manuscript reveals a favorable attitude toward the Indians, which is Garcilaso's position. Herrera, on the other hand, held adverse views of the Indians. In his opinion, the Indians are the aggressors, while the Spaniards are the victims.

WRITING AND CHRONOLOGY

Florida was written in two stages, as has been evidenced by the investigations of Durand (1954, 1962a) and Miró-Quesada (1971): the first, between 1585 and 1589; the second, starting around 1590. The project had been described by Garcilaso in 1586 in the dedication of his translation of the *Diálogos de Amor de León Hebreo*. He announces there that he will dedicate to the King "the journey of the Conquistador Hernando de Soto to Florida." In 1587, Garcilaso mentions that he has "written more than one-fourth" of the book. Without revealing the name, he states that his principal informant is a gentleman who resides in Las Posadas, a little town in southern Spain. It was later discovered, however, that this man was the conquistador Gonzalo Silvestre.

Around 1587, Garcilaso located a manuscript on the Florida expedition written by Alonso de Carmona, entitled *Peregrinaciones*. At about the same time he found still another manuscript, written by Juan de Coles, in a printer's shop in the city of Córdoba. Both Carmona and Coles had been members of Soto's expedition to Florida, but they do not appear to have known Gonzalo Silvestre. Soon afterwards, Garcilaso again revised his account, based on these two manuscripts, and thus we find in the *Florida* information mentioned only by Carmona and Coles. For example, Juan de Coles tells the story of a soldier named Juan Ortiz who had lived several years among the Indians in Florida and had forgotten the Spanish language almost entirely. When he was attacked by a Spanish soldier, Juan Ortiz tried to identify himself but could only utter "Xivilla, Xivilla" (Sevilla, Sevilla) and make the sign of the cross with his bow.

In another instance, described by both Carmona and Coles, Juan Ortiz asked the Indians to come forward, but one of them was wounded by a Spaniard. The manuscript reads: [they fled and] "some did not stop until they reached town; others came by three's and by two's." Garcilaso made only slight changes in the final 1605 edition, providing a few more details and altering the amount to "three's and four's." These and similar texts show that Garcilaso began to incorporate materials from Carmona and Coles into his own version soon after he received them. This strongly suggests that the manuscript may have been written by or before 1587.

It does not seem likely that the *one-fourth part*, mentioned by Garcilaso, corresponds to this manuscript. It is known that Garcilaso sent the one-fourth part to Ambrosio de Morales, the Royal Chronicler. Morales found it acceptable after comparing it with another, still unknown text on the Soto expedition that he had in his possession. It seems unlikely that Garcilaso would have sent a draft with no chapter headings, with corrections and additions between the lines, to a respected friend. Since Morales died in 1591, the one-fourth part must have been completed before that date.

Miró-Quesada and Durand have indicated that a second version of *Florida* was finished in 1592. Garcilaso himself made this announcement in a letter to Francisco Fernández Franco: "I have finished the *History of Florida* . . . the work has stopped for lack of scribes who can rewrite it" (Asensio 1953, 583–593). In 1602, Garcilaso again revised his book, removed the part concerning the origin of the name "Perú," and inserted it in the *Royal Commentaries*. The *Relación de la descendencia de Garci Pérez de Vargas (1596),* which was intended to be *Florida's* prologue, is also removed. The publication was delayed several more years. In 1599 he legally authorized Juan de Morales to make arrangements to publish his book, and the definitive title is mentioned for the first time: *La Florida del Inca*. It was finally printed in Lisbon in 1605, over fifteen years after the first draft had been completed. During this long period of time, the text underwent many corrections and it passed through several hands.

Since Garcilaso wrote "Pirú" instead of "Perú" in the early manuscript, Durand believes it was written before 1590. Since this manuscript cannot be the one-fourth part that was mentioned in 1587, we propose that it was written in that year or even earlier.

THE *DECADES* BY ANTONIO DE HERRERA

Herrera had been named official chronicler of the Indies in 1596. Due to the enormity of the task, he sought information wherever it was available and relied heavily on the chronicles which he found at the Royal Palace. He proceeded to copy from various sources, depending on the subject matter. He obtained geographical data from López de Velasco. He drew information about Columbus from Hernando de Soto and Las Casas. For different regions he selected from appropriate sources: for México, from Cervantes de Salazar, Bernal Díaz, and Gómara; for Perú, from Cieza de León, Zárate, López de Jerez, Diego Fernández, and others.

Herrera's first four *Decades* were published in 1601 and the remaining four in 1615. He devoted *Decades* VI and VII to narrating the expedition of Hernando de Soto to Florida. By comparing the printed edition of *Florida* with the *Decades,* several scholars— Porras Barrenechea 1955, Vargas Ugarte 1930, Durand 1954, and Miró-Quesada 1971—have noted that Herrera's source was Garcilaso. Herrera misleads us, however, because he states that the material about Florida was sent by the Viceroy of México and it was brought by a "friar minor," for whom he requested a remuneration. Herrera also says that this account had been written by a member of the Hernando de Soto expedition, but does not mention his name.

There is strong evidence that around 1602 or 1603 Herrera

had in his possession a copy of a manuscript of Garcilaso's *Florida,*
based on information revealed during the lawsuit initiated by
Count of Puñonrostro, descendant of Pedrarías Dávila, second
governor of the Darien province (presently Panama), against
Herrera. The Count wanted Herrera to rectify his harsh criticism
of Dávila. During the legal proceedings, Herrera was asked about
the historical sources of the *Decades,* and he identified in writing
the authors "who have written on matters of the Indies: Alvar
Núñez Cabeza de Vaca, *Cosas de la Florida;* Garcilas (*sic*) Inga, on
the same subject: it is not yet printed" (Medina 1913, vol. 2, 530).
Herrera, however, never mentioned Garcilaso in his *Decades.* He
then either erred or concealed the truth. It is clear that a manuscript of Garcilaso, based on Silvestre's account of the expedition, is Herrera's direct source. Moreover, textual comparison
strongly indicates that this source was the early manuscript under
discussion.

TEXTUAL COMPARISONS

Numerous events narrated in the early manuscript, and also in
Herrera's *Decades,* appear very briefly and succinctly in comparison with the 1605 edition, as suggested by the following examples. A close textual comparison illustrates the development of
Garcilaso's descriptive and narrative art over time, as well as the
similarity between Herrera's history and the early manuscript.

The scene when Hernando de Soto encounters Juan Ortiz,
mentioned above, is revealing. The identical text appears in both
Herrera and the early manuscript. Garcilaso's 1605 edition, however, is adorned with additional descriptions that pertain to the
psychology of the characters. He narrates that Soto felt "pity and
pain when learning about the travails" of Ortiz, and he even "ca-
resses the Indians who accompanied" him (cf. Herrera 1954, VI,
x; Garcilaso 1951b, II, VII). In another scene, Hernando de Soto
asks Juan Ortiz to report on the conditions of the land where he
had lived with the Indians. Ortiz answers that he knew little because he never strayed away from his second Indian master, so as
not to awake suspicions that he wanted to escape. Garcilaso's per-

tinent comments insinuated that, in spite of the good treatment
by *cacique* Mucozo, Ortiz actually lived in a threatening environment (cf. Herrera 1954, VI, X; Garcilaso 1951b, II, VII).

The scene when *cacique* Mucozo visits Hernando de Soto is described briefly in the early manuscript, and Herrera recalls it in
only two lines. The 1605 edition, however, expands upon it no-
ticeably: Mucozo gives a long speech, after a colorful description
of the welcoming ceremony (cf. Herrera 1954, VI, X; Garcilaso
1951b, II, VII).

In another instance, Hernando de Soto was planning with
an Indian *cacique* to build a bridge across a ravine over a river.
The early manuscript provides succinctly the basic information.
Herrera summarizes the event in three lines. Garcilaso (1605)
elaborates, adds dialogue, increases the number of Indian aggressors, and describes the vociferous Indians on the other side
of the precipice, who shout threats and strong insults at the Spaniards.

Another interesting scene reveals careful elaboration in the
first edition of 1605, introducing an important philosophical
theme (Maticorena 1989). Hernando de Soto receives *cacique*
Guachoya and his entourage. In the early manuscript the *cacique*
sneezed forcefully and all the Indians present lowered their
heads, spread their arms open, and deferentially said, "the sun
keep you, the sun be with you, the sun give you greatness, and
similar expressions." Herrera repeats basically the same words.
This event also appears in the 1605 edition, with an added scene
in which the Spaniards are astonished to discover that the Indians compliment their leader in the same fashion as the Spaniards. Governor Soto explains to his surprised people: "Don't
you see that the whole world is but one?" This is an important
reference to the idea of the unity of the human race and the
world. López de Gómara had expressed a cosmological interpretation by saying that "the world is one and not many." The organic concept of the "whole" and its "parts" was revived by late
Scholasticism. It also appears in León Hebreo: "the final purpose
of the whole is the unifying perfection of all the Universe." Juan

Bautista Avalle-Arce (1964) refers to another text of Garcilaso which also demonstrates Garcilaso's reference to the concept of "uniformism."

CONCLUSION

The date of the early manuscript is probably about 1587, long before Garcilaso had finished the first completed version. In 1587 there seem to have been two extant manuscripts: the one we have described, and on which Herrera relied, was primarily a summary; the other is said to be about one-fourth of the total. In both of them the account of the events proceeded largely from the oral version of Gonzalo Silvestre. Garcilaso later incorporated in the early manuscript information that he obtained from the versions of Juan de Coles and Alonso de Carmona. A comparison of the early manuscript with the final, richer version published in 1605 illustrates the development of Garcilaso's narrative artistry.

NOTE

1. This manuscript belongs to a private collection in Seville, Spain.

Twelve

JOSÉ ANADÓN

History as Autobiography in Garcilaso Inca

CHRONICLERS OF ALL TIMES HAVE provided autobiographical references in their works. There are numerous motives for such autobiographical revelations, but it would seem that some predominate, namely, a desire to disclose one's personal memoirs at a certain point in one's life, a psychological need to confide in others, and perhaps a wish to impress and dazzle the reader by creating a singular image of oneself. An autobiography can express, in various combinations and proportions, self-love or vanity, timidity or insecurity, or even mere self-interest. The chroniclers of the Indies in particular frequently emphasized the personal note, either occasionally or at times even continuously.[1] Circumstances alone prompted some of these chroniclers to assume the role of narrator, and their expertise varied widely, from the quasi-illiterate soldier-writer to the epic poet. The style and tone of their discourse thus reflect an entire human spectrum, ranging from devious self-seeking, to unadorned sobriety, to the heights of veiled subtleties and nuances of meanings. Throughout this vast array of autobiographical voices and forms of expression, Garcilaso Inca de la Vega represents a singular case. He lived during historical moments of extraordinary importance, and his own life was equally remarkable. Under such circumstances, the combination produced a unique view of those times as well as a prescient insight into the future of the mestizo Ameri-

149

can culture. The autobiographical valuation of history in the writings of Garcilaso is therefore a topic which needs to be studied in greater depth.[2]

The history of the Americas unveiled a fertile field for Garcilaso. It offered splendid themes and represented a vehicle through which he would be able to fulfill his inner ambition to obtain recognition and honor. His strong desire to achieve renown through writing becomes obvious in the dedications of his books. Although this activity satisfied an evident and authentic aesthetic vocation, he began to publish only late in life, when he was already past fifty. History, nonetheless, meant much more than this to Garcilaso, since it became the medium whereby his own most intimate conflict would be exorcized. Like many of his Peruvian mestizo contemporaries, he endured the anguished dislocation of his existence as a result of his double heritage, Indian and Spanish. The general wretchedness and poverty of the mestizos of Imperial Inca blood who lived in Spain during the sixteenth and seventeenth centuries is well documented (Dunbar Temple 1948, 112–156). In contrast, Garcilaso appears as a learned scholar of the Renaissance who is dedicated to the reconstruction of the image of his native land. It is an admirable image: serene, mature, balanced, and more estimable because Garcilaso's personal drama was implicated in it. He had witnessed and had been intimately affected by those crucial historical events that had crushed both the Incas and the first Spaniards to arrive in Perú. In a sudden turn of events, the two worlds in which he grew up ceased to exist, and from then on his eyes were to remain fixed on distant memories alone. As Garcilaso narrated the fall of the Incas and the Peruvian conquistadors in his historical work, he was simultaneously recalling and interpreting his own broken existence.

The autobiographical aspects of many passages in Garcilaso's writings reveal a complex process of psychological development and maturation. His recollections are incorporated profusely throughout each of his books, and always with visible distinction. Such an abundance suggests a rich diversity and unbounded nu-

ances of meaning. The recollections are expressed in varied
ways: evocations of incidents personally experienced, confidences about events happening to him at the precise moment of
writing, or abundant news about his family, friends, and distant
lands. It is a wide-ranging display of subject matter, conveyed
through myriad conceptual and emotional intonations, full of
historical significance and literary possibilities.

The unique identification of the self with history, as it appears
in Garcilaso, has yet to attract theoretical attention. Although different facets of autobiography have been studied—the genealogical model, the metaphor of travel or a journey, the confes-
sional mode, the narrative in first person, for example—this
combination in Garcilaso introduces variables which are more
difficult to systematize. Recent studies on autobiography from
the perspective of the social sciences provide a wider framework
within which to develop our exploration. According to this approach, the author's objectives become the principal object of
inquiry: "The autobiographical discourse refers more directly to
the interpretative intents of the subject and to the image it constructs . . . rather than to the description of historical events"
(Piña 1988, 3). An autobiography is thus "a process of compre-
hension and interpretation" around a subject which has been
structured linguistically into the text. Through this process one
is able to glean "attributions of meaning" which conform to the
image of the self. Garcilaso's intent is precisely to impose upon
the reader his own vision of the historical worlds he witnessed,
both maternal and paternal. It must be emphasized, as Piña asserts, that autobiography is not merely a description of particular
historical events, an aspect which Diamela Eltit (1997, 42–43)
has recently explained insightfully:

> Autobiography takes place in the process by which memory is writ-
> ten. For this reason, autobiography cannot be read literally as the
> truth. Instead, it should be taken as . . . a biographical *mise en scène*
> where the "I" activated in the text is, ultimately, a fiction. I'm not
> talking about the traditional opposition between truth and lies, but

the fact that autobiography is an act that impels us to construct another place where it is possible to apprehend another perspective of reality.

In the case of Garcilaso, this perspective is useful in de-emphasizing the question of the historical accuracy of his narrative, thus averting a problem that has traditionally plagued Garcilaso scholarship. Although Garcilaso's subjectivity at times interferes with his historical rendition, his views nonetheless add a depth of understanding to such a vital period.

How is the image of the self created in Garcilaso? What meanings have designed the image of that self? We will first explore his continuous exposure to environments nourished by a propensity towards first-person accounts, in Cuzco and in Spain. We will then examine the abundant autobiographical references in all of Garcilaso's writings. When the image that he formed of himself from his privileged vantage point is finally complete, at the moment he finished his last book (he died shortly thereafter), it contains not only a profound interpretation of historical events but a fundamental message for future generations as well. These perceptions, derived from Garcilaso's life and works, underscore the fact that, ultimately, autobiographical discourse provides a vehicle whereby meanings are apprehended and shared collectively by the readers (Piña 1988, 5).

RECITATIONS: HIS SELF IN THE PAST

Although Garcilaso's biographers have noted his references to childhood stories (most recently Ramírez Ribes 1993, 84–88), we can never meditate enough on the significance of those experiences which took place both in his mother's and his father's milieu. Garcilaso grew up among famous people who eagerly recited their glorious deeds. Those engaging stories, which he began to hear from his earliest years, captivated him forever. "It is my opinion," writes Cieza de León, "that the conquistadors and settlers of these lands while away their time by recalling their battles and their consequences" (Cieza de León 1986, CXIII, 298). Garcilaso often refers to that custom: "I heard them in my own country," he says, "from my father and his contemporaries, whose favorite and usual conversation was to repeat the stirring and notable deeds performed in their conquests" (Garcilaso 1966/1, I, III, 13). Recalling the famous stanza on the Gallo island, he affirms that "as a child, I often heard these lines repeated by Spaniards telling these events in the conquest of the New World. . . . I later in Spain came upon them" in López de Gómara's chronicle, where I "was very glad to find them for the memories they called to my mind" (Garcilaso 1966/2, I, VIII, 650). These words disclose his satisfaction in having been a witness of the story, and at the same time his recollection awakens within him a keen sense of nostalgia. He also reveals the place where he heard most of those tales: "I heard them in my father's house—where, as I have said, this was the main theme of conversation during their leisure" (Garcilaso 1966/2, II, XVI, 774). Recalling Carvajal and the battle of Jauijahuana, he states: "I shall say what I heard from those who were in his company that day, among whom I was reared from the age of nine—my ninth birthday was the day following these events—till I was twenty, when I left Perú" (Garcilaso 1966/2, V, XL, 1206). In this important and characteristic passage, Garcilaso associates at one and the same time the affirmation of the witness, intimate confessions, precise chronological references to his life, and the typical reference to the famous trip that defined his future, when he left Perú never to return again.

Such was the environment which nurtured Garcilaso as a boy and a young man. However, those who narrated their experiences, sitting in a circle of friends, as was customary then among soldiers, were not just the old Spanish warriors. When Indian relatives visited his mother, they would also sit and recall the previous times of prosperity. Then they would mourn "their dead kings, their lost empire, and their fallen state." During those conversations, "I, as a boy, often came in and went out of the place where they were, and I loved to hear them, as boys always do like to hear stories. Days, months, and years went by, until I was sixteen or seventeen" (Garcilaso 1966/1, I, XV, 41). He further elaborates: "they talked to me at length about their laws and

government . . . they told me, as if I were their own son, all about
their idolatry, rites, ceremonies, and sacrifices. . . . In short, I
would say that they told me about everything they had in their
state" (Garcilaso 1966/1, I, XIX, 49–50). And he insists, chapters
later: "it was chiefly with these that I conversed as a child," the
Incas and Pallas of royal blood (I, XXVI, 64). It was a world far
removed from Europe and its culture, and was depicted in elegiac tones—a natural disposition after the catastrophe that had
destroyed the Inca Empire. Those shattering moments must have
registered deeply in Garcilaso's sensibility.[3]

In those verbal testimonies which he heard from both families early in life, we find the latent congenital drama that marked
his entire existence. Both worlds were equally his and were fascinating to his childhood mentality. Invariably, those experiences
became perpetually ingrained. It is a known phenomenon that
childhood memories, and even those from youth, become embedded in people's minds much more easily than recent ones. In
Garcilaso, such abundant autobiographical recollections, voiced
by so many friendly people close to him, Indians and Spaniards
alike, appear to be familiar and daily affairs. They emerge and
are depicted in his writings with the simplicity of spontaneous
occurrences and the vigorous impulse of nature.

MORE RECITATIONS: HIS SELF IN SPAIN

The general atmosphere Garcilaso knew in Cuzco did not vary
in Spain, for this was a century historically charged. Amidst battles and heroic deeds, strong characters abounded. One of them
was Garcilaso's uncle, Alonso de Vargas, the old captain under
Charles V and the former colleague-of-arms of the Marquis-consort of Priego, who also lived in Montilla and was related to Garcilaso. The country during those times was inebriated by continuous political successes and victories on the battlefield, and it must
have been exciting to listen to the military exploits of a family
hero. In Montilla, site of a provincial court, where distractions
and entertainment were scarcely available, family gatherings and
conversations assumed the character of a primary need. This was
the case particularly among noblemen, who were not allowed to

work with their hands or engage in mercantile activities but had rather to occupy their leisure time in "honest occupations," alternating their duties as courtiers with study or the pursuit of pious causes.

Within this context, inevitable chats ensued between the old and experienced captain and his intelligent nephew. The affection the old gentleman had for him was obvious, as he willed him one-half of his fortune. This fondness could have originated from the young Garcilaso's attentiveness and opportune comments, a demonstration of his appreciation and understanding. His uncle Alonso represents in Garcilaso's life one of the strongest bonds with Spain.

The memories recounted by uncle Vargas were augmented by those of Gonzalo Silvestre. Garcilaso had met him in Perú, encountered him again in Madrid, and they saw each other in Montilla. Silvestre then went to live in Las Posadas, a nearby town. Garcilaso's visits to his old friend became more and more frequent, as the "Indiano" dictated to him the events that appear in the *Florida*.

Garcilaso's nostalgia for his distant homeland was somewhat alleviated by talking to travellers coming from Perú, to some who were returning to the viceroyalty, or to an occasional compatriot who dropped by. Among them were a Dominican who lived in Córdoba but who had taught Quechua; a priest who hailed from Quito; a cleric from Montilla who had traveled briefly through the Tahuantinsuyu; his classmate Juan Arias Maldonado; the famous Franciscan writer Luis Jerónimo de Oré, and many others.

Garcilaso held frequent conversations with his neighbors in Córdoba, who inquired about the far-away kingdom of his birth, already legendary soon after its discovery. We now know that scholars from the Andalucia region asked him about matters concerning America. The abbott from Rute, Francisco Fernández de Córdoba, perhaps the most notable genealogist of his time, quotes him three times in his *Didascalia multiplex* (Asensio 1953, 583–593). A famous biblical scholar, the Jesuit Juan de Pineda, quotes him in his *Commentaries on Job*, 1601 (Miró-Quesada 1994, 199–201). The respected philologist Bernardo de Aldrete quotes him in *Origen de la lengua castellana,* 1606, and *Varias antigüedades de España, Africa y otras provincias,* 1614 (Durand 1976, 138 ff.). All of these and many other examples reveal that Garcilaso was a narrator who loved to share his material and discuss it with other persons. He is described by witnesses as being "muy sosegado en sus razones" (very calm in his reasonings) (Vargas Ugarte 1930, 106). It is obvious that this "Antarctic Indian," as he called himself (Garcilaso 1951a, 41), captivated his listeners with his knowledge and intelligence.

Thus, the autobiographical nature of many passsages in Garcilaso's works stem from a complex set of experiences from his early childhood onward. He was an individual who was born and reared amidst verbal communication, who always lived surrounded by oral discourse. After he had achieved a deserved reputation for his historiographical work, he himself addressed "grave and religious persons who have often heard me" (Garcilaso 1966/2, VIII, II, 1419).

PERSONAL TRACES IN HIS WRITINGS

Autobiographical references appear in Garcilaso's very first publication, the *Diálogos,* in the letters to Phillip II and Maximilian which constitute part of the dedication. His main objective was to report services rendered to the Crown and to obtain remuneration from them. References to nonessential but nonetheless interesting minutiae, however, by far surpassed the compulsion to reveal personal information. He stated, for example, that he was about to travel "this fall to Las Posadas, a village in Córdoba," to write the *Florida* (*Diálogos,* "Dedicación," in the "letter to the abbott Maximilian of Austria, March 12 of 1586"). This attention to personal details would seem also to have characterized his private correspondence, at least in the two extant letters written to Fernández Franco (Asensio 1953). This autobiographical trait would reappear in the *Genealogy of Garci Pérez de Vargas* (*Relación de la descendencia . . .*), which is a treatise about his own family. In it, he sought to elucidate to the addressee, namesake of the conqueror of Seville (who defeated the Moors in 1248 and gained the city for Ferdinand the Saint), "the way in which my grandparents are also yours, and also all of us who value your lineage from which we all have come" (Garcilaso 1951a, 34). These intimate digressions appeared repeatedly, up to the final words, which stated that the *Genealogy* had been written "in Córdoba and in this poor rented home" (Garcilaso 1951a, 48). It should be stressed that genealogical studies were his early historical exercises, as he researched parochial and family archives in Extremadura and Andalucia.

In *Florida,* Garcilaso announced repeatedly and with impatience that he was working on his next project on Peruvian history.[4] Moreover, the *Florida* became in large measure the "autobiography" of a friend, Gonzalo Silvestre, who shared with him copious memories from his prodigious mind. Garcilaso subjected Silvestre to a rigorous interrogation process. The series of "questions which I put to him repeatedly" ("preguntas y repreguntas," Garcilaso 1951b, preface, xxxix; and also II, Part 1, XXVII, 157–161) assumed the character of an unexpected exercise in personal memories relative to their historical possibilities. Due to the projection of the work onto his friend, *Florida* can be viewed as a book of an autobiographical nature. It is also truly a monument to friendship, the kind of noble friendship which Garcilaso studied in the Neoplatonic writer Piccolomini, whom he was pleased to quote.[5]

Autobiographical revelations in the *Royal Commentaries* have informed scholars on a variety of subjects and have proven indispensable in the step-by-step reconstruction of the lengthy process in the writing of Garcilaso's books (Durand 1962, 247–266). Similar material is abundant in other authors, for example Cieza de León, but it will never approximate that of Garcilaso's in terms of quantity and detailed descriptions. The *Commentaries* contain poetic depictions of landscapes, fruits, animals, feasts, and entertainments, evocations that have been recognized for their outstanding literary merits.[6] These descriptions provide valuable data about natural as well as folkloric history. Garcilaso's astute mind and penchant for observation have, moreover, furnished information of indisputable value on the social and economic organization of the Incas.[7] In like manner, his writings render extensive observations concerning the social life of Spaniards, Indians, and mestizos, which are of interest not only for their richness but also for the quality of the nuances observed.

Autobiography and nostalgic evocation often go hand in hand. "That I saw," "that I knew," are expressions that frequently occur in his writings when referring to events, things, or persons. These are autobiographical signs as well as certifications from an eyewitness. In some cases, the reiteration of these words denotes contentment, reaching a level of nostalgic delight. Thus, for example, when he described the Inca purification ceremony called *Citua:*

> *I remember* having seen part of this celebration in my childhood. *I saw* the first Inca come down with his spear, though not from the fort, which was already abandoned, but from one of the Incas' houses on the skirt of the hill where the fortress is. The place of this house is called Collcampata. *I saw* the four Indians running with their spears. *I saw* the common people shaking their clothes and making the other gestures, and *saw them* eat the bread called *çancu*. *I saw* the torches or *pancuncu,* but *did not see* the nocturnal rite, because it was very late and *I had* already gone to bed. *I remember* having afterwards *seen* a *pancuncu* in the stream running through the middle of the square. It lay near the house of my fellow pupil in the grammar school Juan de Cellorico, and *I recall* how the Indian boys passing down the street avoided it. *I did not* avoid it because *I did not* know why; if they had told me, I should certainly have fled too, for *I was* a child of six or seven. (Garcilaso 1966/1, VII, VII, 416, emphases mine)

The numerous anecdotes that Garcilaso recalled are either amusing, incredible, or unusual. He may describe whole scenes, isolated incidents, or individual characters. He paints an incredible image of Girón on the night of the uprising: "I saw Francisco Hernández in a room giving onto the street, sitting on a chair with his hands crossed on his breast, and his head bowed, more pensive and brooding than Melancholy itself. He must have been brooding on the deed he was to do that night" (Garcilaso 1966/2, VII, II, 1318). On other occasions, he would make statements in-

duced by a mixture of affection and pride, as when he emphasized: "In witness thereof I may say that I knew a gentleman, a
grandee of Spain" (Garcilaso 1966/2, v, XLIII, 1218). His feeling of pride attained its apogee when he spoke to his readers
knowing that he was the privileged witness of the birth of a
new era. With biblical grandeur he bore witness to events which
might appear to be only minor, for example, the scene when the
first yoked oxen trod Peruvian lands ("one of the most beautiful
scenes that he wrote," according to Durand 1976, 49). That moment was witnessed with great rejoicing by the Spaniards and "a
whole army of Indians, who gathered from all sides for the purpose," and who, with Garcilaso in their midst, were "amazed and
bewildered by so monstrous a spectacle, which was new to them
as it was to me" (Garcilaso 1966/1, IX, XVII, 582). A whole new
world unearthed by virtue of the word. So few words, and yet such
depth of meaning.

The whole design and construct of the *Royal Commentaries* appear explicitly linked to Garcilaso's life. Garcilaso felt that the
existence of his people together with that of his own were so
intimately intertwined that he could not describe Perú if he were
not somehow part of the picture. The twenty years that Garcilaso
lived in Perú were tenaciously to occupy his thoughts forever. The
history of Perú in the *Royal Commentaries* did not extend beyond
those twenty years, except for a key episode with which the book
ended: the execution of Túpac Amaru by Viceroy Toledo. This,
however, was a longstanding idea. While writing the first book of
the *General History* and narrating the death of Atahualpa, he did
not feel sure that he would be able to finish his work. He thus
stated: "we shall briefly relate the events concerning the life and
death of the Inca kings up to the last of them *and their descendants,*
which was our first intention. Later, if occasion offers, we shall
set down the most notable events that occurred during the wars
between the Spaniards" (Garcilaso 1966/2, I, XXVII, 694, emphasis mine). He explained in this passage that, if he were to have a
final choice, he would discard the Civil Wars but never the be-
heading of Túpac Amaru. He wanted to conclude the second
part of the *Royal Commentaries* with the death of the last Inca,

suggesting thereby the notion that it also represented the end of his own ancestry. And in the prologue to the *Commentaries,* he mentioned the still embryonic second part, or *General History:* "I am still writing two other books about the events that took place in my land among the Spaniards, down to the year 1560 when I left it" (Garcilaso 1966/1, "Preface to the Reader," 4). When Garcilaso briefly alluded to affairs that happened after he had left Perú (e.g., the end of Marquis of Cañete's term of office, and some activities by his son, don García), he excused himself for those additions and reconfirmed his initial plan: "This particular point has been anticipated in time and place: it is not my intention to go beyond the death of the heir to the Empire of Perú" (Garcilaso 1966/2, VIII, XV, 1470).

During his residence in Spain, Garcilaso felt a sense of detachment from current events in his native country. Those were generally prosperous times in colonial Perú. Occasionally, the news from home would relate an event of a more singular nature: a pirate had been sighted along the coast, preparations were being made to receive a viceroy, or ceremonies were being planned to memorialize the death of a Spanish king. Garcilaso was not interested in writing about those affairs; he preferred rather to explore the difficulties of the past. After Girón's uprising, he states, "there have followed fifty-seven years of peace, up to the time of writing this chapter in 1611" (Garcilaso 1966/2, VIII, I, 1415). And then he adds categorically: "My own intention is only to deal with the events of those days, and to leave those of today to whoever is willing to take the trouble to write about them" (ibid.). Since he was so wholly absorbed by his historical projects, it would seem that he was not the least bit interested in the new Spanish literary currents, and he never once mentioned the works of creative writers from the Spanish Golden Age. Garcilaso's eventual escape from the world by entering a religious order coincides with his strange withdrawal from the present moment and his resolute devotion to his own past through his historical work. To withdraw from the world was a common resolve among many Spaniards at the time, but in Garcilaso's case the influence of America played a fundamental and decisive role.

It should not be surprising, therefore, that scholars have repeatedly compiled the autobiographical passages from Garcilaso, particularly those from the *Royal Commentaries*. One of the earliest collections was gathered by Rafael Ramírez de Arellano (1922, vol. 2, 118–125). Then followed other anthologies, such as Porras Barrenechea's *Recuerdos de infancia y juventud* (1957) and Avalle-Arce's *Antología vivida* (1964). Due to the sheer volume of autobiographical references in each of Garcilaso's works, these and other similar editions could be significantly augmented.

In summary, Garcilaso's historical narrative is peculiarly personal, involving both form and content. This personal aspect is displayed in a variety of tones throughout his works: it can be at times confidential (Porras Barrenechea 1986, 395), affable, nostalgic, ebullient, joyful, or pathetic. Although autobiographical elements appear frequently in the chroniclers of the Indies and other historical authors whom Garcilaso read in Spain,[8] these features appear more accentuated in Garcilaso because of a profound commitment on his part to his family, both maternal and paternal, his own intimate experiences, and to the historical past he is writing about. Structurally, his old plan to finish the history with events around 1560, when he left Perú forever, was executed without vacillation. The decision to conclude the second part of the *Royal Commentaries* with the death of the last Inca can also be seen as portraying the end of his own lineage. Yet Garcilaso's discourse cannot be reduced to mere personal confidences and testimonies, or to structural designs, because it also reflects elements which are rooted deeply in Hispanic America itself.

Although today we may dispute the accuracy of some of his facts or may disagree on the way he understood history, one indisputable fact remains: history had for him a unique and profound meaning. If the *Royal Commentaries* are appreciated for what they intended to accomplish as a humanistic historical project, we encounter a great work that offers an organic and integral conception of a world and an era.[9] We discover, principally through the autobiographical passages in his works, that this historical conception derives from a person who is very represen-

José Anadón

tative of those turbulent years. His own human existence is intimately related to the historical times which he narrates. History and autobiography become equivalent in the depth of his spirit. Furthermore, Garcilaso's voice deserves to be heard for its intuitions about the destiny of Perú, proclaiming at an unusually early moment, towards the end of the sixteenth century, that the future nationality would include "Indians, Mestizos and Creoles," and would comprise all of the old Inca Empire. He was thus the first in the New World to foresee a new ethnically-mixed American culture.

NOTES

1. Sylvia Molloy's groundwork study (1991) recognizes that very little has been done with respect to autobiography in the Colonial period, save for some few and well-known figures. The observations which follow are derived from a lengthier and still unpublished study on autobiography and the chronicles of the Indies.

2. José Durand (1948, 33) noted this distinctive feature over four decades ago and also briefly alluded to it in subsequent articles. More recently, several authors, including Enrique Pupo-Walker (1982), William D. Ilgen (1974), Julio Ortega (1978), Susana Jákfalvi-Leiva (1984), and José Miguel Oviedo (1995), have repeatedly emphasized the importance of autobiographical elements in Garcilaso's historical works.

3. As he was growing up, he naturally drew closer to his father's side, but he never lost contact with his Indian world. When he was a young man, for example, he recalls that when Inca Sairi Túpac arrived at Christian-held territory, "I went in my mother's name, and asked his permission for her to go" and kiss his hands (Garcilaso 1966/2, VIII, XI, 1443).

4. Miró-Quesada (1994, 193) underscores Garcilaso's continuous references to Perú while writing about the North American territory. He notes Garcilaso's proclivity to introduce Quechua words like *curaca* (lord of vassals) and *zara* (corn) instead of the preferred indigenous words *cacique* and *maíz*, as well as his use of *apu* (captain general) and Quechua locutions or *frasis* (which is not equivalent to "phrase"). It is interesting to recall that Ercilla used Quechua expressions in *La Araucana*, such as *apu, palla* (woman of royal blood), *mita* (forced labor by the Indians), *llauto* (a cord, part of the royal headdress), *yanacona* (ser-

vant), etc. It is quite likely that reading Ercilla's poem piqued Garcilaso's patriotic zeal and prompted him to introduce Quechua words into the Spanish language.

5. In the *Diálogos*, in the letter to Maximilian, Garcilaso noted: "Alexandro Picolomini [*sic*], that honorable gentleman, worthy of all praise, in the *Institución moral* [*Della Instituzione Morale*, 1542] which he wrote, and where he talked about friendship, admonished the translator" of the *Dialoghi D'Amore* because he believed that the original version had been written in Hebrew. In effect, Alessandro Piccolomini dedicated book 9 to the theme of friendship. Garcilaso read the works of this Neoplatonic humanist, and this particular book was in his library when he died.

6. Picón Salas (1962, 82): "the two most delightful narratives by seventeenth-century authors born in Spanish America and composed far away from the Indies" were Garcilaso's *Royal Commentaries* (1609) and the *Historical Account of the Kingdom of Chile* (1646) by the Jesuit Alonso de Ovalle.

7. Murra (1980) extensively uses Garcilaso's information about the economy of ancient Perú, and also the Valera passages that he transcribes.

8. The influence of the many autobiographical writers whom he read, some of whom he even knew personally, will constitute the subject of an entirely different study.

9. For insights into Garcilaso's profound mode of interpretation as a humanist historian, cf. Durand 1976, 79 ff.; Miró-Quesada 1994, 263 ff.; and Pease G. Y. 1995, 378.

APPENDIX A

Debating Garcilaso

Gathered here are the ideas expressed in spirited verbal exchanges following the three principal sessions of the symposium on Garcilaso Inca held at the University of Notre Dame from March 31 to April 2, 1996. After the speakers had summarized the contents of their essays (which appear complete in this volume), an enthusiastic response ensued from the audience composed of fellow participants, colleagues, and students from Notre Dame and institutions across the country. The answers of panelists clarified or added new insights to their presentations. They contribute to the appreciation of the written essays and thus are worth recording. Except for minor stylistic changes, modifications have been kept to a minimum to preserve the spontaneity of these exchanges.

I

Panelists: Franklin Pease G. Y., Sabine MacCormack, Juan
    Bautista Avalle-Arce
Moderator: Iván A. Jaksić

José Anadón: When Garcilaso compares the Incas to the Romans, a theme with echoes in antiquity, as you have so precisely and expertly demonstrated, he is also subscribing to a providentialist notion of history, that is, that the Incas, just like the Romans, had prepared the advent of Christianity. Could you tell us which classical authors, whom Garcilaso may have read and drawn from, espoused a providentialist view of Rome?

Appendix A

Sabine MacCormack: That is actually and curiously quite hard to do. The proposition that the Romans are in one way or another the instrument of God as they were preparing the way for the Gospel, is extremely problematic in late antiquity. It was first proposed in a major way by Eusebius of Caesarea, the Greek Church historian and biographer of the emperor Constantine, who really did believe that the conversion of Constantine opened the road for a millennial kingdom of some kind, and that that kingdom was Rome. And there are repercussions of this Eusebian view in the West, for example in the Christian Latin Church historian Orosius, often described as the student of Augustine. But here is the problem. If you say that the Roman Empire was the vehicle of Christianity, you are going to commit yourself to one particular kind of political organization and one particular kind of authority. The one who saw that problem more sharply than anyone else was Augustine of Hippo, to whom is often attributed the idea that the Church is the Kingdom of God, although that is not what he said. The Church cannot be the Kingdom of God because no one can know who will be chosen, which is God's decision. Similarly, it cannot be said that any one political organization is especially the instrument of divine providence. So the early Middle Ages inherited this incredible tension between the Eusebian and Orosian views on the one hand, and the Augustinian view on the other. Now, Isidore of Seville, whom Garcilaso read, was a sort of modified Augustinian. On the one hand, he really did want to say that the Visigoths, who converted to Catholic Christianity from Arianism, were in some way the Kingdom that should dispense, as it were, the "economies of Christ"—I am using a late antique phrase. But on the other hand, he was too honest a bishop to be truly convinced that this would really work. And so if one is a careful reader of documents and of historical texts in sixteenth-century Spain, one will encounter the repercussions of both of these views. And I think that this ambiguity does, in one way or another, exist in Garcilaso because he writes as a dutiful historian within the Spanish Empire. How could he act otherwise? The issue is not one of coercion or of advocating a fashionable view, but it rather pertains to a certain obligation to sustain the society which has nourished an individual, whatever that society may be like. Garcilaso felt that way. So this is the source of his providentialism. It is a convenient doctrine. It will justify conquests. But Garcilaso, as you all perfectly well know, at the same time does not want to justify the conquest. He will say that the fall of the Inca Empire was "indeed a tragedy." So, in a sense, I cannot answer your question because I do not know exactly what he did read. But I do think that he reflects this major and pervasive tension in Spanish historical writing as well as in Spanish political theory. It is in the legislation—and Spanish legislation is not what critics of Spanish imperialism say it is. It is indeed a sort of self-justificatory legislative exercise, but throughout the legislation there is this constant questioning: Is what we are doing really right? And I think that is also found in Garcilaso.

Luis Cortest (University of Oklahoma): Very often we hear mentioned the importance and influence of Ambrosio de Morales, the royal chronicler of Phillip II, on the *Royal Commentaries* and other works. But I have often wondered if Garcilaso knew the work of another *cordobés* (a native of Córdoba), Juan Ginés de Sepúlveda? Although ideologically he is quite different from Morales, nevertheless Sepúlveda was the royal chronicler of Charles V at the time of the conquest, and as an official chronicler he wrote about all of those events. I also wonder about Pietro Martire d'Anghiera, because anthropologists have shown us that he had a kind of an unfiltered view, since he received reports of events that were written just as they were happening. Of course it was filtered, in a sense, since it was an official history. However, I really think that these chroniclers must have been important for Garcilaso, and I ask you, what is your opinion on this subject?

Franklin Pease: In the example that I gave, the influence of Morales resides in the way he approaches antiquity, and in the exemplary nature of its representation. I am not so sure that I have new arguments that would explain the influence of authors such as Sepúlveda, and the others. Your suggestions are interesting; however, we have to remember that in antiquarians, such as Morales, the image of an exemplary and almost mysterious past functions more adequately.

James Turner (University of Notre Dame): I would like to ask Sabine MacCormack to specify a little more clearly the kinds of analogies to Rome which are and are not made by Garcilaso. It seems to me that in your paper there are two types of analogies to Rome: (1) specific analogies between the Inca Empire and Rome, i.e., the imperial setting, the Roman roads compared to the Inca's, and so forth; and (2) the use of categories drawn from Roman history or political theory to try to explain the Inca Empire, i.e., the Polybian notion of cyclical history, the Ciceronian notion of a state of nature, the Livian notion of a legendary prehistory, etc. Yet, while those categories were developed in an effort to explain Rome, they are meant to be universal in their application; for example, Polybian history applies to Greece as well as to Rome. So, it is that first type of analogy that I am interested in. Where is the Inca Empire seen as like Rome, and where is it seen as not like Rome? For example, I should think that the Polybian notion of the Roman polity as a mixture of aristocracy, democracy, and monarchy does not apply to the Incas.

Sabine MacCormack: That is precisely right; the three constitutions of Polybius—monarchy, aristocracy, and democracy—are indeed part of the Polybian cyclical model that is not applicable to the Incas. It is not applicable for historians and political theorists in the sixteenth- and seventeenth-century Spanish world, because they are convinced, for a variety of reasons, that monarchy is the best form of government. It is an undeniable fact that cannot be argued; they are not interested in anything else. The question about how the Incas are not like Rome is in some ways extremely hard to answer. And here might be a reason why it is so difficult to respond. I think that the primary concern of sixteenth-century Spanish historians and political thinkers is to define what an empire is. They are not interested in city-states, nor in national territorial monarchies, nor in a republic of one kind or another. They are only interested in imperial structures, and in the kind of sovereignty that it is possible to have in an empire. That is why they were interested in the Romans. As they saw it, the Roman Empire was not held together by one single language, even though Latin was the imperial language. So they are not thinking about what makes the Romans different. They are thinking about what you need to have when you have an empire like theirs. They go round and round on this issue because it determines what you can say about sovereignty. In the Spanish kingdoms themselves, sovereignty has become an exercise whereby the king of Spain rules over several entities that had been autonomous kingdoms before, so that imperial model had spread across the world. The one area where a difference is clearly perceived is in the area of written documents. There are lengthy dicussions throughout the sixteenth century regarding the Inca system of recording events: to what extent one can say that there was writing in the Andes, to what extent the *quipus* constitute a historical memory, to what extent the narratives that are encoded in *quipus* are really handed down from one generation to the next, and to what extent they represent a shared memory. These are big questions, but herein lies, I think, the major and fundamental difference between the Incas and classical antiquity.

Efraín Kristal: I would like to ask whether the comparisons that Garcilaso makes between Spain and Rome, the Spanish conquistadors and the Romans, shed any light on the comparisons that he then makes between the Inca Empire and Rome.

Sabine MacCormack: A both searching and important question. I think the answer is yes. The easy answer is that the comparisons articulate Garcilaso's argument that the Incas are a political society. Then one would say that his argument is further confirmed by the comparison between Spain and the Romans. And here is why. I think we have tended to see in Garcilaso the dimension of the ideal. So there is the ideal of the Spanish conquistador who is a hero of the kind that one reads about in Roman histories. There is also the Inca ruler who is a Caesar Augustus. But the Roman analogies also underpin a series of arguments that see

flaws in both of these societies. Thus one can juxtapose the flaws
of the Spanish conquest, such as in aspects of the evangelization,
with the flaws of the Inca conquest. On the other hand, one can
juxtapose the benefits of the Spanish conquest with the benefits
of Inca governance and the ability of the conquistadors to make
friends and to rule by conciliation. I think I will stop here because there is more to be said but I am not sure that I can express
it clearly.

Jeff Barrow (Purdue University): A question for either Sabine
MacCormack or Franklin Pease. In responding to an earlier question you mentioned Garcilaso's tragic vision of history. Can we
see here a reflection of Greek historians, in particular Thucydides?

Franklin Pease: I think we need to think in broader terms. According to recent investigations, we find, in addition to Thucydides'
view of a tragic present, elements that come from other Greek
authors. In other chroniclers, but not concretely in Garcilaso
Inca, it is easier to find structural images from Greek society
which have been taken from early sixteenth-century translations.
Your question becomes more interesting when applied to the
General History rather than to the *Royal Commentaries,* where we
find something similar to Thucydides' concept of a heavily bur-
dened present. Garcilaso twice represents the losing side. He is
not only speaking for the Andean population, but also, to a certain extent, in the name of the losers of the so-called Civil Wars
between the Spaniards in Perú. In this added context, the tragic
dimension acquires a larger meaning.

Iván Jaksić: Thank you. Sabine, would you like to add to Franklin's
comments?

Sabine MacCormack: Yes. I think that that is absolutely right, and
perhaps if one looked at the Peruvian Civil Wars one might find
there some reception by Garcilaso of the concept of stasis and a
sort of self-generating destruction that is so fundamental a theme

in Thucydides, a theme that he sets up with the civil strife in Corcyra.

Carmela Zanelli: I would like to comment on the last question, because it addresses my current research. As Franklin Pease has remarked, it has become obvious at least to me that the tragic dimension is even more important in the *General History* than in the *Royal Commentaries.* This is due to Garcilaso's perspective on the Civil Wars, where he attaches great importance to Gonzalo Pizarro's rebellion and subscribes to the notion that any political project is doomed to fail, even Viceroy Toledo's. I am trying to prove that the concept of tragedy in the *General History* comes from a complex medieval historical tradition. He is not drawing the concept of tragedy directly from Aristotle, but basically from medieval authors. Henry Kelly's book about ideas and forms of tragedy provides useful examples. By the sixteenth century, the concept of tragedy no longer applies exclusively to a literary form, but also to historical events. Even prose narratives can be called tragedies. The overthrow of kingdoms are tragic events because whole lineages are destroyed. We can thus see two different concepts of tragedy in Garcilaso: (1) the historical dimension of tragedy, as when he describes the death of the last Inca, Túpac Amaru. The placement of this event at the end of the book reinforces a concept from medieval times, which is not present in Aristotle. It was a condition for a medieval text to end tragically; and (2) the personal dimension of tragedy, which is present in the depiction of the Civil Wars and in Garcilaso's own life.

Iván Jaksić: Thank you. Any comments on the comments about the medieval sources of tragedy, Professor Avalle-Arce?

Juan Bautista Avalle-Arce: Well, whatever was meant in the Middle Ages by tragedy has little to do with the semantics in the sixteenth century. So when the Inca uses the word *tragedia,* he's definitely putting it into the Renaissance context. It was, therefore, quite clear to any reader of the time as to what was meant.

Appendix A

Panelists: Pierre Duviols, Carmela Zanelli, José A. Rodríguez
    Garrido
Moderator: María Rosa Olivera-Williams

Sabine MacCormack: Professor Duviols, I have read an interpretation of Viracocha in which the god is nothing more than a phantom, and not something real. Do you think that it is a wrong reading? I have also understood this passage as an expression that Garcilaso understands the philosophical dilemma of Thomism, which states that one can imagine things that do not exist.

Pierre Duviols: Garcilaso is very careful not to use the supernatural in his works. He could have read similar examples in previous historians, who described how the god Viracocha defended the Incas against the Chancas, or the vision of the cross that Constantine saw before the battle with Maxentius, whose victory conquered Rome and led to the founding of Christianity. What we see here, however, is a complex passage or progression from a symbolic plane (an appearance which is not real) to a real plane (when king Viracocha orders that a statue be built of that appearance) which nevertheless maintains its symbolic character (the Incas imagine that the Spaniards resemble that statue) and which has future projections (the eventual creation of *mestizaje*).

Sabine MacCormack: I have also thought that as a phantom Viracocha represents, in a certain sense, an ironic commentary by Garcilaso, by suggesting that a phantom is the ancestor of the Spaniards.

Pierre Duviols: I do not see anything ironic in this episode. I see rather that he tries to make it believable. Garcilaso is a historian who is a creator of myths, although he is not naive. He is writing a literary history. I do not believe that the matter of truths or lies plays any part in this instance.

Efraín Kristal: My question relates to the apparition and Viracocha. The young man in the story has been banished by his father, and told never again to return to Cuzco. The father has decided, in fact, that somebody else will inherit the title of Inca, and I say this because of the importance you attribute to this title in Garcilaso. Garcilaso, furthermore, is careful to narrate the episode using a language of uncertainty, so it is not really known whether it happened or not. The young man, then, confronts a moral dilemma, because the apparition could be the devil, a malignant phantom, or someone who is lying to him. He does not really know whether the information he has concerning the Chanca rebellion is true or false, but he realizes that it is a serious threat to the Incas. What shall he do? He decides to return to Cuzco and warn them. My question is: to what extent do the moral dilemmas of the young man, who is not yet an Inca and who is not destined to become one according to his father's will, play a part in the way you have interpreted Garcilaso's lineage?

Pierre Duviols: It is a subtle question. An important detail to remember is that the young man does not have any doubts that the apparition really happened. I do not see in the text that he doubts the truth of that event. He knows that he has been banished, you are correct, that the Inca his father has rejected him, and that he cannot return to Cuzco. But he believes that the apparition did occur.

Sabine MacCormack: This question is for José Rodríguez. Do you see any connection between Garcilaso's insistence on traditional concepts of nobility and virtue, and the ongoing transformation of the Spanish government and governmental staff into a much more professional workforce? The *letrados,* for example, had nothing to do with nobility but were governmental officials who had certain technical qualifications. Isn't Garcilaso positioning himself, inasmuch as he would have liked to have served the king of Spain and been recognized in that capacity? But yet he did not succeed in obtaining a court appointment. Instead, he finds himself in exile, in a sort of second exile in Córdoba. He then writes history, exalting a more old-fashioned concept of virtue and nobility. Could this be interpreted as a critique of his own times?

José A. Rodríguez Garrido: As I see it, in the prologue [to the second part of the *Commentaries*] at least, the source of his reflection comes from a tradition of *viri illustres* which starts with Petrarch, is remodeled by Boccaccio, and then continued in the fifteenth century. His political position is separate from his humanistic position. My impression is that Garcilaso favors a humanistic position and this choice, if I understand your question correctly, may be the result of his disillusionment over his unsuccessful attempts at court to receive the recognition of his paternal and maternal merits. In the prologue, Garcilaso resorts to a historical rendition of this theme with the purpose of articulating a unitary vision of Perú.

Sabine MacCormack: The ideals espoused by the authors that you have mentioned correspond to an epoch long gone. I would like to ask whether you see in this somewhat old perspective of Garcilaso a criticism directed toward the bureaucratic government of Phillip II, a government run by people like Polo de Ondegardo, for example, who are not nobles but rather *letrados,* or *licenciados.* It is a very different style of government in which there is no room for any kind of nobility, whether it is achieved by theological, civic, or by virtuous means. This criticism appears in the Spanish historiography of the late sixteenth century, for example, in *Las guerras civiles de Granada* by Diego de Mendoza. Mendoza blasts the decisions made by the *letrados* during the war. The *letrados* who live in Madrid, he says, do not understand the war, or the idiosyncracies of the Moors. Do you place Garcilaso in that kind of historiographical tradition, which is also a political tradition, and which in Perú ends somewhat later with Viceroy Toledo? Wouldn't this perspective help to explain your critical view of Viceroy Toledo?

José A. Rodríguez Garrido: If we contextualize it historically, the tradition of *viri illustres* in Garcilaso, with strong references first to Petrarch, and then to other models is, obviously, a political response as well. Your comments indeed serve to contextualize these models. The fact that Garcilaso chose this textual tradition can have a political connotation directed against the imperial political practices of the preceding decades.

Efraín Kristal: Although many texts of *viri illustres* illustrate the qualities that you have noted, starting with Boccaccio the *viri illustres* are all portrayed as sinners and failures. How do you situate Boccaccio's model in your argument?

José A. Rodríguez Garrido: When I began to study the theme of *viri illustres* in Garcilaso, I realized that it was very vast. Different passages required different approaches. I finally decided to focus only on the prologue, where the treatment of the tradition differs from that of the rest of the text. The biographical sketches of Gonzalo Pizarro, Francisco Pizarro, or Diego de Almagro come closer to Boccaccio's model. I have thus called the prologue and the dedication "utopian textual spaces," although I am not saying that the *Commentaries* reflect a Utopia. I would assert that these two texts present an "essential history," or history as it should be, a model history. As history unfolds within the text, however, it ends in tragedy. I see a clear contradiction between the historical vision designed in the prologue and the historical reality described in the second part of the *Commentaries*. The tradition of *viri illustres* thus needs to be studied differently depending upon the text being scrutinized. The influence of Boccaccio's model appears strong in the text, while Petrarch is stronger in the prologue.

Efraín Kristal: I do not think that the contradictions remain unresolved. As you have said, the idealized vision reconciles the contradictory elements.

Appendix A

José A. Rodríguez Garrido: Exactly. The prologue is obviously a text of reconciliation, as opposed to what happens in the body of the text.

Carmela Zanelli: It must also be taken into consideration that both the prologue and the dedication were possibly the last texts that Garcilaso wrote. His state of mind at that moment may have altered his previous perception of the entire work.

José Antonio Mazzotti: Do you find that the epic tradition is an important influence, with its concept of "elevation" of the epic hero, in accordance with the original meaning of the word (*héroe/aéreo*)? Would Garcilaso's preference towards Boiardo and Ariosto influence his appreciation of the conquistadors as *viri illustres?* Also, would you consider the mythification aspect from the viewpoint of an Andean cultural trajectory? For example, does Gonzalo Pizarro's trip from Huarina to Pucara and Cuzco, where he is received as an Inca, have any resonance with Viracocha's foundational journey?

José A. Rodríguez Garrido: Yes, the epic tradition is also present in the formation of the concept of *viri illustres,* and Garcilaso does indeed quote Boiardo and Ercilla. But I think that Garcilaso's intention is to place the tradition of *viri illustres* within a historical discourse, outside the poetic tradition. When he refers to Juan de Castellanos' book—whose title, *Elegía de varones ilustres,* is obviously connected to the same tradition—he praises its historical content while deploring that it is written in verse. Thus he sees the epic poem as poetic discourse. This is a clear indication that he views the tradition of *viri illustres* as part of a historical discourse.

Student: This is a question about the theme of the Virgin. I am a little confused. It seems that you literally believe that the Indians saw the Virgin. Would it not it be more accurate to say that the Indians probably misinterpreted some phenomenon of nature as the apparition of the Virgin, and mistook thunderstorms for celestial weapons? These phenomena were then manipulated by the Catholic priests so as to convert them more easily after a defeat of such magnitude.

Carmela Zanelli: The miraculous apparitions and celestial phenomena mark important episodes in historical reconstruction. Garcilaso uses them because it is easier for him to justify the conquest within the framework of the so-called providentialist conception of history. I was looking at this subject from that viewpoint.

Mathew Riley (University of Notre Dame, junior): It has been stated that Garcilaso criticized Gómara and other writers for not including in their histories these miracles and supernatural events. Humanists like Gómara never traveled to the New World but wrote about the conquest while living in Spain, relying on eyewitness accounts and other direct sources. I have also read that Gómara would resort to anything to attract the favors of the Crown. Why then wouldn't he include those miraculous stories, as Garcilaso did, since the Crown would have been delighted to hear stories concerning the evangelization of the Indian people?

Carmela Zanelli: The interesting part of your question is that the exact opposite occurs in the *Historia verdadera de la conquista de Nueva España* by Bernal Díaz del Castillo. When Gómara describes the supernatural intervention of the Apostle Santiago (St. James), Bernal Díaz contradicts him, stating that he was there and did not see anything. In the case of Garcilaso, he basically follows Blas Valera and José de Acosta, who describe in their historical accounts the same providential vision. I would just like to add that the intervention of the Virgin and St. James in these narratives also suggests that although the Spaniards were sinners and often misbehaved during the conquest, nevertheless the evangelization efforts had to continue.

Appendix A

Panelists: Miguel Maticorena Estrada, Efraín Kristal, José
    Antonio Mazzotti
Moderator: Julio Noriega

José Anadón: Efraín Kristal has vividly shown us the problematic
nature of the terminology that was used to describe the inhabitants of the New World after the conquest. My question refers
to one of those words discussed, *infidel,* and precisely how Garcilaso Inca understood it. Collaterally, it is interesting to recall that
Bartolomé de Las Casas introduces a provocative view of the concept of infidels. He argues, for example, that the Pope is the head
of all infidels. In another instance, in one of his treatises, which
we now know that Garcilaso Inca read, he studies papal power
and says that the infidels represent the body of the Church "in
potentiality" (*in potencia*). Could you please comment on the similarities, or differences, or similarities and differences, between
Las Casas and Garcilaso in the way they employ the term infidel?

Efraín Kristal: You are asking me to write a book. I will just say
that there is a part of Las Casas that Garcilaso shares. Yet Garcilaso also criticizes Las Casas very aggressively in the *General History* for supporting the kind of laws that will chastise the conquistadors in a way that will create more strife. Although different
authors use different paradigms of the *infidel,* I think that, in a
way, they basically share the same premise. The reason why persons would choose to use one orientation instead of another is a
very complicated matter that involves political and other factors.
I am not a specialist in the theological intricacies of all of this, I
am merely detecting a pattern. I have done research on sixteenth-
century Spanish historiography that does not deal directly with
America in order to obtain an insight into the paradigms available to anybody who wanted to understand these matters in the
period. It seems that there was a horizon of possibilities. On the
one side you have the Goths, on the other side you have the
Turks, in the middle there is a great variety. An understanding
of these differences, however, could be very illuminating when it

comes to clarifying certain texts in Ercilla and Garcilaso. So then, going back to your question, I think that the premises and some of the conclusions in Las Casas and Garcilaso are actually shared by the two, at least from the perspective that interests me.

Luis Cortest: I would like to comment on José Anadón's question. Perhaps a key consideration in order to understand Las Casas' position appears in his *Defense* of the Indians. When Las Casas discusses in the *Apologética* the four types of barbarians, I think that those arguments can begin to answer the question asked. Because the whole discussion of that topic among other thinkers of the time is not nearly as sophisticated. For example, Suárez's *De Triplice Virtute* and Domingo de Soto's *De Iustitia et Iure* are not very elaborated treatises on this matter. Francisco Suárez offers a very simple explanation. I think that Las Casas actually has in that text one of the most sophisticated discussions of the notion of the idolater and the barbarian. But my question is simpler. You pointed out in your talk, Professor Kristal, the influence of some medieval sources, yet it seemed to me that you were really talking about sixteenth-century sources in relation to the paradigm that you outlined. Which specific medieval histories do you have in mind? My own view is that medieval Spanish histories are not that important for Garcilaso. I would argue, for example, that a writer like Fray Jerónimo Román y Zamora is far more relevant to Garcilaso than any of the medieval historians. I would say the same of Ambrosio de Morales.

Efraín Kristal: I had in mind several medieval histories, beginning with San Isidoro. The first history of the Goths is a very short text in Latin, and it is a basic source. Then the whole medieval tradition that culminates in Jiménez de Radas, a compendium which then becomes the source of the *Primera Corónica* as well. I take your point. I think that the book by Juan de Castillo is much more interesting to me in order to see the connections with Garcilaso Inca, than the sources just mentioned. What fascinates me, however, is that these medieval works are the ones that Juan de Castillo quotes and reinterprets in the sixteenth century. Jiménez de Rada says, for example, that through divine intervention God punished the Roman Empire, and through divine intervention He has punished us. He is making those comments while the reconquest is still going on. So by the time you reach the sixteenth century and the reconquest is over, then the story can be told in a way that was not possible before. I agree with you that it is more relevant to read sixteenth-century authors in order to appreciate the full story of that century. But to see how the story develops, I think it is fascinating to look at the medieval sources, most of which are cited in sixteenth-century texts. So, in a way, the story that matters to Garcilaso Inca cannot really be told before the advent of the Catholic Kings of Spain.

Carlos Jerez-Farrán (University of Notre Dame): Your presentation seemed to me very pertinent and also applicable to the theories of Foucault. For example, the way in which sin or vice become well-defined categories, created in order to better define virtue or purity. Have you thought of applying Foucault's theories to the analysis of the Incas and the paratext of the Visigoths?

Efraín Kristal: Not in a direct way. I appreciate your question because in some ways my argument is in line with Foucault's ideas, although I do not share his epistemological assumptions. At rock bottom, Foucault sees a level of arbitrariness in the paradigms which are used to exclude, include, separate, catalog, etc. I am also interested in determining paradigms in that sense, but not in unmasking the claims of knowledge by showing the arbitrariness of paradigms. I do not think, as your question suggests, that the paradigms are ultimately tautological. I think, rather, that the paradigms I am discussing were reasonable attempts to gain knowledge about the "other" in the Renaissance. I am interested in reconstructing the possibilities for making sense out of the indigenous population of the Western Hemisphere given Spanish Renaissance assumptions about non-Christian peoples.

María Rosa Olivera-Williams (University of Notre Dame): A brief comment to Efraín Kristal, related to the ideas expressed by

Carmela Zanelli. It seems to me that your comparison between the Incas and the Goths was excellent, especially the tragic concept of history due to the blindness of the Spaniards which precipitated the fall of the Incas. The inability of the Spaniards to see the Incas as intermediaries, as a group which was willing to convert to Christianity, reminded me of Sor Juana Inés de la Cruz, who did think of America and the Indians as being in an intermediary stage, as expressed by the female characters in her "Loa para el auto sacramental de *El Divino Narciso.*" The tragic concept, which starts with Aristotle, thus appears not only in the *écriture* but can also be seen in the interpretation of historical events. In Garcilaso as well as in Sor Juana there is a tragic concept of history.

Efraín Kristal: I thought that the comments of Carmela Zanelli in response to Sabine MacCormack's presentation were very relevant. As we know, Aristotle floats through the Spanish Middle Ages in a translation of a summary by Averroës, which produces very interesting interpretations. One of these, which was quite influential, equates tragedy with the end of a lineage, or the fall of an empire. In a strict sense, the concept of tragedy in late medieval times, for example, did not apply to the drama but to historical events. A tragedy is also understood within a context of divine interventions. Thus I find fascinating José Durand's proposition of another type of divine intervention when he describes the influence of Stoicism in Garcilaso. I think that the idea of divine intervention to evangelize peoples has to be complemented with the idea of divine chastisement related to the fall of empires.

Paul Firbas: I would like to ask José Antonio Mazzotti about the "real" receptors whom he has identified—Creoles, mestizos, and Indians. Do you believe that in the *Royal Commentaries* any of these subjects becomes an "ideal" receptor who can be followed throughout the text, or is the text generally open to any of these three groups, or do you see that in some parts one is preferred over the other?

Appendix A

José Antonio Mazzotti: Thank you for your question, which allows me to amplify some of the premises stated in my presentation. Any discourse must have a receptor; in other words, any subject-*écriture* supposes a subject-reader. The problem is how to define the subject-*écriture* within the text, and beyond the historical subject which the discourse enunciates. I disagree with all the critical traditions that present Garcilaso as the subject of knowledge and reconstruction. When we propose reading a subtext which evokes, or simulates, the Indian tradition, Garcilaso would represent one of those functions. It would be a fractured subject, as revealed by the name Inca that he has chosen to use. Thus, readings can be fractured or they can have intentionality. While in the case of the Creoles we would have an "ideal" reading, with respect to the Indian and mestizo elites (the descendants of the Incas) it would be more difficult to explain what kind it is. This would have to be verified by meticulous archival research. It can be more easily verified during the eighteenth century because of the rebellion of Túpac Amaru. There was a clear reception then, especially following the publication of the second edition of the *Royal Commentaries*. All readings of a text of this complexity will be partial. The multiple and thus partial readings of the *Commentaries* could have motivated references to an authority, which would be a descendant of the conquistadors according to the Creoles, or a descendant of the Incas according to the "ideal" receptors, the mestizos. They would be contained, however, from the moment the subject-*écriture* constitutes itself as a fractured entity.

APPENDIX B

PAUL P. FIRBAS

The Inca of Durand:
Annotated Bibliography on Garcilaso Inca
and Other Topics in the Work of José Durand

The present bibliography brings together the works of the Peruvian Professor José Durand (1925–1990), which were published both during his life and posthumously. With few exceptions, it excludes book reviews and articles which appeared in newspapers or cultural supplements. Durand wrote for the Mexican newspapers *Novedades, Excélsior, El Sol,* and *Sábado.* He also contributed to the Peruvian dailies *El Comercio* and *La Prensa,* serving for the latter as editor of the cultural supplement from 1953 to 1956 and then as a regular contributor until 1961.

There are various references that Durand sent to press two ballet scripts, one of them entitled *La manda,* which was an adaptation of Juan Rulfo's short-story "Talpa." Since these texts are not available, they have not been included in the bibliography.

The descriptions of the forty-two articles which Durand dedicated to Garcilaso Inca are comprehensive. It should be stressed, however, that they represent my own understanding of Durand's texts. In the remaining sections, as the topics move away from the Colonial period, the notes become merely brief guides to the items described. The entries within each thematic section are arranged in chronological order.

The initial point of departure for this annotated bibliography was an unpublished and imprecise bibliography which José Durand himself prepared in 1974 and updated ten years later. I

Paul P. Firbas

would like to thank Professor José Anadón for making these and other materials available to me, and also express my gratitude for the excellent service that I received from the Main Library of the University of Arizona. The major part of this investigation was accomplished during the 1995–1996 academic year, which I spent at that institution.

1. "La biblioteca del Inca." *Nueva Revista de Filología Hispánica* (México) 2, no. 3 (1948): 239–264. [A reference is also included concerning José Durand's comment on the note "Sobre la biblioteca del Inca" by Bruno Migliorini and Giulio Cesare Olschki in *Nueva Revista de Filología Hispánica* 3, no. 2 (1949): 168–170.]

The list of 188 books in Garcilaso's library is based on the inventory made by his executors in Córdoba in 1616. The catalog reflects the books he possessed late in life. The general categories in the collection are composed of historical, classical (ancient and Renaissance), religious-moral, and scientific works. Each entry is explained and/or augmented with bibliographical references and information obtained from the works of such noted bibliographers as Nicolás Antonio, Brunet, La Viñaza, Medina, Palau, Pérez Pastor, Valdenebro, Escudero, Haebler, O'Gorman, Leonard, Millares Carlo, Torre Revello, etc. Whenever certain titles are doubtful, several probabilities are suggested. First editions are indicated whenever possible, especially those which seemed to be in Garcilaso's library. The article comments on material that was not listed in the catalog but which was very likely read and owned by Garcilaso: manuscripts, romances of chivalry, and books by Pineda, Zárate, Oré, Morales, Román y Zamora, Cabeza de Vaca, etc. Spanish translations of Latin and Italian works are mentioned. In a note written by Durand one year later in the same journal, six entries are corrected and clarified.

2. "Dos notas sobre el Inca Garcilaso." *Nueva Revista de Filología Hispánica* (México) 3, no. 3 (1949): 278–290.

The first note refers to Garcilaso's friendship with the humanist Bernardo de Aldrete. Aldrete was very interested in the Indies and quoted Garcilaso twice, the first time in a marginal note in his *Origen y principio de la lengua castellana* (1606) on the origin of the name Perú, and the second time in *Varias antigüedades* (1614), in a discussion of the first account of the New World by Alonso de Sánchez. The extent of Aldrete's influence upon Garcilaso is still unknown. The second note concerns both Garcilaso's use of the words "Perú" and "Pirú," and his linguistic ideas on the Quechua language. "Perú" was the oldest form that Garcilaso used, probably before 1596, when he was describing its etymology (derived from "Berú" and "Pelú") and planning to include the explanation in his book about Florida that he was then writing. He finally decided, however, to insert the text in the *Royal Commentaries*. It is believed that sometime between 1598 and 1600, Garcilaso received Blas Valera's "torn" papers, in which he found, among other things, confirmation of the pronunciation and spelling of many Quechua words. Garcilaso's linguistic ideas, however, were not influenced by any chronicler of the Indies but were rather the result of personal experience and his humanistic formation.

3. "El duelo, motivo cómico." *Mar del Sur* (Lima) 4 (1949): 30–33.

Garcilaso's ideas underwent a long process of maturation, as exemplified in this particular theme. Duels represent laughable situations for Garcilaso. Ridicule thus becomes a form of condemnation, yet at the same time he makes good use of the anecdotes and the colorful circumstances pertaining to duelling. Garcilaso's library contained two books entitled *El duelo,* one of which was probably written by Girolamo Muzio. This book, which disapproved of duels, was translated into Spanish. Durand's article then describes and comments on two duels in the *Royal Commentaries*—one between Pablo Meneses and Martín de Robles, the other between the *Corcobado* (the hunchbacked), Rodrigo de Salazar, and Pedro de Puelles.

4. "Garcilaso el Inca, platónico." *Las Moradas* (Lima) 3, nos. 7–8 (1949): 121–129.

This article refers to Mariano Iberico's hypothesis, expounded in 1939, about the essentially idealistic character of the *Royal Com-*

mentaries. Durand adheres to Iberico's position but also stresses the importance of Garcilaso's constant striving for historical truth. Nevertheless, Garcilaso's Platonism and syncretism allow him to reconcile poetry and history, the Spanish conquest and the Inca Empire. Although Garcilaso strives to be historically exact, he constructs a kind of utopian Inca Empire. As a Platonist and an Indian, he characterizes the Tahuantinsuyu as an idealized Golden Age period. Thus, Garcilaso's work cannot be judged exclusively in historical terms, but must also be viewed in terms of its poetic and humanistic dimensions.

5. "El Inca Garcilaso, historiador apasionado." *Cuadernos Americanos* (México) 4 (1950): 153–168.

Disillusioned with the present, Garcilaso concentrates on reliving the past. He becomes a writer by probing into his own experiences. He is a man without a homeland; drastic changes had occurred in Perú—the original conquistadors and the Inca Empire no longer existed. In Spain he lived on his early memories and studied in solitude, showing no interest in popular literature or culture. He became disillusioned with life. The three main goals of the conquest (evangelization, wealth, and honor) had not been realized. The conversion of the natives to the Christian faith had stalled because of constant wars in Perú, and the wealth of the Indies raised the cost of living in Spain. Garcilaso articulated two key perceptions in his historical works: the reconstruction of the spiritual climate surrounding the events narrated, and the feeling that he was the privileged witness of the monumental and "cruel transition" between two epochs. Around 1612, after having finished his work and feeling redeemed by it, Garcilaso expresses optimistic views about the future of America in his final words written in the dedication to the *General History of Perú.*

6. "La idea de la honra en el Inca Garcilaso." *Cuadernos Americanos* (México) 6 (1951): 194–213. [This article was part of Durand's doctoral thesis, completed in Lima, 1949, at the National University of San Marcos; a corrected version appeared in *Panorama* 1 (1952): 67–83.]

According to Garcilaso, honor resides in the virtue of an individ-ual and not in the opinions of others. Different emphases on val-ues in the new American societies caused a change in the tradi-tional Spanish concept of honor. This article studies four aspects of Garcilaso's thought on the subject: (1) Honor-Nobility. Gar-cilaso defends the honor of the conquistadors on the premise that deeds determine nobility; (2) Honor-Fame-Virtue. Accord-ing to humanist thought, honor was not bestowed in accordance with the opinions of the common people, and fame was achieved solely by leading a virtuous life; (3) Honor-King. The most val-ued kind of honor is found both on a personal and an abstract level, and this is superior to the tenets of a monarchy. Loyalty and great deeds deserve honor, even if this means going against the king. The political ideas of Garcilaso coincide with those of Ribadeneyra and Mariana, who opposed those of Macchiavelli; and (4) The King and the Indies. Garcilaso admires Gonzalo Pizarro, the Contreras and Carvajal, all of whom rebelled against the king. Garcilaso's concept of honor was thus shaped by hu-manist ideas and his own experiences.

7. "Historia y poesía en el Inca Garcilaso." *Humanismo* (México) 1, no. 6 (1952): 25–28.

The "historian-poet" was an ideal model during the Renaissance. Garcilaso did not directly intervene in this contemporary po-lemic concerning the nature of history and poetry, and it was quite clear that he preferred a historian's perspective. He be-lieved *La Araucana* should have been written in prose rather than in verse, so that it would be more believable from a historical point of view. He realized that history and poetry have their own and distinct themes. Although he introduced poetic elements into his writings, Garcilaso believed that a "truthful and exem-plary" work can be realized only through historical discourse. The article points out structural parallels between *La Araucana* and the *Florida* and briefly examines some critic's notions on the theme of fiction in Garcilaso's works [cf. no. 4].

Paul P. Firbas

8. "El Inca Garcilaso, clásico de América." [Written in 1952, it was first published in English in 1953 (see no. 10); the Spanish version appeared in 1976 (see no. 36).]

This article provides biographical information about Garcilaso, stressing his constant yearning for the past, and his Renaissance style of writing while already living in the age of the Baroque. It also describes his fatalistic thought as the ultimate result of several causes, among them his readings of the Stoic philosophers, the circumstances in which he lived, the Civil Wars of Perú, and his Indian background. In spite of this, Garcilaso possessed an understanding spirit, the consequence of the philosophical harmony that he advocated, and a desire to reconcile the Spanish and the Indian cultures. Garcilaso's soul is a good barometer by which to better understand those historical times. He was a disillusioned individual with a very complex spirit. For example, he would at times sustain two contradictory theses about the same topic. He was both timid and audacious. Sometimes he was reserved and would not talk about his family nor about books that he had read (by the influential Las Casas, for example). On other occasions he would eagerly communicate details about his early life. He was a diligent worker, somewhat candid, but yet with a sharp critical sense. Although his character was melancholic and nostalgic, he could narrate anecdotes in a very lively manner. The shyness, silences, omissions, and evasions which are found in his writings are also characteristic of the Peruvian Indians, who are by nature suspicious and distrustful of others. Garcilaso's tragic life parallels the situation of Perú at that time. His life and works, therefore, are symbols of his time and project optimism and hope in the destiny of the New World.

9. "Un sermón editado por el Inca Garcilaso." *Nueva Revista de Filología Hispánica* (*Homenaje a Amado Alonso*) (México) 7, nos. 3–4 (1953): 594–599.

In 1900, Valdenebro Cisneros announced in his book *La imprenta en Córdoba* the existence of a pamphlet in the Biblioteca Provincial de Sevilla, bound in a volume called *Varios,* and entitled *Sermón que predicó el Reverendo P. F. Alonso Bernardino . . . en la ciudad de Málaga . . .* (Córdoba: Francisco de Çea, 1612). It had been published at the request of the "Indio Garcilaso de la Vega." Garcilaso is thus highlighting his Indian origin as well as his profound faith. The author was Alonso de Montilla, a Franciscan from Montilla, and it is unlikely that Garcilaso ever met him, although he was a friend of one of the friar's relatives. The pamphlet was dedicated to "don Alonso Fernández de Córdoba, Marqués de Priego, señor de la casa de Aguilar," Garcilaso's relative, who owed him a substantial amount of money. The article reviews Garcilaso's relationship with the Marquis and transcribes the text of the sermon's dedication, which was written by Garcilaso in 1612. In September of that same year, Garcilaso bought a chapel in the Cathedral of Córdoba, where his remains are still buried today. In March 1613, Garcilaso reports that he received 433,928 maravedís from the Marquis as a substantial installment on his debt. Both shyness and courtesy are involved in his peculiar manner of requesting the payment of the debt. Yet Garcilaso never mentions his edition of this sermon, nor does it appear in the catalog of his private library.

10. "The Spanish Inca." *Américas* (Washington, D.C.) 5, no. 4 (1953): 6–8, 30–31. [This is the English version of "El Inca Garcilaso, clásico de América" (no. 8). The English title was not given by Durand (cf. no. 16: 49).]

11. "La redacción de la *Florida del Inca:* Cronología." *Revista Histórica* (Lima) (1954): 288–302.

Durand recognizes that he mistakenly thought that the *Florida* was practically finished by 1589. Instead, it was written in three stages: (1) between 1585 and 1589 a first whole draft was completed; (2) around 1590 Garcilaso obtained the manuscripts of Alonso de Carmona and Juan de Coles and wrote a second version of *Florida,* which he finished in 1592. A disillusioned tone permeates this version, as a result of a bad year in 1591; and (3) between 1593 and 1603 he introduces final corrections, while at the same time he was writing the *Royal Commentaries* and the as yet untranslated *Genealogía de Garci Pérez de Vargas.* In 1604 he wrote the dedication to the Duke of Teodosio de Braganza, and it was probably at this time that he added sections concerning the activities of Portuguese soldiers in America. The available historiographical information confirms Garcilaso's accurate use of his sources in *Florida,* which consisted of three eye-witness accounts and one document which the royal chronicler Ambrosio de Morales had in his possession.

12. "A dos siglos y medio de la *Florida* del Inca Garcilaso." Universidad de México (México) (1955): 27–29.

The first two paragraphs deal briefly with the literary and historical value of the *Florida* and the problems of the three Spanish editions of the text. The article reproduces with minor variants pages 288–290 and 143–145 of the two articles published in Lima in *Revista Histórica* and *Letras,* respectively (see no. 11 and no. 14).

13. "Garcilaso y su formación literaria e histórica." In *Nuevos estudios sobre el Inca Garcilaso de la Vega,* 63–85. Lima: Banco de Crédito del Perú, 1955.

Durand identifies the primary lines of investigation that ought to be undertaken concerning Garcilaso and his works: more biographical studies, studies on the chronology of the works, their sources, as well as stylistic and linguistic analyses. The archaic expressions present in his prose are attributed to his long residence in Montilla. Garcilaso's literary vocation seems to have appeared without any known preconceived design. Durand reveals that those parts in the *Royal Commentaries* which deal with political history and the wars and conquests of the Incas were not part of the original plan but rather later additions. [In item no. 20, Durand refers to "inexplicable errors" in this printed version based on a lecture given in Lima, but he neither identifies nor corrects those mistakes.]

14. "Veracidad y exactitud en la *Florida* del Inca." *Letras* (Lima) 54–55 (1955): 143–150.

Garcilaso accurately uses his sources and informants in *Florida.* A substantial amount of the surprising information he gives has been subsequently confirmed by other chroniclers, for example, in Fidalgo de Elvas' *History* and the accounts by Rodrigo de Rangel and Luis Hernández de Viedma. He is concerned that the authenticity of his information could be questioned, since it was provided by an anonymous informant, who, as it was discovered during this century, was the conquistador Gonzalo Silvestre. In order to show the exactness of his account, he even left the vagueness and gaps just as they appeared in his sources. He also fears being accused of partiality because of his Indian origin. To anticipate any doubts, Garcilaso solemnly swore on several occasions that he was telling the truth. [This article is reproduced in pages 298–300 of item no. 11.]

15. "Ediciones de la *Florida*. Estudio bibliográfico." In *La Florida del Inca* by Garcilaso Inca de la Vega. Ed. and notes by Emma Susana Speratti Piñero; prologue by Aurelio Miró-Quesada. México: Fondo de Cultura Económica, 1956.

Durand compiles a new bibliography of the editions of Garcilaso's *Florida*. It is based on an earlier work by Ventura García Calderón with later additions by Raúl Porras Barrenechea. Previous information is corrected, and unknown editions and translations are added. Twenty-one copies of the first edition of *Florida* are identified and their present locations are indicated. The bibliography also includes Spanish anthologies, as well as translations into French, German, English, and Flemish.

16. "Estudio preliminar y notas." In *Comentarios reales* by Garcilaso Inca de la Vega, 1: 11–56. Lima: Universidad Mayor de San Marcos, 1959 [2d. ed. Lima: Cultura popular, 1967].

Reproduces the articles "El Inca Garcilaso, clásico de América" [no. 8] and "El Inca Garcilaso, historiador apasionado" [no. 5]. The latter title is changed to "La historia como autobiografía," without changing any of its contents; and Durand also adds two notes: "Perennidad de los *Comentarios reales*" (49–51) and a chronology of Garcilaso (51–56).

17. "Los dos autores de *La Florida*." *Letras* (Lima) 64 (1960): 19–27.

Paul P. Firbas

This article reviews some aspects of Gonzalo Silvestre's life according to contemporary accounts. Concerning his residence in Perú, it recalls Iñigo López Carrillo's accusation against Silvestre's involvement in Pedro de Hinojosas' assassination, and also the rape of Anton de Roda's wife, which was confirmed by two additional testimonies. Back in Spain, after participating in Hernando de Soto's ill-fated expedition to Florida, Silvestre sought royal compensation for his travails in the Indies. The central part of the, article concerns Silvestre's friendship with Garcilaso, and their collaborative work in writing the history of that expedition to Florida, which was finished while Silvestre was still alive. [Some of the ideas in this article are extensively developed in no. 11 and no. 27.]

18. "Blas Valera y el jesuita anónimo." *Estudios Americanos (Homenaje a Raúl Porras Barrenechea)* (Sevilla) 22, nos. 109–110 (1961): 73–94.

The purpose of the article is "to study the personality of the author of the anonymous manuscript entitled *De las costumbres antiguas de los naturales del Pirú*," and to examine the hypothesis proposed by Raúl Porras Barrenechea that Blas Valera was the actual writer. Durand indicates that the author was neither Peruvian nor mestizo, but rather a Jesuit *chapetón* (that is, a recently arrived Spaniard) missionary. This affirmation is based on several facts: the different interpretation of the name "Perú," the chronology of the anonymous text established from an overlooked reference to missions in Chachapoyas (the text would have been written by 1594, although its content focuses on the years 1568–1583), the anonymous author's partial mastering of Quechua language, his silence about mestizos and Creoles, his statements against *encomenderos* (Spaniards who had been granted land and inhabitants), his censure of the Peruvian rebellions, and his typically Spanish blame of Spanish people. Durand reviews biographical aspects of Blas Valera and the reference to his father, Luis Valera, in the anonymous text. Finally, the article anticipates the hypothesis that the author was Luis López, a Jesuit who was prosecuted by the Inquisition at the time of Viceroy Toledo.

19. "Estudio preliminar y notas." In *Historia general del Perú. Segunda parte de los Comentarios reales* by Garcilaso Inca de la Vega. Lima: Universidad Mayor de San Marcos, 1962–1963 [reprinted in no. 36].

The following aspects of the *General History of Perú* or *Second Part of the Royal Commentaries* are studied: (1) the years of composition: from 1603 to 1612. The prologue was written in 1615. This is Garcilaso's longest book and the one with the most brilliant historical thesis. It narrates the "tragedy of the father's side, the world of the conquistadors"; (2) the Inca and the Stoics: the work and its topic are tragic. Garcilaso's Indian soul and his readings disposed him to fatalism. Christian thought and Stoicism harmonized with Indian patience and resignation. Garcilaso's writings had a clearly Renaissance character until about 1600, but then a fatalistic and resigned *Weltanschauung* informed his last works; (3) the Neoplatonic influence: the concept of love in Garcilaso's work. Although tragedy is present, there will always be place for hope and for balance between the two worlds of his origin; (4) literary and historical conception: fourfold perspective of Garcilaso's narration, as a man intimately related to the deeds he relates, as a chronicler, as a writer to whom history is a literary genre, and as a humanist historian, preoccupied with the inner meaning of the events he narrates; and (5) the look to the future: in his prologue he addresses all Peruvians and clarifies his purpose for writing about "our *patria*, people, and nation." The Inca understood that, because of his work, his life was not meaningless.

20. "El proceso de redacción de las obras del Inca Garcilaso." *Annales de la Faculté des Lettres et Sciences Humaines d'Aix* (Aix-en-Provence) 36 (1962): 247–266.

Garcilaso was an outstanding student of grammar and Latin during his early days of instruction in Cuzco. In Montilla, Spain, he met wise persons and started to read historical works while he was still young. The project of writing the history of Florida seems to be related to the French Huguenot attempts to colonize that region of America. This scenario could have encouraged Gonzalo Silvestre's memories of his life as a soldier. Garcilaso and Silvestre probably worked together in the history of de Soto's expedition since 1567. The Inca finished his translation of León Hebreo's *Dialoghi d'Amore* between 1585 and 1586, after five years of work, without being aware of Carlos Montesa's or Guedalla Yahia's translations, but he did know the Latin translation done by Juan Carlos Sarraceno. Garcilaso asked scholars and wise men like Jerónimo de Prado, Agustín de Herrera, Pedro Sánchez de Herrera, and Fernando de Zárate to clarify his doubts. His method of writing was slow and careful. The *Genealogía de Garci Pérez de Vargas* was completed in 1594 with some addenda in 1596. At first he conceived of it as a prologue-dedication to his *Florida,* but then he put it away and it remained in manuscript form. This project harmonized with the autobiographical inclination of his works. Part of the sources for this genealogy were kept in Extremadura (especially Badajoz), so it is likely that Garcilaso made a trip to this Spanish region. [No references to the *Royal Commentaries.*]

21. "Un rasgo humanístico del Inca Garcilaso." *Cuadernos* (Paris) 64 (1962): 36–42.

Garcilaso always writes as a humanist, regardless of the topic. His ideas about fame, honor, nobility, fortune, etc., were part of the thought of his time, except for Erasmianism. With true humanist curiosity he discussed in detail various forms of manual labor, which was something unusual for a Peninsular gentleman, but not for a Spanish-American or a member of the Indian nobility. His language is at one and the same time old (because of his residence in Cuzco and Montilla) and new (containing many neologisms of Latin origin). He was proud of his knowledge of the specific vocabulary of every occupation: horse breeding, hunting, falconry, sailing, music (he could play various instruments and was versed in Pythagorian thought) and architecture (Renaissance and Indian). He uses with precision terms like "barbarians," "infidel," and "gentile," applying the latter to the Incas. All his humanist knowledge serves the historical purpose of his work.

Because of his disillusion with the world, he was a representative man of the late Renaissance.

22. "Las enigmáticas fuentes de la *Florida del Inca*." *Cuadernos Hispanoamericanos* (Madrid) 168 (1963): 597–609.

In opposition to positivist criticism, this article asserts the historical accuracy of the *Florida*. Some details of this book, apparently without any documentary support, have been corroborated by later historical research: the naval battle in Cuba before de Soto's arrival, the matter between the soldier Sanjurje and the viceroy, the existence of the *lugarteniente* (second-in-command) Rojas, Diego de Muñoz's captivity, etc. The whole work is rich in historical material. About the veracity of the sources, the article maintains that: (1) as a consequence of the close relation between Garcilaso and book printers in Córdoba, it is more than likely that Juan Coles' papers were found in one of those printers' houses; (2) there is no doubt that the *Florida* was compared with Ambrosio de Morales' manuscript chronicle; (3) Alonso de Carmona was historically real and his memoirs were used by Garcilaso after Silvestre's death and helped him to fill in the gaps left by the first informant. Carmona's and Coles' information is of a clear historical intent, as they usually minimize the literary aspects of the book; and (4) Garcilaso underscores Silvestre's heroic deeds and makes him one of the protagonists in the history, which is somewhat questionable. However, different sources agree that Silvestre was a good and loyal soldier. Finally, the article affirms that from the known accounts of de Soto's expedition, the one written by the anonymous gentleman of Helvas is the most credible, but Garcilaso's account is the most beautiful and detailed.

23. "Garcilaso entre el mundo incaico y las ideas renacentistas." *Diógenes* (Paris) 43 (1963): 17–33.

Garcilaso Inca, a first-generation mestizo, enters the Florentine Neoplatonic world with his translation of León Hebreo's *Dialoghi* and his readings of Marsilio Ficino and, perhaps, Pico della Mirandola. He also read many humanists with Platonic ideas.

Paul P. Firbas

Among the Spanish authors, he read the complete works of Fray Luis de Granada and, while residing in Montilla, he met the Jesuits of the city and became personally acquainted with Juan de Avila. The Neoplatonism in Garcilaso is generally related to utopian concepts, especially through Saint Augustine, although he never quotes this author. His favorable vision of the Inca Empire reflects an indirect intervention in the debate about the legitimacy of the Spanish possessions in America. Garcilaso's Neoplatonic thought could have germinated within the Inca spirit of his maternal home or, more likely, his contact with this European doctrine could have shaped his memories from his childhood. In any case, Garcilaso was eclectic in thought, which allowed him to conciliate different ideas: Neoplatonism, Stoicism (in its relation to the Jesuits), Petrarchism, and Senecan thought (in his *Proemio* to the *Florida*). Other Renaissance aspects can be seen in his historical providentialism, the humanist reflections on wealth, and his disillusionment with and tragic vision of reality (as in Seneca and metaphysical Stoicism). At the same time, these aspects can also be related to Inca culture.

24. "El nombre de los *Comentarios Reales.*" *Revista del Museo Nacional* (Lima) 32 no. 3 (1963): 321–331.

The title *Royal Commentaries of the Incas* reveals historical, literary, psychological, biographical, and stylistic aspects. "Commentaries" refers to its value as "commentary" with respect to other chronicles of the Indies and to the influence of Julius Caesar and the biblical commentaries of the Andalucian Jesuits Jerónimo de Prado, Juan Bautista Villalpando, and Juan de Pineda y Pedro Maldonado de Saavedra, all three residents of Córdoba and personally known by Garcilaso. Thus, the commentary cannot be understood as a minor form of historical writing, as Agustín de Zárate considered it. Garcilaso does not have a modest project, like Alvar Núñez Cabeza de Vaca, neither does he imitate Julius Caesar or biblical commentaries. He possesses his own literary identity. The adjective "royal" in the title seems to stress the work of a "royal chronicler" (Inca royalty), while the phrase "of the Incas" avoids a dangerous singular ("of the Inca") with which

Garcilaso would have named himself a "royal chronicler," an official title that he never had.

25. "Les deux univers de l'Inca Garcilaso." *Annales de la Faculté des Lettres et Sciences Humaines d'Aix* (Aix-en-Provence) 38 (1964): 23–55.

This article is based on conferences held in Austin, Texas, Princeton, and Lima in 1953, on articles that are already published (especially no. 5) as well as on unpublished material. It reviews the relation between Garcilaso's biography and his writings, especially with respect to their complexities, their reception, and the essential contradictions in his thought, a dualistic reality that Garcilaso strives to reconcile. In this sense, Garcilaso's position concerning the debate about the legitimacy of the Spanish conquest and Las Casas' ideas is also contradictory and reflects the mestizo nature of the author. He accepts the conquest and defends the Inca government against Viceroy Toledo. He does not reject Las Casas' ideas but he considers them impossible to apply and the cause of many disasters. Garcilaso's portraits of de Soto and Pizarro are the opposite of those of Las Casas.

26. "El Inca llega a España." *Revista de Indias* (Madrid) 25, nos. 99–100 (1965): 27–43.

This article is about the life of Garcilaso in Montilla, Spain, and his relationship with his paternal family. Garcilaso Inca, formerly named Gómez Suárez de Figueroa, was sent from Perú to his paternal home in Badajoz when he was twenty years old. The article attempts to re-create, via indirect sources, the arrival of Garcilaso in that city in Extremadura. The meeting of the Peruvian mestizo and his family in Badajoz soured, which resulted in Garcilaso's trip to Montilla in search of his uncle Alonso de Vargas and the protection of the Marquis-consort of Priego. Garcilaso's unsuccessful claims at the Spanish court consumed his wealth and brought disgrace upon him, and thus he attempted, also unsuccessfully, to return to Perú in 1563. After his experience at the court, Garcilaso participated in the Battle of Alpujarras under the protection of the Marquis of Priego. Alonso de Vargas died in 1570 and Garcilaso inherited half of his possessions, which solved his monetary difficulties. The Inca changed his name to Garcilaso de la Vega because his uncle, the *mayorazgo* (eldest son) Gómez Suárez de Figueroa and the first Duke de Feria, bore hostility to the Marquis of Priego. By adding "Inca" to his new name he created his literary identity.

27. "La memoria de Gonzalo Silvestre." *Cahiers du Monde Hispanique et Luso-Brésilien* (Toulouse) 7 (1966): 43–52.

This article reviews the accuracy of the recollections of the soldier Gonzalo Silvestre, Garcilaso's informant in the *Florida*. Silvestre did not rely on written notes but rather on continuous questions posed by Garcilaso. He remembered the names of 121 expeditionary soldiers, and in fifty-four instances the Christian names, family names, and places of origin are correct; on the other hand, Rodrigo Ranjel used written notes but registered only forty-seven names, of which twenty-two are incomplete; the Fidalgo de Elvas in his *Relaçam* mentions forty-one soldiers; and Luis Hernández de Viedma, although good in naming places, mentions only seven persons. Some names are mistaken in Silvestre but correct in the Fidalgo, which means that the *Relaçam* was not used to refresh the memory of the soldier. In spite of mistakes, Silvestre did not invent any member of the expedition. Thus the *Florida* is an important historical source which, however, like all sources, requires critical examination. The article concludes with comments by Marcel Bataillon and Aurelio Miró-Quesada, both of whom stress the importance of José Durand's work.

28. "Los silencios del Inca Garcilaso." *Mundo Nuevo* (Paris) 5 (1966): 66–72.

This study concentrates on the importance of intentional omissions in Garcilaso's work. Garcilaso conceals some unpleasant facts about his family (marriages between brothers and sisters in his maternal family, and dishonored relatives on the side of Garci Pérez); he is reserved about Peruvian rebels and about his sources (i.e., his readings of Las Casas and Polo de Ondegardo) and he contradicts Alonso de Ercilla, without mentioning him, regarding the figure of Pedro de Valdivia. He adheres to certain aesthetic rules such as quoting sparingly (he mentions neither Petrarch nor León Hebreo, although their influence is obvious in his writings) and avoiding unnecessary discussions (he does not engage Cieza and Palentino concerning pre-Inca history and minor Inca rulers). Some silences are inexplicable, for example, his failure to mention Leonor de Soto or Tocto Chimpu, or Hernando de Soto's and Huayna Capac's daughters, respectively. His reticence about Francisco de Solano, called "the Peruvian apostle," and Juan de Avila is astonishing. He also consistently avoids mentioning Gonzalo Silvestre. There seem to be moral reasons for not mentioning those who have been dishonored. As a historian, Garcilaso shows respect for the honor of others and holds high "the concept of the historian as a minister of Fame." His explicit censures of Viceroys Marquis de Cañete and Francisco Toledo thus constitute strict chastisements. Condemnation through forgetfulness was also usual among the Incas, and the Quechua language is especially rich in elusive terms. Garcilaso's silences therefore contain features from both the Andean people as well as from the culture of the Renaissance.

29. "El Inca en los años aciagos." *Anuario de Filología* (Maracaibo) (1967): 137–155.

The article explains how the feeling of disillusionment evolved in Garcilaso Inca as a result of several tragic incidents in his life. "Three stages of misfortune" are identified: (1) the time spent at the Spanish court presenting his claims, (2) his military activities, and (3) "the disfavor of the new Marquis of Priego." From 1586 to 1589, his letters to the Marquis were written in a pleasant tone, but by 1592 complaints predominate. The transitional years until 1593 were economically and intellectually rewarding, but his pessimism became extreme between 1600 and 1604. The years from 1594 to 1604 constituted Garcilaso's "bad period": his *Florida* was still waiting to be printed, there was uncertainty whether the *Royal Commentaries* would ever be published, and he had quarreled with the Marquis don Pedro. The region of

Andalucia suffered a terrible plague (1599–1600) and drought (1605), and the two parts of the *Royal Commentaries* were written under these disastrous conditions in the area. The Spanish Invincible Armada was defeated in 1588 and Cádiz was sacked in 1596. On the other side of the Atlantic, Peruvian conditions were sad: the Civil Wars were raging and the Inca Empire was in ruins. Thus, the *Royal Commentaries* reflect a specific period in time which was rife with pessimism but also fertile with hope. The factors of Garcilaso's disillusionment are varied and complex, coherent and yet enigmatic.

30. "El Inca, hombre en prisma." In *Studi di Letteratura Ispano-Americana*, 41–57. Milano: Istituto Editoriale Cisalpino, 1967.

There are three possible approaches to understanding Garcilaso's work: (1) he can be considered exclusively as part of European culture; (2) European culture is conceived merely as a means of expression in his work; or (3) he and his work belong both to the Indian and to the Hispanic worlds. The context within which the author places himself in his writings offers the best means to understanding the indigenous aspects of his nature. The article emphasizes the differences between a "converso" and an American mestizo in Spain. Representing two cultures, Garcilaso is in a position of "harmonious instability." Mestizos lived in social disarray. Garcilaso's indirect opinions sometimes favor and at other times oppose "just wars." He never quoted or adhered to Sepúlveda's ideas, but he was a good friend of the latter's friend, Ambrosio de Morales. Garcilaso also pretended to ignore Las Casas' ideas, yet he owned his *Tratados* and could have known his *Apologética* through Román y Zamora's *Repúblicas del mundo*. Garcilaso equates the New Laws, which were supported by Las Casas, with the devil, and he justifies the Spanish conquest, just as the Anonymous of Yucay. However, he never censured the writings of the Dominican friar, although he believed that it was impossible to apply his doctrine to realistic conditions (in this he followed three chroniclers: Gómara, Zárate, and the Palentino). For Garcilaso, the evangelization of the Indies and the messianic concept of history justified the conquest.

31. "El influjo de Garcilaso en Túpac Amaru." *Copé* (Lima) 2, no. 5
    (1971): 2–7 [reprinted in *Cuadernos Americanos. Nueva época*
    (México) 18 (1989): 172–177].

A brief review of Garcilaso's secret adherence to Las Casas' ideas:
his defense of the "legítimo señorío de los Incas" (legitimate
lordship of the Incas), his arguments in favor of the "restitution"
of the empire (especially related to the fate of Túpac Amaru I),
his criticism of Felipe II, and his favorable attitude towards the
Peruvian rebels against royal authority. The Inca mestizo José
Gabriel Condorcanqui could have assumed his name, Túpac
Amaru, after reading the *Royal Commentaries*. Garcilaso inspired
the national consciousness through his concept of a Peruvian
homeland (*patria*—the former Tahuantinsuyo) dating back to
late sixteenth century. Condorcanqui, like Garcilaso, did not re-
fuse his Hispanic legacy. Both of them defined themselves as
Catholics, addressed their ideas to a Perú with no divisions due
to class, and demanded the integral unity of the country.

32. "Montería indiana: el chaco." *Anuario de Letras* (México) 10
    (1972): 75–104.

A study of the *chaco,* the great hunting game of the Incas. No
author examines this topic in as much detail as Garcilaso Inca.
The first sources that describe the chaco were: Estete, Pedro
Pizarro, Trujillo, Gómara (misleading information), Cieza (excellent account), Antonio de Herrera, Zárate (better informed
than Gómara, though they use a common source), Polo de
Ondegardo (interested in the rules and the economic, social, and
political effects of the chaco), Juan de Matienzo, Gonzalo Argote
de Molina (in *Discurso de la montería* he follows his personal account of the chaco after the conquest), and Acosta (he does not
mention llamas, only pumas). In the *Royal Commentaries*, the description of the chaco was written before 1600. Garcilaso does
not mention his sources, and his account is independent and con-
fined to pre-Hispanic times. He describes it as a solemn hunting
ceremony characterized by nobility of action. He refers to its rigorous bans, rules, the inventory which is kept in *quipus,* the dis-

tribution and storage. It is a realistic but idealized account, the product of a mestizo who was a hunter himself. By the mid-seventeenth century, Bernabé Cobo offers new information and completes the account given by Estete concerning the chaco ordered by Manco Inca in 1534. The number of Indians involved in the chaco according to different sources is compared and the number given by Cieza, i.e., "between 3,000 and 100,000," is considered "reasonable."

33. "Juegos ecuestres en el Inca Garcilaso." *Cuadernos Americanos* (México) 2 (1973): 159–181.

An article about the equestrian knowledge of Garcilaso, and the games and festivities related to horses and bull fights in Garcilaso and other sources, e.g., the Mexican Juan Suárez de Peralta, the knight commander Chacón, Luis Buñuelos, Bernardo de Vargas Machuca, etc. The differences between the use of bridle and riding "a la jineta," the latter preferred in the Indies while in Europe it was becoming obsolete. Garcilaso had been present at cane games ("juegos de cañas") since his childhood. He actively participated in these games in Perú (the participation of mestizos like Garcilaso in these games proves their social acceptance). Bull fights deserved brief mentions in the *Royal Commentaries*. Garcilaso is cautious with respect to bull fights since they were condemned by Pope Pius V. Regarding public horse races, there is just one reference in Garcilaso, a "delightful passage," whereas he does not even mention other less famous contests.

34. "De bibliografía indiana." *Revista Iberoamericana* (Pittsburgh) 11, no. 86 (1974): 105–110.

Includes two notes: the first one about a "dirty and incomplete" copy of Alonso de Ovalle's *Histórica relación,* with the date MDCXLVIII added to the title page (reproduced in the article). The second note refers to the first edition of the *Royal Commentaries* printed in Lisbon, 1609, which usually lacks the drawing of Garcilaso's coat of arms. Durand offers the hypothesis that the page with the coat of arms was posthumously added to the five hundred copies of the *Royal Commentaries* which, according to the inventory made by his executors, Garcilaso had in his home. The *princeps* of Garcilaso and Ovalle which lack the pre-title pages (the coat of arms, and the page entitled "Varias y curiosas noticias del reino de chile . . . ") should be considered the oldest editions, rather than incomplete ones.

35. "Los *Comentarios reales* y dos sermones del doctor Pizaño." *Nueva Revista de Flología Hispánica (Homenaje a Raimundo Lida)* (México) 24, no. 2 (1975): 292–307.

Renaissance Neoplatonism and the Counter-Reformation, although opposing tendencies, influenced Garcilaso Inca and others like Cervantes. In Spanish letters, Neoplatonism flourished slowly and remained dominant throughout the sixteenth century. Plato was read in Ficino's Latin translation and commentaries. The Spanish editions of León Hebreo were made late during the Counter-Reformation. Garcilaso wrote at the same time that Campanella composed his *Citá del Sole*. Dr. Alvaro Pizaño de Palacios, canon at the cathedral of Córdoba and outstanding preacher, reflects in his sermons many ideas related to the *Royal Commentaries*. Garcilaso and Pizaño were friends and shared an interest in Plato. Pizaño quotes Plato about rulers of governments and develops ideas similar to those of Garcilaso. In another sermon Pizaño refers extensively to the Heliopolis. The topic of the Sun is important in the *Dialoghi d'Amore* and appears in various Renaissance authors. In Córdoba, towards the beginning of the seventeenth century, this topic was related to ancient Perú; in 1629, the Jesuit Martín de Roa used but did not quote the *Royal Commentaries* regarding the idolatry of the Sun.

36. *El Inca Garcilaso, clásico de América.* México: Sepsetentas, 1976 [Lima: Biblioteca Nacional, 1988, partial edition].

This book presents nine articles—slightly modified—which were originally published between 1949 and 1962 in journals and books in Lima, México, Paris, and Washington, D.C.: "El Inca Garcilaso, historiador apasionado" (1950) [no. 5], "Garcilaso el Inca, platónico" (1949) [no. 4], "El Inca Garcilaso, clásico de América" (1952/3) [nos. 8, 10], "Introducción a los *Comentarios*

Paul P. Firbas

reales" (1962) [no. 19, renamed], "La idea de la honra en el Inca Garcilaso" (1951) [no. 6], "El duelo, motivo cómico" (1949) [no. 3], "Un rasgo humanístico del Inca Garcilaso" (1962) [no. 21], "Dos notas sobre el Inca Garcilaso" (1949) [no. 2], and "Un sermón editado por el Inca Garcilaso" (1953) [no. 9].

Reviews: Luis Alberto Sánchez, *El Sol de México* (México), cultural supplement, 22 August 1971; Armando Zubizarreta, *Cuadernos Americanos* (México) 219 (1978): 177–179; Franklin Pease, *Anuario de Letras* (México) 17 (1979): 366–369.

37. "Perú y Ophir en Garcilaso Inca, el jesuita Pineda y Gregorio García." *Revista Histórica* (Lima) 3, no. 2 (1979): 35–55.

From the time of Columbus, authors like Pedro Mártir, Francisco Vetablo, and Benito Arias Montano maintained the thesis that Perú was the biblical region of Ophir, where gold was plentiful. In the second volume of his *Commentariorum in Job* (1601), Juan de Pineda gathered information received from Garcilaso Inca in late 1593 or early 1594 about the etymology of the word *Perú*. The article reviews Pineda's biography and his relation to Garcilaso. By 1603, Fray Gregorio García came to Spain from México. In his *Origen de los indios* (1607), García discusses different opinions about this topic, and although he shows great esteem for Garcilaso, whom he probably met in 1603, he disagrees with him. García also believes that Perú derives from Ophir, contradicting Garcilaso and Pineda. In his book *Salomon praevitus* (1609), the latter author diplomatically replies to García, leaving the conclusion to the reader's judgment, although asserting that "Ophir bears no resemblance to the name Perú." Garcilaso could possibly be referring to García in the first part of the *Royal Commentaries,* book 2, chapter 5, when he describes the meaning of the Quechua term *pacha*. Garcilaso, perhaps influenced by Blas Valera and his eclectic Neoplatonism, wrote his own conciliatory version of the etymology of Perú, which he thought was derived from "Berú" and "Pelú," an Indian proper noun and a generic noun for river, respectively [cf. no. 2]; but he avoids further debate.

204

38. "Andanzas del Padre Maldonado y su *privado* ejemplar." *Nueva Revista de Filología Hispánica (In memoriam Raimundo Lida)* (México) 29, no. 2 (1980): 312–342.

A study of the manuscript, context, and biography of the Augustinian friar Pedro Maldonado, who had previously been a Jesuit, author of *Tratado del perfecto pribado* (presumably written in 1603), which he dedicated to the Duke of Lerma. Garcilaso Inca identifies him as "Pedro Maldonado de Saavedra," the person who, in Córdoba around 1599, gave him the "torn papers" of the Jesuit Blas Valera, one of his principal sources. Maldonado moved to Valladolid after that date, and by 1603 he was held in great esteem by the king's favorite ("el valido"), the Duke of Lerma. In the following year he lost the Duke's esteem. In 1606, when he entered the Augustinian order, he anonymously published the *Discurso del choro y officio divino,* a praise of vocal and communal prayer.

39. "Los últimos días de Blas Valera." In *Libro de homenaje a Aurelio Miró Quesada Sosa,* 1:409–420. Lima: P. L. Villanueva, 1987.

This article focuses on Blas Valera, the Peruvian mestizo and Jesuit, and his banishment from Perú to Spain until his death in 1597, soon after the sack of Cádiz and his escape to Málaga. He was punished and sent to Spain after being accused of having had a sexual liaison with an Indian woman. The article reviews briefly the debate between Manuel González de la Rosa and José de la Riva-Agüero concerning the historical truth in Garcilaso's works and his use of the "torn papers" of Father Blas Valera, which he had obtained from Father Pedro Maldonado. Printed sources and manuscripts are used to describe the sack of Cádiz and the destruction of the Jesuit House, which lends credibility to Garcilaso's version of how he obtained Valera's papers, which, according to the article, had been in Garcilaso's possession since 1599. The *Royal Commentaries* thus saved the Peruvian Jesuit from oblivion and vindicated him to his Order. Valera's friendship with the Andalucian Jesuit Luis López is explored. The account written by the "Anonymous Jesuit" is attributed to López; it coincides with fragments of Valera's work and was written sometime after his death (cf. no. 18).

40. "En torno a la prosa del Inca Garcilaso. A propósito de un artículo de Roberto González Echevarría." *Nuevo Texto Crítico* (Stanford) 1, no. 2 (1988): 209–227.

Criticism of the article "The Law of the Letter: Garcilaso's *Commentaries* and the Origins of Latin American Narrative," written by Roberto González Echevarría (*The Yale Journal of Criticism* 1 [1987]). Durand disputes the accuracy of several terms used by González Echevarría, such as "letrados," "bastard," "restitution," "encomenderos," etc. Mistakes are pointed out in the biography of Garcilaso's father, for example the statement that Garcilaso Inca was never legally recognized by his father, and that Gasca participated in the battle of Huarina. Durand criticizes and refutes the hypothesis that the rhetoric of notary-writing explains the excellent prose of Garcilaso and that his motivation to become a writer derives from his failure to receive compensation from the Spanish court. Durand asserts that Garcilaso's prose style was already mature by the time he finished translating the *Dialoghi* of León Hebreo, a text which bears no resemblance to notarial prose. Durand finally stresses the importance of variety in the composition of the *Commentaries* and its relationship to the picaresque. He speculates on Garcilaso's vocation as a writer and points out the social and intellectual prestige that Garcilaso enjoyed in Córdoba.

41. "Garcilaso Inca jura decir verdad." *Crítica Hispánica* (Pittsburgh) 10, nos. 1–2 (1988): 21–39.

This article sounds a note of alarm about the critical tendency in the United States to see only literary value in the "historical works of Garcilaso Inca." It focuses on the narrative concerning the mythical origin of the Incas in the *Commentaries* and compares it with other chronicles. Garcilaso describes legends knowing full well that they are fiction. The article further studies the solar origin of the Incas in Betanzos (a source which Garcilaso seems to ignore); in Sarmiento, Gómara, Zárate, Cieza de León (whose conclusions coincide with those of Garcilaso, although it is very unlikely that Garcilaso had ever read Cieza's manuscript), in the *Relación de las muchas cosas acaecidas en el Perú* of 1552 (*Account of the many things that occurred in Perú*), in Cristóbal de Molina, el Cuzqueño (close similarities), in José de Acosta, and in Bernabé Cobo (who never doubted Garcilaso's veracity). Cobo also states that during the government of Tupac Yupanqui (the grandfather of Garcilaso's informant), the solar temple located on one of the islands in Lake Titicaca was remodeled. Durand affirms that Garcilaso's rendering of the myth, although it is a late and adorned version, is based on authentic native elements from older accounts. The mastery of Garcilaso's prose does not affect the veracity of his narrative. [Durand published three articles in Lima's newspaper *El Comercio* in reply to María de Rostworoski's *Historia del Tahuantinsuyu* (Lima, 1988), all of which are closely related to this entry: "El sol envía a sus hijos," 20 September 1988, p. 2; "Filiación de una leyenda del Inca Garcilaso," 22 September 1988, p. 2; and "Garcilaso Inca en el banquillo," 7 November 1988, p. 2. These brief articles insist on the veracity and complexity of Garcilaso Inca.]

42. "Rodrigo Niño, el de los galeotes." *Nueva Revista de Filología Hispánica* (México) 37, no. 2 (1989): 383–404.

A brief review of the bibliography that treats as fictitious the adventures of Captain Rodrigo Niño in the second part of the *Royal Commentaries*, and a study of the possibility of their veracity and the historical and literary consequences which can be derived from this assumption. The article reviews the references to Rodrigo Niño in the chronicles of Zárate and Palentino, texts which are Garcilaso's sources for the characterization of Niño. Several new documents are revealed: an unpublished account in the Archivo de Indias that clarifies the identity of Rodrigo Niño's namesake; a letter of the Viceroy and first Marquis of Cañete sent to the King on 3 November 1556, that reveals the imprisonment of suspects of conspiracy, among whom were Rodrigo Niño and Gonzalo Silvestre (this conspiracy would have taken place six years after the voyage with the galley slaves); the interrogations-

Paul P. Firbas

confessions conducted by Doctor Cuenca, in which Niño gives information about the distribution of lands and his ambition to obtain territory as *encomiendas;* the document written by the viceroy on November 2, ordering the suspects to go to Spain to testify in front of the king; and correspondence between the Duke of Alba and Licenciado Rodrigo Niño, the captain's uncle. The article concludes by speculating on the estate inherited by Licenciado Niño, and stating that despite the lack of evidence for the voyage of Rodrigo Niño with the galley slaves, it very likely occurred.

SPANISH-AMERICAN CHRONICLES AND
EPIC POEMS

43. "Gómara: encrucijada." *Historia Mexicana* (México) 2, no. 2 (1952): 210–222.

Studies the purposes of Gómara's *History,* the style of his prose, and the reception of his historical work during his time.

44. "El chapetón Ercilla y la honra Araucana." *Filología* (Buenos Aires) 10 (1966): 113–134.

Discusses the relationships among Ercilla, the old conquistadors, and the "otros *chapetones* notables" (other distinguished and recently arrived Spaniards): Francisco Falcón, Diego Alvarez, the soldier Cieza de León, and the Jesuit Luis López; delineates the position of *La Araucana* with respect to the Hurtado de Mendoza family; and refers to the themes of honor, the Indians, and the just war.

45. "Caupolicán, clave historial y épica de *La Araucana.*" *Revue de Littérature Comparée (Hommage à Marcel Bataillon)* (Paris) 2, nos. 2–4 (1978): 367–389.

Reviews the circumstances surrounding the publication of *La Araucana,* its sources and reception in its time; compares the character of Caupolicán in *La Araucana,* with other texts such as Jerónimo de Vivar's *Crónica* (although it is never mentioned by

Ercilla), the *Account* by Licenciado Herrera (written before
Ercilla's poem), and others.

46. *"La Araucana* en sus 35 cantos originales." *Anuario de Letras*
    (México) 16 (1978): 291–294.

The posthumous version of *La Araucana* with its thirty-seven cantos undermines the climactic ending of the poem. The article
questions the authenticity of all the added verses, since their in-
clusion in the poem did not express the last will of the poet. The
poem should thus be read in its original thirty-five cantos until
new evidence indicates otherwise. [The article summarizes a lecture given at a colloquium about Ercilla held at the University of
Michigan in 1969 (no. 47: 166, n. 6).]

47. "Oña y su defensa del *mozo capitán acelerado.*" In *Studia humanitatis:*
    homenaje a Rubén Bonifaz Nuño, ed. Aurora M. Ocampo et al., 165–
    174. México: Universidad Nacional Autónoma de México, 1987.

The article studies the *Arauco domado* by Pedro de Oña as a response to Ercilla's verses (*La Araucana,* canto 35) against García
Hurtado de Mendoza. It also examines the theme of the just
war, the figure of Galvarino, and Oña's insistence on presenting
García as a prudent young man.

48. "Peculiaridad de la literatura colonial: el caso de Ercilla." In *Rup-*
    tura de la conciencia hispanoamericana (Época colonial), 77–85. Ma-
    drid: Fondo de Cultura Económica, University of Notre Dame,
    1993.

"We do have a Colonial Literature, but we lack ideas to order it."
A study of Ruiz de Alarcón and especially Ercilla in their complex
position as belonging to both Peninsular and Colonial literature.

COLONIAL JOURNALISM

49. "Edición, prólogo y apéndices." In *Guía política, eclesiástica y mili-*
    tar del virreinato del Perú, para el año de 1793 by Hipólito Unánue,
    ix–xxxiii. Edición facsimilar. Lima: COFIDE, 1985.

The *Guide* of the Peruvian doctor Hipólito Unánue "appears as
a direct derivation of the *Mercurio Peruano*" and is considered an

example of the "journalism of the Enlightenment period during a time of growing nationalism" in Perú. The prologue discusses calendars and "guías de forasteros" (guides written for foreigners), the "Guías" by Unánue, and journalism in Lima as exemplified in such writers as Lecuanda, José María Egaña, and Unánue. The facsimile edition of the *Guía* is enlarged and is a reproduction of the copy owned by José Durand.

50. "Compilación y prólogo." In *La Gaceta de Lima. De 1756 a 1762. De Superunda a Amat,* edición facsimilar, xiii–xxxiv. Lima: COFIDE, 1982.

The *Gaceta* "constitutes an irreplaceable document for the Colonial history of the eighteenth century," and it is considered the oldest regular newspaper in South America. The volume gathers forty-five issues (ten were unknown) and one supplement.

51. "Compilación, prólogo y apéndice." In *La Gaceta de Lima. De 1762 a 1765. Apogeo de Amat,* edición facsimilar, xi–lv. Lima: COFIDE, 1982.

The prologue deals with Viceroy Amat and with Doctor Ortega y Pimentel, who was responsible for the *Gaceta*. The "long sequence" of the periodical (1762–1772) is divided into three periods: the good beginning (up to number 28, published in March 1767), the careless period, and the anarchical period. The volume compiles "most of the first period, up to number 21, where the year 1765 ends."
Review (of the first two volumes): César Pacheco Vélez, *Debate* (Lima) 18.

52. "Compilación, prólogo y apéndice." In *La Gaceta de Lima. De 1793 a junio de 1794. Gil de Taboada y Lemos,* edición facsimilar, xi–lvii. Lima: COFIDE, 1983.

The *Gaceta* reappeared in 1793 and was devoted almost exclusively to foreign matters. This third volume includes: the "prospecto," thirty-five issues, and six supplements which cover an uninterrupted period of ten months; "28 of these issues and one supplement were completely unknown." The prologue studies the "new *Gaceta*," "the prospecto," "the periodicals of international affairs," the image of Lima and America in the *Gaceta* (which includes two chronicles related to the new "literature about customs"), the figures of del Río, Unánue, and Egaña and their relationship to the periodical, and the "correos y redactores" (messengers and writers). As in the other two volumes, the prologue ends with a description of the contents of the facsimile edition.

SOCIETY AND THE TIMES IN SPANISH AMERICA:
SIXTEENTH TO NINETEENTH CENTURIES

53. "El afán nobiliario de los conquistadores." *Cuadernos Americanos* (México) 1 (1953): 175–192.

It advances some fragments and expands chapters 3, 4, and 6 (about the Indies and the Reconquest) from the book *The Social Transformation of the Conquistador* [no. 54].

54. *La transformación social del conquistador.* 2 vols. Serie "México y lo mexicano," número 15. México: Porrúa y Obregón, 1953.

The book is presented as "an essay of interpretation on historical phenomena" about the conquistadors and their Creole lineage. The first volume includes six chapters, and the second volume eight: 1. Caracteres y causas de la transformación; 2. El hombre, la familia y la tierra; 3. Ir a valer más; 4. El ansia de oro; 5. El afán de honra; 6. La ambición de nobleza; 7. Rechazo y protesta; 8. Una aristocracia de guerreros; 9. La usurpación de tratamientos; 10. Aseñoramiento de los plebeyos; 11. Los hidalgos de Indias y los oficios manuales; 12. Los hidalgos y el comercio; 13. Justificación de la nobleza indiana; and 14. Refinamientos y cortesía.

55. "Colonial Etiquette." *Américas* (Washington, D.C.) 5, no. 10 (1953): 21–46.

English translation of chapter 14 of the second volume of *The Social Transformation . . .* [no. 54].

56. "El ambiente social de la conquista y sus proyecciones en la colonia." *Historia Mexicana* (México) 3, no. 4 (1954): 497–515.

Reproduces fragments plus rewritten and expanded parts of chapters 10, 11, and 12 of *The Social Transformation . . .* [no. 54]

57. "Baquianos y gachupines, criollos y chapetones. Albores de la sociedad americana colonial." *Cuadernos Americanos* (México) 87 (1955): 148–162.

Discusses the rivalry between "indianos" and "peninsulares," the situation of poor Creoles, the vanities and disillusionment of the sons of the conquistadors, and the protests in Lima and México on account of unjust rewards given to the conquistadors.

58. "Conquistadores y libertadores. Orígenes remotos de la independencia americana." *Fanal* (Lima) 11, no. 44 (1955): 7–11.

The independence of the American countries is understood as a long process of differentiation between "baquianos" and "chapetones," or between "criollos" and "gachupines." The article studies the first rebellions in the sixteenth century, the medieval aspect of the conquest, the social transformation and motives of the conquistadors, and the fact that merely 5,000 Spaniards achieved the conquest.

59. "El lujo indiano." *Historia Mexicana* (México) 6, no. 1 (1956): 59–74.

A study of the great temples of the sixteenth century, Colonial luxury and etiquette, Mexican grandeur, and the distribution of wealth.

60. *La transformación social del conquistador.* 2da. edición parcial. Lima: Nuevos rumbos, 1958.

Reprint "with some additions and a few corrections" of the first volume of the 1953 edition [no. 53].

61. "Trujillo en el XVII: un manuscrito ignorado." *Revista del Museo Nacional* (Lima) (1981): 215–233.

Edition of the first three chapters of the unpublished manuscript by Luis Joseph de Castro Domonte, *Vida de D. García de Toledo Bracamonte Natural de la Ciudad de Truxillo del Perú* (Trujillo, 1708), an old account of the history of the Peruvian city Trujillo. A brief study of the manuscript and the historical characters mentioned precedes the edition.

SPANISH-AMERICAN LITERATURE: NINETEENTH AND TWENTIETH CENTURIES

62. "Siempre con Alfonso Reyes." *Estaciones* (México) 5, no. 18 (1960): 12–15.

Written in honor of Alfonso Reyes, the article is a memorial to "a great humanist."

63. "La última literatura hispanoamericana." *Cuadernos* (Paris) 53 (1961): 153–158.

The figure of Borges; the phenomenon of "Borgism"; the influence of Kafka; the individual peculiarities of Arreola and Cortázar; the "truth and intensity" of Juan Rulfo; the Americanism of Alejo Carpentier; Miguel Angel Asturias. "The center of gravity [in Spanish-American literature] is now located in its narrative, as it previously occurred with poetry during the Modernismo."

64. "Julio Cortázar: Storytelling Giant." *Américas* (Washington, D.C.) 15, no. 3 (1963): 39–43.

Biographical review of Cortázar, the importance of jazz in his life, the diversity of his themes, and his declared influences.

65. "Julio Cortázar: los cuentos del gigante." *Américas* (Washington, D.C.) 15, no. 4 (1963): 39–43.

Spanish version of no. 64.

66. "Octavio Paz. A Mexican Poet-diplomat." *Américas* (Washington, D.C.) 15, no. 7 (1963): 30–33.

Biographical review, his relationship with surrealism, his multiple literary interests, his poetry. A recollection of Durand's last visit to the poet's home in Paris.

67. "Octavio Paz. Un mexicano poeta y diplomático." *Américas* (Washington, D.C.) 15, no. 8 (1963): 30–33.

Spanish version of no. 66.

68. "Letras de la Independencia. Un panorama literario y de ideas: de los precursores al romanticismo," *La Prensa* (Lima), 28 July 1971, p. 3.

Studies several topics: the first manifestations of nationalism, liberals against "ilustrados" (enlightened thinkers), neoclassical and "costumbrista" (local customs) writers, Mariano Melgar's "yaravíes" (poems inspired by Indian songs), Pardo y Segura, and the Romantic generation.

69. "Palma y las *Tradiciones*." *La Prensa* (Lima), 28 July 1971, p. 11.

Reviews the importance of Ricardo Palma's *Tradiciones* in Peruvian literature. Description of the first "tradiciones" (Traditions, a literary sub-genre), their variety of forms, the typical structure, and Palma's relationship to Modernismo.

70. "La realidad mágica de Asturias: *Los brujos de la tormenta primaveral.*" In *Narradores hispanoamericanos de hoy. Simposio,* ed. Juan Bautista Avalle-Arce, 41–54. Chapel Hill: University of North Carolina, 1973.

Study of the short story "Brujos," which was added to the second edition (1946) of *Leyendas de Guatemala* (*Legends From Guatemala*), defined as a narrative of poetic pre-history. Comparisons with *Hombres de maíz.*

71. "La realidad plagia dos cuentos fantásticos de Augusto Monterroso." In *Augusto Monterroso.* Anejo 1 de *Texto crítico,* 20–23. Xalapa: Universidad Veracruzana, 1976.

A news item published in the London *Times* reproduced the plot of Monterroso's short-story "Centenario." The news about the abuses of a U.S. company in Honduras and the suicide of its director also "plagiarized" another short story by Monterroso entitled "Mr. Taylor."

72. "Nota al pie de Monterroso." In *Augusto Monterroso*. Anejo 1 de *Texto crítico*, 64–69. Xalapa: Universidad Veracruzana, 1976.

Article about Monterroso, the man and the writer, his "curious" success, and the "firmness of his fervor for Cervantes." Evocation of a friend and his literary work.

73. "Años de transición: *Las batallas del desierto* de José Emilio Pacheco." In *Cambio social en México, visto por autores contemporáneos*, 141–146. México: Sociedad de escritores de México, Universidad de Notre Dame, 1984.

Historical perspectives of México are captured through the experiences of a child.

POPULAR POETRY AND THEATER

74. "Décimas peruanas de la guerra del Pacífico." *Revista de la Universidad Católica* (Lima) 6 (1979): 79–106.

An introduction and annotated edition of five popular "décimas" (ten-verse poems): (1) "Aunque el Huáscar se perdió"; (2) "Me dicen que hay un pacae"; (3) "Bolognesi defendió," text 1; (4) "Bolognesi defendió," text 2 and the corrected version; and (5) "Piérola, querido amigo." Transcriptions of two fragments about Bolognesi, décimas by Emiliano Niño, and décimas from Chile about Grau and Cáceres.

75. "Romances y corridos de los *Doce pares de Francia*." In *El romancero hoy: nuevas fronteras*, 159–179. Madrid: Gredos, 1979.

Discusses the differences between the Carolingian ballads, of remote origin, and the cycle of the Twelve Peers of France which was derived from the *Historia del Emperador Carlomagno . . . y . . . de los Doce Pares de Francia* (Sevilla, 1521). Reviews modern studies about décimas of Puerto Rico, "vidalas" from Tucumán, and a ballad from Venezuela. During the eighteenth century in Spanish

America, the Carolingian ballad began to lose popularity by the time the first décimas of the cycle of the Twelve Peers appeared.

76. "Los *Doce pares* en la poesía popular mexicana." *Cuadernos Americanos* (México) 233 (1980): 167–191.

The medieval topic of the Twelve Peers of France was part of the repertoire of singers in their poetic competitions. The cycle of the Twelve Peers is more alive in México. The article discusses "glosas" from Veracruz, a "quintilla" from Tabasco, a "serie potosina," "décimas de arte mayor," "desafíos" (popular competitions among singers); and two décimas by Vega Zamarón. The article also offers samples from New México.

77. "Teatro popular nicaragüense: los *Doce pares de Francia* en Niquinohomo." *Anuario de Letras* (México) 20 (1982): 287–330 [written in collaboration with Ernesto Mejía Sánchez].

Edition and a brief study of the Niquinihomo manuscript of the piece of popular theater entitled *Historia de Carlo Magno. Los doce pares de Francia.*

78. "Para un romancero limeño del XVIII." In *Homenaje a Ana María Barrenechea*, 387–404. Madrid: Castalia, 1984.

Brief study and edition of the text of a "convite" (an invitation). The imprint lacks date and place of publication, but it is "undoubtedly from mid-eighteenth-century Lima." The text is an anonymous ballad which is divided in quatrains. The Mercedarian Castillo is indicated as its probable author.

MUSIC, DANCE, AND FOLKLORE

79. "Musicalia." *Revista de la Universidad de Buenos Aires* 2, no. 5 (1948): 7–21.

A study of the essay bearing the same title which was written by José Ortega y Gasset in 1918.

80. "*La pavana del moro.* Una coreografía del mexicano José Limón." *Nuestra Música* (México) 5, no. 19 (1950): 226–235.

A study of the choreographic work of José Limón, especially his mature work. *La Pavana* was inspired by Shakespeare's *Othello* and was performed for the first time in New York in 1949.

81. "Ideas musicales de Ortega y Gasset." *Nuestra Música* (México) 7, nos. 27–29 (1952): 188–197.

Reprint of article no. 79.

82. "Del fandango a la marinera." *Fanal* (Lima) 16, no. 59 (1961): 10–15.

A study of the Peruvian national dance, the "marinera" or "zamacueca," its origin in the old "fandango," its regional differences, the "mozamala," and the continental diffusion of the marinera.

83. "De la zamacueca a la marinera." *Mensajes* (Lima) 15 (1971): 23–27.

The article studies the mixed origin of this Peruvian song-and-dance artistic expression in the nineteenth century, its continental diffusion, and eventual decline. It reproduces some stanzas of old zamacuecas and marineras.

84. "La marinera: baile nacional." *La Prensa* (Lima), 28 July 1971, p. 5.

Written on the occasion of the anniversary of Peruvian independence, this article contrasts the folklore of Lima in 1921 and in 1971.

DIVERSE TOPICS

85. "Manatí, mato, manato." *Nueva Revista de Filología Hispánica* (México) 4, no. 3 (1950): 274–276.

Linguistic note on the origins and ambiguities of the terms *mato* and *manato*.

86. *Ocaso de sirenas. Manatíes en el siglo XVI.* México: Tezontle, 1950.

An essay about "America in the European imagination," and an annotated anthology of quotes referring to "manatíes," or sea cows, from Christopher Columbus to Alexander von Humboldt.

Paul P. Firbas

Reviews: Alberto Salas, *Buenos Aires Literaria* (Buenos Aires) 1, no. 4 (1953): 53–56; Washington Delgado, *Letras Peruanas* (Lima) 2, no. 5 (1952): 27.

87. "El problema canónico del manatí." *Mar del Sur* (Lima) 4, no. 10 (1950): 80–81.

Reprint of the pages under the same subtitle in *Ocaso de Sirenas* (1950: 53–56), entry no. 86.

88. "Castas y clases en el habla de Lima." *Cahiers du Monde Hispanique et Luso-Brésilien* (Toulouse) 2 (1964): 99–108.

This study includes the commentaries of Mme. Trouvé, M. Diaz, and M. Borricaud. The author reviews the vocabulary of Lima reflecting different racial types, the mestizo culture, the differences in social classes, in economical and educational aspects, and allusions to regional expressions. Brief diachronic study of some terms.

89. "El amor a la lectura." *Revista de Bellas Artes* (México) 3 (1982): 65.

Closing words in the International Forum of Writers at the University of Notre Dame, Indiana.

90. "Mar de piratas." *Revista Peruana de Cultura. Segunda época* (Lima) 1 (1982): 37–49.

A study of the image of the sea cow in the writings of Charles de Rochefort, Jean Baptiste Du Tertre, Alexander Oliver Exquemelin, Jean Baptiste Labat, and William Dampier.

91. *Ocaso de Sirenas. Esplendor de manatíes.* 2d. ed., aumentada y revisada. México: Fondo de Cultura Económica, 1983.

Second edition, a corrected and expanded version of entry no. 85.
Reviews: Luis Miguel Aguilar, *Nexos* (México) 7, no. 75 (1983): 45; Guillermo Niño de Guzmán, *Cielo Abierto* (Lima) 10, no. 28 (1984): 62–63.

92. *Desvariante.* Serie "Tierra Firme." México: Fondo de Cultura Económica, 1987.

Eleven short stories: "La cita," "Desvariante," "Después de la siesta," "La ventaja," "Travesía," "Señor Abrigo," "El prisionero de la torre," "Gatos bajo la luna," "El retorno," "Ensalmo del café," and "El árbol perdido."

Reviews: Rosella di Paolo, *Debate* (Lima) 9, no. 46 (1987): 69–70; Luis Ignacio Helguera, *Vuelta* (México) 12, no. 137 (1988): 44–45.

WORKS CITED

Acosta, José de. 1954. *De procuranda Indorum Salute o Predicación del Evangelio en las Indias* (1588). In *Obras*. Biblioteca de Autores Españoles, vol. 73, pp. 389–608. Madrid: Ediciones Atlas.

———. 1962. *Historia natural y moral de las Indias* . . . (1590). Edición preparada por Edmundo O'Gorman. México: Fondo de Cultura Económica.

Aldrete, Bernardo de. 1972–1975. *Del origen y principio de la lengua castellana o romance que oi se usa en España*. Edición facsimilar y estudio por Lidio Nieto Jiménez. Madrid: Consejo Superior de Investigaciones Científicas.

Alighieri, Dante. 1966. *Il Convivio*. Ed. Maria Simonelli. Bologna: Casa Editrice Prof. Pàtrom.

Almarza, Sara Costa. 1990. *Pensamiento crítico hispanoamericano: Arbitristas del Siglo XVIII*. Madrid: Pliegos.

Anderson, Benedict. 1983. *Imagined Communities: Reflections on the Origin and Spread of Nationalism*. London: Verso.

Anónimo (¿Alonso de Barzana?). 1586. *Arte, y vocabulario en la lengua general del Perú llamada Quichua, y en la lengua Española*. Lima: Antonio Ricardo, Impresor.

Asensio, Eugenio. 1953. "Dos cartas desconocidas del Inca Garcilaso." *Nueva Revista de Filología Hispánica* (México) 7, nos. 3–4: 583–593.

Augustine, St. (Aurelius Augustinus). 1895–1904. *Epistulae*, recensuit et commentario critico instruxit Alois Goldbacher. Corpus Scriptorum Ecclesiasticorum Latinorum, vols. 34, 44, 57, 58. Vindobonae (Vienna): F. Tempsky.

Avalle-Arce, Juan Bautista. 1964. *El Inca Garcilaso en sus 'Comentarios.' Antología vivida*. Madrid: Gredos.

Bajtin, Mijail. 1991. *Teoría y estética de la novela*. Madrid: Taurus.

Baron, Hans. 1966. *The Crisis of the Italian Renaissance*. Princeton: Princeton University Press.

Bernal, Alfredo Alejandro. 1982. "*La Araucana* de Alonso de Ercilla y Zúñiga y *Comentarios Reales de los Incas* del Inca Garcilaso de la Vega." *Revista Iberoamericana* (Pittsburgh) 120–121 (July-December): 549–562.

Boccaccio, Giovanni. 1983. *De casibus virorum illustrium. Tutte le opere.* Vol. 9. Ed. Pier Giorgio Ricci and Vittorio Zaccaria. Milano: Arnoldo Mondadori Editore.

Bosio, Luciano. 1983. *La Tabula Peutingeriana. Una descrizzione pittorica del mondo antico.* Rimini: Maggioli.

Botero, Giovanni. 1598. *Mundus Imperiorum sive de Mundi Imperiis Libri Quatuor.* . . . Coloniae Agrippinae (Cologne): Excudebat Bertramus Buchholtz.

Brading, David A. 1986. "The Incas and the Renaissance: *The Royal Commentaries* of Inca Garcilaso de la Vega." *Journal of Latin American Studies* (Cambridge) 18: 1–12.

———. 1991. *The First America. The Spanish Monarchy, Creole Patriots and the Liberal State 1492–1867.* Cambridge and New York: Cambridge University Press.

Bremmer, J. N., and N. M. Horsfall. 1987. *Roman Myth and Mythography.* London: University of London, Institute of Classical Studies.

Buntinx, Gustavo, and Luis Eduardo Wuffarden. 1991. "Incas y reyes españoles en la pintura colonial peruana: La estela de Garcilaso." *Márgenes* (Lima) 8: 151–210.

Burga, Manuel. 1988. *Nacimiento de una utopía. Muerte y resurrección de los incas.* Lima: Instituto de Apoyo Agrario.

Burke, Kenneth. 1984. *Counter-Statement.* Berkeley: University of California Press.

Calancha, Antonio de la. 1639. *Chronica Moralizada del Orden de San Agustín en el Perú con sucesos exemplares vistos en esta Monarchia.* Barcelona: Por Pedro de Lacavalleria.

Calvet, Louis-Jean. 1981. *Les langues véhiculaires.* Paris: Presses Universitaires de France.

Caro Baroja, Julio. 1992. *Las falsificaciones de la Historia (en relación con la de España).* Barcelona: Seix Barral.

Carrera, Fernando de la. 1644. *Arte de la lengua yunga de los valles del Obispado de Truxillo del Peru, con un Confessionario, y todas las Oraciones Christianas, traducidas en la lengua, y otras cosas.* Lima: Por Joseph de Contreras.

Castillo, Julián del. 1582. *Historia de los Reyes Godos.* Burgos.

Cerrón-Palomino, Rodolfo. 1987. "Unidad y diferenciación lingüística en el mundo andino." *Lexis* (Lima) 11, no. 1: 71–104.

———. 1991. "El Inca Garcilaso o la lealtad idiomática." *Lexis* (Lima) 15, no. 2: 133–178.

———. 1993. "Los fragmentos de gramática quechua del Inca Garcilaso." *Lexis* (Lima) 17, no. 2: 219–257.

———. 1995. *La lengua de Naimlap (reconstrucción y obsolescencia del mo-*

chica). Lima: Pontificia Universidad Católica del Perú, Fondo Editorial.

Cicero, Marcus Tullius. 1976. *Two Books on Rhetoric commonly called On Invention (Rhetorici libri duo que vocantur De inventione)*. In *Cicero in Twenty-Eight Volumes*, vol. 2. Loeb Classical Library. Cambridge: Harvard University Press; London: William Heinemann.

———. 1988. *The Republic (De re publica)*. In *Cicero in Twenty-Eight Volumes*, vol. 16. Loeb Classical Library. Cambridge: Harvard University Press; London: William Heinemann.

Cieza de León, Pedro de. 1986. *Crónica del Perú. Primera parte.* 2d ed. corregida. Introducción de Franklin Pease G. Y. Nota de Miguel Maticorena E. Lima: Pontificia Universidad Católica del Perú, Fondo Editorial, Academia Nacional de la Historia.

Córdoba Salinas, Diego de. 1957. *Coronica de la Religiosissima Provincia de los Doze Apóstoles del Perú. De la Orden de nuestro Serafico P. S. Francisco de la Regular Observancia; con relación de las Provincias que della an salido, y son sus hijas.* Ed. y notas de Lino E. Canedo, O.F.M. Washington, D.C.: Academy of American Franciscan History.

Cornell, T. 1995. *The Beginnings of Rome. Italy and Rome from the Bronze Age to the Punic Wars (c. 1000–164 B.C.)*. London: Routledge.

Covarrubias Orozco, Sebastián de. 1994. *Tesoro de la lengua castellana o española* (Madrid 1611). Madrid: Editorial Castalia.

Domingo de Santo Tomás. 1994a. *Grammatica o Arte de la lengua general de los indios de los reynos del Perú* (Valladolid 1560). Edición facsimilar, con un prólogo, por Raúl Porras Barrenechea, Lima: Ediciones del Instituto de Historia, 1951; transliteración y estudio por Rodolfo Cerrón-Palomino, Madrid: Agencia Española de Cooperación Internacional.

———. 1994b. *Lexicon o vocabulario de la lengua general del Perú* (Valladolid 1560). Edición facsimilar. Lima: Instituto Historia, 1951; reprint, Madrid: Agencia Española de Cooperación Internacional.

Ducci, Lorenzo. 1974. *Trattato della nobiltà*. Sala Bolognese: Arnaldo Forni Editore.

Dunbar Temple, Ella. 1948. "Azarosa existencia de un mestizo de sangre imperial incaica." *Documenta* (Lima) 1, no. 1: 112–156.

Durand, José. 1948, 1949a. "La Biblioteca del Inca." *Nueva Revista de Filología Hispánica* (México) 2, no. 3 (1948): 239–264; and 3 (1949): 166–170.

———. 1949b. "Dos notas sobre el Inca Garcilaso." *Nueva Revista de Filología Hispánica* (México) 3: 278–290.

———. 1954. "La redacción de la *Florida del Inca:* Cronología." *Revista Histórica* (Lima) 21: 288–302.

———. 1955. "Garcilaso y su formación literaria e histórica." In *Nuevos estudios sobre el Inca Garcilaso de la Vega*, 63–85. Lima: Centro de Estudios Histórico-Militares.

———. 1962a. "El proceso de redacción de las obras del Inca Garcilaso." *Anales de la Faculté des Lettres et Sciences Humaines d'Aix* (Aix-en-Provence) 36: 247–266.

———. 1962b. "Un rasgo humanístico del Inca Garcilaso." *Cuadernos del Congreso por la Libertad de la Cultura* (Paris) 64: 36–41. Reprinted in Durand 1976.

———. 1963. "Garcilaso entre el mundo incaico y las ideas renacentistas." *Diógenes* (Buenos Aires) 10, no. 43 (July-September): 17–33.

———. 1966. "La memoria de Gonzalo Silvestre." *Caravelle. Cahiers du monde hispanique et luso-brésilien* (Toulouse) 7: 43–52.

———. 1971. "El influjo de Garcilaso Inca en Túpac Amaru." *Copé* (Lima) 2, no. 5: 2–6.

———. 1976. *El Inca Garcilaso, clásico de América*. México: Secretaría de Educación Publica.

———. 1983. *Ocaso de Sirenas. Esplendor de Manatíes*. México: Fondo de Cultura Económica.

———. 1990. "Garcilaso Inca jura decir verdad." *Revista Histórica* (Lima) 14, no. 1: 1–25.

Duviols, Pierre. 1964. "The Inca Garcilaso de la Vega, humanist interpreter of the Inca religion." *Diógenes* (Buenos Aires) 44: 36–52.

———. 1979. "Datation, paternité et idéologie de la *Declaración de los quipucamayoc a Vaca de Castro*." In *Cultures en devenir.* Paris: Fondation Singer-Polignac.

———. 1983. "Guaman Poma, historiador del Perú antiguo: una nueva pista." *Revista Andina* (Cuzco) 1, no. 1: 103–115.

———. 1988. "Los cultos incaicos y el humanismo cristiano en el Inca Garcilaso." In *Historia y crítica de la literatura hispanoamericana*, Cedomil Goić, vol. 1, *Época Colonial*. Barcelona: Editorial Crítica.

———. 1994. "Les *Comentarios reales de los Incas* et la question du salut des infidèles." *Caravelle. Cahiers du monde hispanique et luso-brésilien* (Toulouse) 62: 69–80.

Ercilla, Alonso de. 1979. *La Araucana*. 2 vols. Edición, introducción y notas de Marcos A. Morínigo e Isaías Lerner. Madrid: Castalia.

Escandell Bonet, Bartolomé. 1953. "Repercusión de la piratería inglesa en el pensamiento peruano del siglo XVI." *Revista de Indias* (Madrid) 51: 81–87.

Estete, Miguel de. 1924. *Noticia del Perú*. Colección de libros y documentos para la historia del Perú, vol. 8, 2d series. Lima: Sanmartí y Cía.

Eusebius, Bishop of Caesarea. 1989. *The History of the Church from Christ to Constantine.* Trans. G. A. Williamson; ed. with a new introduction by Andrew Louth. London and New York: Penguin Books.

Fox Morcillo, Sebastián (Sebastiano Fox Morzillo). 1557. *De historiae institutione. Dialogus.* Parisiis: Apud M. Juvenem.

Frankl, Víctor. 1963. *El "Antijovio" de Gonzalo Jiménez de Quesada y las concepciones de realidad y verdad en la época de la contrarreforma y del manierismo.* Prologue by José Antonio Maravall. Madrid: Ediciones Cultura Hispánica.

Frenk, Margit. 1982. "Lectores y oidores. La difusión oral de la literatura en el Siglo de Oro." In *Actas del Séptimo Congreso de la Asociación Internacional de Hispanistas* 1: 101–123. Roma: Bulzoni.

García, Gregorio. 1981. *Origen de los Indios de el Nuevo mundo, e Indias Occidentales.* . . . Edición por A. González de Barcía Carballido y Zúñiga, Valencia: En casa de Pedro Patricio Mey, 1607; segunda impresión, Madrid: En la imprenta de F. Martínez Abad, 1729; facsimilar de la 2a., Estudio preliminar de Franklin Pease G. Y., México: Fondo de Cultura Económica.

Garcilaso de la Vega. 1590. *La traduzión del Indio de los tres Diálogos de Amor de León Hebreo.* Madrid: En casa de Pedro Madrigal.

———. 1944. *Historia General del Perú (Segunda parte de los Comentarios Reales de los Incas).* Edición al cuidado de Angel Rosenblat. Buenos Aires: Emecé Editores S.A.

———. 1951a. *Relación de la descendencia de Garci Pérez de Vargas (1596).* Reproducción facsimilar del manuscrito original, con un prólogo por Raúl Porras Barrenechea. Lima: Ediciones del Instituto de Historia.

———. 1951b. *The Florida of the Inca.* Trans. and ed. John Grier Varner and Jeannette Johnson Varner. Austin: University of Texas Press.

———. 1966. *Royal Commentaries of the Incas and General History of Perú.* 2 vols. Translated with an introduction by Harold V. Livermore. Foreword by Arnold J. Toynbee. Austin and London: University of Texas Press.

———. 1982. *Commentaires Royaux des Incas.* Preface by Marcel Bataillon, "L'historien Garcilaso." Paris: Maspero.

———. 1986a. *La Florida.* Ed. Cassa di Risparmio di Verona. Prologue by Gabriella Airaldi, "Il tempo e la storia." Verona: Vicenza e Belluno.

———. 1986b. *La Florida del Ynca.* Facsimile of the 1605 first edition. Introduction and notes by Sylvia-Lynn Hilton. Madrid: Historia 16.

———. 1991. *Comentarios Reales de los Incas.* Edición, prólogo, índice temático y glosario de Carlos Araníbar. 2 vols. México and Lima: Fondo de Cultura Económica.

Genette, Gérard. 1982. *Palimpsestes. La littérature au second degré.* Paris: Éditions du Seuil.

——. 1987. *Seuils*. Paris: Editions du Seuil.

Gil, Juan, ed. 1992. *El Libro de Marco Polo*. Madrid: Alianza Editorial.

Gisbert, Teresa. 1980. *Iconografía y mitos indígenas en el arte*. La Paz.

González Holguín, Diego. 1952. *Vocabulario de la lengua general de todo el Perú llamada lengua qquichua o del Inca* (Lima, 1608). Nueva edición. Lima: Imprenta Santa María.

——. 1975. *Gramatica y arte nueva de la lengua general de todo el Perú, llamada lengua qquichua, o lengua del Inca* (1607). Cabildo Vaduz-Georgetown, Druck: Franz Wolf, Hepopenheim a.d.B.

——. 1989. *Vocabulario de la lengua general de todo el Perú llamada lengua qquichua o del Inca* (1608). Lima: Universidad Nacional Mayor de San Marcos.

Greer Johnson, Julie. 1981. "A Caricature of Spanish Women in the New World by the Inca Garcilaso de la Vega." *Latin American Literary Review* (Pittsburgh) 19, no. 18: 47–51.

Guamán Poma de Ayala, Felipe. 1993. *Nueva corónica y buen gobierno*. Edición y prólogo de Franklin Pease G. Y., vocabulario y traducciones de Jan Szemiñski. Lima: Fondo de Cultura Económica.

Guardiola, Juan Benito. 1591. *Tratado de nobleza y de los títulos y ditados que oy día tienen los varones claros y grandes de España*. Madrid: por la viuda de Alonso Gómez.

Guíbovich, Pedro. 1993. "Lectura y difusión de la obra del Inca Garcilaso en el virreinato peruano (siglos XVII–XVIII). El caso de los *Comentarios reales*." *Histórica* (Lima) 37: 103–120.

Gutiérrez, Gustavo. 1993. *Las Casas: In Search of the Poor of Jesus Christ*. Maryknoll: Orbis Books.

Hampe Martínez, Teodoro. 1994. "El Renacimiento del Inca Garcilaso revisitado: los clásicos greco-latinos en su biblioteca y su obra." *Revista Histórica* (Lima) 18, no. 1 (July): 69–94.

Hernández, Max. 1993. *Memoria del bien perdido. Conflicto, identidad y nostalgia en el Inca Garcilaso de la Vega*. Madrid: Sociedad Estatal Quinto Centenario, 1991; 1ª edición peruana, corregida y aumentada por el autor, Lima: IEP (Instituto de Estudios Peruanos) and BPP (Biblioteca Peruana de Psicoanálisis).

Herrera, Antonio de. 1954–1955. *Historia general de los hechos de los castellanos en las islas y tierra firme del Mar Océano*. 12 vols. Madrid: Real Academia de la Historia.

Husson, Jean-Phillipe. 1985. *La poésie Quechua dans la chronique de Felipe Guamán Poma*. Série Etnolinguistique Amerindiene. Paris: L'Harmattan.

——. 1993. "La poesía quechua prehispánica: sus reglas, sus categorías, sus temas a través de los poemas transcritos por Waman Puma de Ayala." *Revista de Crítica Literaria Latinoamericana* (Lima) 37: 63–86.

Ilgen, William D. 1974. "La configuración mítica de la historia en los *Comentarios reales* del Inca Garcilaso de la Vega." In *Estudios de literatura hispanoamericana en honor a José J. Arrom,* ed. Andrew P. Debicki and Enrique Pupo-Walker, 37–46. Chapel Hill: University of North Carolina.

Isidoro de Sevilla (Saint Isidore of Seville). 1975. *Las Historias de los Godos, Vándalos y Suevos de Isidoro de Sevilla.* Estudio, edición crítica y traducción por Cristóbal Rodríguez Alonso. León: Centro de Estudios e Investigación "San Isidro."

Jákfalvi-Leiva, Susana. 1984. *Traducción, escritura y violencia colonizadora. Un estudio de la obra del Inca Garcilaso.* Syracuse, New York: Maxwell School of Citizenship and Public Affairs.

Jiménez de Rada, Rodrigo. 1989. *Historia de los hechos de España.* Madrid: Alianza.

Jolowicz, Herbert Felix. 1952. *Historical Introduction to the Study of Roman Law.* 2d ed. Cambridge: Cambridge University Press.

Julien, Katherine J. 1982. "Inca Decimal Administration in the Lake Titicaca Region." In *The Inca and Aztec States 1400–1800: Anthropology and History,* ed. George Collier, Renato Rosaldo, and John Wirth, 119–151. New York: Academic Press.

Keen, Maurice Hugh. 1984. *Chivalry.* New Haven: Yale University Press.

Kellas, James G. 1991. *The Politics of Nationalism and Ethnicity.* New York: St. Martin's Press.

Kohl, Benjamin G. 1974. "Petrarch's Prefaces to *De viris illustribus.*" *History and Theory* (Middletown, Conn.) 13, no. 2: 132–144.

Kohn, Hans. 1944. *The Idea of Nationalism. A Study in Its Origins and Background.* New York: The MacMillan Company.

Las Casas, Bartolomé de. 1987. *Brevísima relación de la destrucción de las Indias.* Introducción por André Saint-Lu. Madrid: Cátedra.

Leonard, Irving A. 1953. *Los libros del conquistador.* México: Fondo de Cultura Económica.

———. 1990. *Ensayos y semblanzas: Bosquejos históricos y literarios de la América Latina Colonial.* México: Fondo de Cultura Económica.

Livy (Titus Livius). 1988. *From the Founding of the City (Ab urbe condita).* In *Livy in Fourteen Volumes,* vols. 1–3. Loeb Classical Library. Cambridge: Harvard University Press; London: William Heinemann.

López de Gómara, Francisco. 1993. *Historia General de las Indias* (1555). Ed. Franklin Pease G. Y. Edición facsimilar. Lima: Comisión Nacional del V Centenario del Descubrimiento de América.

MacCormack, Sabine. 1991. *Religion in the Andes. Vision and Imagination in Early Colonial Peru.* Princeton: Princeton University Press.

———. 1992. "History, Memory and Time in Golden Age Spain." *History and Memory* (Bloomington, Ind.) 4, no. 2: 38–68.

Works Cited

——. Forthcoming. "History and Law in Sixteenth-Century Peru. The Impact of European Scholarly Traditions." In *Cultures of Scholarship*, ed. S. C. Humphreys. Ann Arbor: University of Michigan Press.

Maravall, José Antonio. 1975. *La cultura del barroco*. Madrid: Ariel.

Mariana, Juan de. 1950. *Historia de España*. Biblioteca de Autores Españoles, vol. 30. Madrid: Ediciones Atlas.

Maticorena Estrada, Miguel. 1967. "Sobre las *Décadas* de Antonio de Herrera: *La Florida*." *Anuario de Estudios Americanos* (Sevilla) 24: 29–62.

——. 1989. "Un manuscrito de *La Florida* del Inca Garcilaso." *El Comercio* (Lima), 9 April.

——. 1992. "La nación de Garcilaso." *El Peruano* (Lima), 13 April.

Mayberry, Nancy. 1991. "The Controversy over the Immaculate Conception in Medieval and Renaissance Art, Literature, and Society." *The Journal of Medieval and Renaissance Studies* (Durham, N.C.) 21, no. 2: 207–224.

Mazzotti, José Antonio. 1993. *Subtexto andino y discurso sincrético en los Comentarios Reales del Inca Garcilaso de la Vega*. Ph.D. dissertation, Princeton University.

——. 1995. "*En virtud de la materia*. Nuevas consideraciones sobre el subtexto andino de los *Comentarios Reales*." *Revista Iberoamericana* (Pittsburgh) 61, nos. 172–173: 385–421.

——. 1996a. "*Sólo la proporción es la que canta:* poética de la nación y épica criolla en la Lima del XVIII." *Revista de Crítica Literaria Latinoamericana* (Berkeley) 43: 29–75.

——. 1996b. "The Lightning Bolt Yields to the Rainbow: Indigenous History and Colonial Semiosis in the *Royal Commentaries* by El Inca Garcilaso de la Vega." *Modern Language Quarterly* (Seattle, Wash.) 57, no. 2.

Medina, José Toribio. 1913. *El descubrimiento del Océano Pacífico. Vasco Núñez de Balboa*. Vol. 2. Santiago: Imprenta Universitaria.

——. 1965. *La Imprenta en Lima (1584–1824)*. 3 vols. Amsterdam: N. Israel.

Meléndez, Juan. 1681. *Tesoros verdaderos de las Yndias. En la Historia de la gran Provincia De San Ivan Bautista del Perú de el Orden de Predicadores*. Roma: En la Imprenta de Nicolas Angel Tinassio.

Menéndez Pidal, Ramón. 1906. *Leyenda del último rey Godo*. Madrid.

Mexía, Pedro. 1989. *Silva de varia lección*. Edición de Antonio Castro. Madrid: Cátedra.

Miller, Konrad. 1916. *Itineraria romana. Römische Reisewege an Hand der Tabula Peutingeriana*. Stuttgart: Strecker und Schröder.

Miró-Quesada Sosa, Aurelio. 1948. "Un Amigo del Inca Garcilaso." *Mar del Sur* (Lima) 2: 20–26.

———. 1971. *El Inca Garcilaso y otros estudios garcilacistas.* Madrid: Instituto de Cultura Hispánica.

———. 1977. "Las ideas lingüísticas del Inca Garcilaso." In *Tiempo de leer, tiempo de escribir.* Lima: n.p.

———. 1994. *El Inca Garcilaso.* Lima: Pontificia Universidad Católica del Perú, Fondo Editorial.

Molloy, Sylvia. 1991. *At Face Value: Autobiographical Writing in Spanish America.* Cambridge and New York: Cambridge University Press.

Momigliano, Arnaldo. 1975. *Alien Wisdom. The Limits of Hellenization.* Cambridge and New York: Cambridge University Press.

———. 1977. *Essays in Ancient and Modern Historiography.* Middletown, Conn.: Wesleyan University Press.

Monzón, Luis de. 1965. "Descripción de la tierra del Repartimiento de San Francisco de Atunrucana y Laramati (1586)." In *Relaciones geográficas de Indias. Perú,* ed. Marcos Jiménez de la Espada. Biblioteca de Autores Españoles, vol. 1, pp. 226–236. Madrid: Ediciones Atlas.

Morales, Ambrosio de. 1792. *Las antigüedades de las ciudades de España.* . . . Vol. 10 of Corónica General de España, 15 vols., 1791–1793. Madrid: En la oficina de don Benito Cano.

Mugaburu, Josephe de, and Francisco de Mugaburu (son). 1917. *Diario de Lima (1640–1694). Crónica de la Época Colonial.* 2 vols. (1640–1670 and 1671–1694). Ed. Horacio H. Urteaga and Carlos A. Romero. In Colección de Libros y Documentos Referentes a la Historia del Perú, vol. 7. Lima: Sanmartí y Cía.

Murra, John V. 1980. *The Economic Organization of the Inka State.* Greenwich, Conn.: JAI Press.

Murra, John V., Nathan Wachtel, and Jacques Revel, eds. 1986. *Anthropological History of Andean Polities.* Cambridge and New York: Cambridge University Press; Paris: Éditions de la Maison des Sciences de l'Homme.

Murúa, Martín de. 1946. *Historia del origen y genealogía real de los reyes Incas del Perú.* Edición de C. Bayle. Madrid: Consejo Superior de Investigaciones Científicas, Instituto Santo Toribio de Mogrovejo.

———. 1987. *Historia general del Perú* (1613). Madrid: Historia 16.

Navagero, Andrés. 1983. *Viaje por España, 1524–1526.* Traducción y notas por Antonio María Fabié. Prólogo por Angel González García. Madrid: Turner.

Nebrija, Elio Antonio de. 1495. *Introductiones latinae.* Salmaticae (Salamanca).

Oré, Luis Jerónimo de. 1992. *Symbolo Catholico Indiano* (1598). Edición facsimilar. Lima: Ediciones Australis.

Orosius, Paulus. 1983(?) *Historia contra los paganos (Historiarum adversum paganos libri septem)*. Estudio preliminar, versión y notas de Enrique Gallego-Blanco. Barcelona: Puvill.

Ortega, Julio. 1978. *La cultura peruana. Experiencia y conciencia.* México: Fondo de Cultura Económica.

Oviedo, José Miguel. 1995. *Historia de la literatura hispanoamericana.* Vol. 1, *De los orígenes a la Emancipación.* Madrid: Alianza Editorial.

Pailler, Claire, and Jean-Marie Pailler. 1992. "Une Amérique vraiment latine. Pour une lecture 'Dumezilienne' de l'Inca Garcilaso de la Vega." *Annales. Économies, sociétés, civilisation* (Paris) 47, no. 1 (January-February): 207–235.

———. 1993. "Una América verdaderamente latina. Por una lectura 'duméziliana' del Inca Garcilaso de la Vega." *Revista Histórica* (Lima) 17, no. 2: 179–222.

Pease G. Y., Franklin. 1994. "Las lecturas del Inca Garcilaso y su información andina." *Revista Histórica* (Lima) 18, no. 1 (July): 135–157.

———. 1995. *Las Crónicas y los Andes.* Lima: Pontificia Universidad Católica del Perú, Instituto Riva-Agüero, Fondo de Cultura Económica.

Peralta y Barnuevo, Pedro de. 1723. *Descripcion de las Fiestas Reales. Noticia de los Augustos Casamientos y Aparato de su Celebracion.* Lima.

———. 1732. *Lima Fundada o Conquista del Perú.* 2 vols. Lima: Imprenta de Francisco Sobrino y Bados.

Pérez de Guzmán, Fernán. 1965. *Generaciones y semblanzas.* Ed. R. B. Tate. London: Tamesis Books.

Pérez Fernández, Isacio. 1995. *El anónimo de Yucay frente a Bartolomé de Las Casas: estudio y edición crítica del Parecer de Yucay, anónimo (Valle de Yucay, 16 de marzo de 1571).* Cuzco: Centro de Estudios Regionales Andinos "Bartolomé de Las Casas."

Petrarca, Francesco. 1955. *De viris illustribus.* In *Prose,* ed. G. Martellotti et al. Milano-Napoli: Riccardo Ricciardi Editore.

Piccolomini, Alessandro. 1542. *Della institutione di tutta la vita de l'huomo nato nòbile e in città libera.* Venetiis: Hieronymun Scotum.

———. 1560. *Della institutione morale.* Venice: n.p.

Picón Salas, Mariano. 1962. *A Cultural History of Spanish America, from Conquest to Independence.* Trans. Irving A. Leonard. Berkeley: University of California Press.

Piña, Carlos. 1988. *La construcción del 'sí mismo' en el relato autobiográfico.* Santiago: FLACSO.

Pino Díaz, Fermín del. 1992. "¿Literatura, historia o antropología? A propósito del mestizaje en los Andes y la obra del Inca Garcilaso." *Anthropológica* (Lima) 10: 55–77.

Pizarro, Pedro. 1978. *Relación del descubrimiento y conquista de los reinos del Perú* (1571). Lima: Pontificia Universidad Católica del Perú, Fondo Editorial.

Plutarch. 1989. "Cato the Younger (Cato minor)." In *Plutarch's Lives in Eleven Volumes,* vol. 7. Loeb Classical Library. Cambridge: Harvard University Press.

Plutarco. 1551. *Vidas de illustres y excellentes varones griegos y romanos . . . traduzidas en estilo castellano.* Argentina: Augustín Frisio.

Polo de Ondegardo. 1916–1917. *Informaciones acerca de la religión y gobierno de los Incas* (1571). 2 vols. Lima: Sanmartí y Cía.

Polybius. 1992. *The Histories in Six Volumes.* Loeb Classical Library. Cambridge and London: Harvard University Press.

Porqueras Mayo, A. 1957. *El prólogo como género literario. Su estudio en el Siglo de Oro español.* Madrid: Consejo Superior de Investigaciones Científicas.

———. 1968. *El prólogo en el Manierismo y Barroco españoles.* Madrid: Consejo Superior de Investigaciones Científicas.

Porras Barrenechea, Raúl. 1955. *El Inca Garcilaso en Montilla, 1561–1614.* Lima: Ediciones del Instituto de Historia.

———. 1986. *Los Cronistas del Perú (1528–1650) y Otros Ensayos.* Edición, prólogo y notas de Franklin Pease G. Y., bibliografía de Félix Alvarez Brun y Graciela Sánchez Cerro, revisada, aumentada y actualizada por Oswaldo Holguín Callo. Biblioteca Clásicos del Perú, vol. 2. Lima: Banco de Crédito del Perú.

———, ed. 1957. *Inca Garcilaso de la Vega. Recuerdos de infancia y juventud.* Selección y prólogo de RPB. Lima: Patronato del Libro Peruano.

Pulgar, Fernando del. 1923. *Claros varones de Castilla.* Ed. Domínguez Bordona. Madrid: Ediciones de "La Lectura" (Clásicos Castellanos).

Pupo-Walker, Enrique. 1982. *Historia, creación y profecía en los textos del Inca Garcilaso de la Vega.* Madrid: Ediciones J. Porrúa Turanzas.

Raleigh, Sir Walter. 1751. *The Works of Sir Walter Raleigh, Kt. Political, Commercial and Philosophical, together with his Letters and Poems* (1596). 2 vols. London: R. Dodsley.

Ramírez de Arellano, Rafael. 1921–1922. *Ensayo de un catálogo biográfico de escritores de la provincia y diócesis de Córdoba con descripción de sus obras.* 2 vols. Madrid: Tip. de la Revista de archivos, bibliotecas y museos.

Ramírez Ribes, María. 1993. *Un amor por el diálogo: el Inca Garcilaso de la Vega.* 2d ed. Prólogo de Arturo Uslar Pietri. Caracas, Venezuela: Monte Avila Editores.

Riva Agüero, José de la. 1952. *La Historia en el Perú.* 2d ed. Madrid: Imprenta y Editorial Maestre.

Rodríguez Garrido, José A. 1995. "La identidad del enunciador en los

Comentarios reales." *Revista Iberoamericana* (Pittsburgh) 61, nos. 172–173: 371–383.

Román, Hieronymo (Jerónimo). 1575. *Repúblicas del mundo,* divididas en XXVII libros, ordenadas por F. Hieronymo Román. En Medina del Campo, por F. del Canto.

Rostworowski de Diez Canseco, María. 1953. *Pachacutec Inca Yupanqui.* Lima: n.p.

——. 1993. *Ensayos de historia andina. Elites, etnias, recursos.* Lima: IEP (Instituto de Estudios Peruanos).

Rowe, John Howland. 1976. "El movimiento nacional inca del siglo XVIII." In *Túpac Amaru II—1780,* comp. Alberto Flores Galindo. Lima: Retablo de Papel Ediciones.

Salinas [y Córdoba], Buenaventura de. 1630. *Memorial de las Historias del Nuevo Mundo Pirú: Méritos y Excelencias de la Ciudad de Lima, Cabeça de sus Ricos, y Estendidos Reynos, y el estado presente en que se hallan. Para inclinar a la Magestad de su Catholico Monarca Don Felipe IV Rey Poderoso de España, y de las Indias, a que pida a Su Santidad la canonizacion de su Patron Solano.* Lima: Por Geronimo de Contreras.

Sallust (Caius Sallustius Crispus). 1984. *Sallust's Bellum Catilinae.* Ed. with an introduction by J. T. Ramsay. Textbook Series, American Philological Association, no. 9. Chico, California: Scholars Press.

Santa Cruz Pachacuti Yamqui Salcamaygua, Joan de. 1993. *Relación de antigüedades deste reyno del Pirú.* Estudio etnohistórico y lingüístico de Pierre Duviols y César Itier. Lima: Institut Français d'Études Andines; Cuzco: Centro de Estudios Regionales Andinos "Bartolomé de Las Casas."

Sarmiento de Gamboa, Pedro. 1965. *Historia Indica.* Edición de P. Carmelo Sáenz de Santa María. Lima: Universidad Nacional Mayor de San Marcos (1964); Biblioteca de Autores Españoles, vol. 135. Madrid: Ediciones Atlas.

Sedeño, Juan. 1590. *Suma de varones ilustres.* Madrid: Juan Rodríguez.

——. 1986. *Coloquios de amor y bienaventuranza.* Ed. Pedro M. Cátedra. Barcelona: "Stelle dell'Orsa."

Smith, Anthony D. 1981. *The Ethnic Revival.* Cambridge: Cambridge University Press.

—— 1986. *The Ethnic Origins of Nations.* London: Basil Blackwell.

Solano, Francisco de. 1991. *Documentos sobre política lingüística en Hispanoamérica (1492–1800).* Madrid: Consejo Superior de Investigaciones Lingüísticas.

Spalding, Karen. 1974. *De indio a campesino. Cambios en la estructura social del Perú colonial.* Lima: IEP (Instituto de Estudios Peruanos).

Suardo, Juan Antonio. 1935. *Diario de Lima (1629–1634).* Introducción y notas de Rubén Vargas Ugarte, S.J. Lima: Imprenta C. Vásquez L.

Suetonius (Gaius Suetonius Tranquillus). 1989. "The Deified Augustus (Divus Augustus)." In *The Lives of the Caesars (De vita caesorum)*, vol. 1, book 2. Loeb Classical Library. Cambridge and London: Harvard University Press.

Tacitus, Publicus Cornelius. 1925. "The Life of Julius Agricola (De vita et moribus Iulii Agricolae)." In *Dialogus, Agricola, Germania*. Loeb Classical Library. London: William Heinemann; New York: G. P. Putnam's Sons.

Tate, Robert B. 1970. *Ensayos sobre la historiografía peninsular del siglo XV*. Madrid: Gredos.

Tercer Concilio Limense (Third Council of Lima). 1985. *Doctrina Christiana, y catecismo para instruccion de los Indios . . . con un Confessionario, y otras cosas . . .* (1584–1585). Facsimilar edition. Madrid: Consejo Superior de Investigaciones Científicas.

Tovar, Antonio. 1963. "Español, lenguas generales, lenguas tribales, en América del Sur." *Studia Philologica*. Homenaje ofrecido a Dámaso Alonso por sus amigos y discípulos con ocasión de su 60 aniversario, vol. 3, pp. 509–525. Madrid: Gredos.

Triana y Antorveza, Humberto. 1987. *Las lenguas indígenas en la historia social del Nuevo Reino de Granada*. Bogotá: Instituto Caro y Cuervo.

Valdés de la Plata, Juan Sánchez. 1548. *Corónica general del hombre*. Madrid.

Vargas Ugarte, S.J., Rubén. 1930. "Nota sobre Garcilaso." *Mercurio Peruano* (Lima) 137–138: 106–108.

———. 1938. *Manuscritos peruanos en el Archivo de Indias*, vol. 2. Lima: Biblioteca Peruana.

———. 1956. *Historia del culto de María en Iberoamérica y de sus imágenes y santuarios más celebrados*. 3d ed. Madrid: n.p.

Varro, Marcus Terentius (M. Terenti). 1964. *Varronis de lingua latina quae supersunt*. Ed. G. Goetz and F. Schoell. Amsterdam.

Vega, Antonio de. 1948. *Historia del Colegio y Universidad de San Ignacio de Loyola de la ciudad del Cuzco*. Vol. 6. Ed. Rubén Vargas Ugarte, S.J. Lima: Biblioteca Histórica Peruana.

Vergil (Virgil) (Publius Vergilius Maro). 1986. *Aeneid*. In *Virgil*, 2 vols. Loeb Classical Library. Cambridge and London: Harvard University Press.

Walbank, Frank William. 1972. *Polybius*. Berkeley: University of California Press.

Yates, Frances A. 1983. *Giordano Bruno y la tradición hermética*. Trans. Domenec Bergada. Barcelona: Ariel.

Works Cited

Zamora, Margarita. 1988. *Language, Authority, and Indigenous History in the 'Comentarios reales de los Incas.'* Cambridge and New York: Cambridge University Press.

Zárate, Agustín de. 1995. *Historia del descubrimiento y conquista del Perú* (1555). Edición, notas y estudio preliminar de Franklin Pease G. Y. y Teodoro Hampe Martínez. Lima: Pontificia Universidad Católica del Perú, Fondo Editorial.

CONTRIBUTORS

José Anadón, Professor of Hispanic Literature at the University of Notre Dame, is the author, among other texts, of *Pineda y Bascuñán, defensor del araucano* (1977), *La novela colonial de Barrenechea y Albis* (1983), and *Historiografía literaria de América Colonial* (1988), and is the editor of *Ruptura de la conciencia hispanoamericana* (1993).

Juan Bautista Avalle-Arce, José Miguel de Barandiaran Professor of Basque Studies at the University of California at Santa Barbara, a leading Hispanist of his generation, specializes in the Spanish Golden Age, particularly Cervantes. He has also studied Latin American Colonial figures such as Columbus, Las Casas, and Fernández de Oviedo. On Garcilaso, he has published *El Inca Garcilaso en sus 'Comentarios.' Antología vivida* (1964) and "Perfil ideológico del Inca Garcilaso," in *Dintorno de una época dorada* (1978).

Rodolfo Cerrón-Palomino, Professor of Linguistics at the Universidad Nacional de San Marcos, has prepared important editions of Quechua grammars and vocabularies and numerous articles on the Quechua language; among these are "Unidad y diferenciación lingüística en el mundo andino" (1987), "El Inca Garcilaso o la lealtad idiomática" (1991), and "Los fragmentos de gramática quechua del Inca Garcilaso" (1993).

Pierre Duviols, Professor Emeritus of the University of Aix-in-Provence, France, has published numerous works on Colonial ethnohistory and Andean pre-Columbian subjects, including *La lutte contre les religions autochtones du Pérou Colonial (L'Extirpation de l'idolâtrie entre 1535 et 1660)* (1971, Spanish translation 1977), and *Cultura andina y represión. Procesos y visitas de idolatrías y hechicerías. Cajatambo, siglo XVII* (1986). He is coeditor of Joan de Santa Cruz Pachacuti Yamqui Salcamaygua, *Relación de antigüedades deste reyno del Pirú* (1993).

Paul P. Firbas graduated in Linguistics and Literature from the Pontificia Universidad Católica del Perú, and received his master's degree at the University of Notre Dame with a thesis entitled "Pirates, Maroons, and Indians in Spanish-American Colonial Epic Discourse: A Study of *Armas antárticas,* a poem by Juan de Miramontes y Zuázola (1995). He is currently completing his doctoral dissertation on Colonial epic poetry at Princeton University.

Eduardo Hopkins-Rodríguez, Professor of Latin American Literature at the Pontificia Universidad Católica del Perú, has written a number of arti-

Contributors

cles on Colonial topics, among them, "El desengaño en la poesía de Juan del Valle Caviedes" (1975), "Poética de Espinosa Medrano en el *Apologético en favor de D. Luis de Góngora*" (1978), "Virtuosismo en Juan del Valle Caviedes" (1993), and "Teoría de la épica y crítica literaria en preliminares de *Lima fundada*" (1994).

EFRAÍN KRISTAL, Professor of Hispanic Literature at the University of California at Los Angeles, has published on Latin American Colonial and contemporary authors. Among his works are *The Andes Viewed from the City: Literary and Political Discourse on the Indian in Peru, 1848–1930* (1988) and "Fábulas clásicas y neoplatónicas en los *Comentarios reales de los Incas*" (1993).

SABINE MACCORMACK, A. F. Palmer Professor of History at the University of Michigan, is a classicist as well as a specialist in the Colonial period of Latin America. Among her publications are *Art and Ceremony in Late Antiquity* (1981), "Antonio de la Calancha: un agustino del siglo XVII en el Nuevo Mundo" (1982), "The Fall of the Incas: A Historiographical Dilemma" (1985), and *Religion in the Andes: Vision and Imagination in Early Colonial Peru* (1991).

MIGUEL MATICORENA ESTRADA is Professor Emeritus of History both at the Universidad de San Marcos and the Pontificia Universidad Católica del Perú. After years of research in Seville's Archivo de Indias, he unearthed vital documents relating to early Latin American chroniclers, which provided the basis of many articles, including "Cieza de León en Sevilla y su muerte en 1554. Documentos" (1955), "Sobre las *Décadas* de Antonio de Herrera: *La Florida*" (1967), and "Cieza de León y Las Casas" (1978).

JOSÉ ANTONIO MAZZOTTI, Professor of Hispanic Literature at Harvard University, has written widely on Latin American Colonial narrative and modern poetry. Among his recent publications are "Betanzos: de la épica incaica a la escritura coral" (1994); an anthology of Peruvian poetry, *El bosque de los huesos* (1995); a co-edition, *Asedios a la heterogeneidad cultural. Homenaje a Antonio Cornejo Polar* (1996); and a volume based on his doctoral dissertation, *Coros mestizos del Inca Garcilaso. Resonancias andinas* (1996).

AURELIO MIRÓ-QUESADA SOSA, Dean of "garcilacistas," is currently the director of *El Comercio*, Perú's leading newspaper. He has been Rector of the Universidad de San Marcos and President of the Peruvian National Academy of History. Among his distinguished publications on Garcilaso are *El Inca Garcilaso y otros estudios garcilacistas* (1971), "Las ideas lingüísticas del Inca Garcilaso" (1977), "Creación y elaboración de *La Florida del Inca*" (1989), and *El Inca Garcilaso* (1994, 3rd edition).

FRANKLIN PEASE G. Y., Professor of History and Dean of the College of Arts and Sciences at the Pontificia Universidad Católica del Perú, has written extensively on the Colonial period. His recent books include *Del Tawantinsuyu a la Historia del Perú* (1989), *Los últimos incas del Cuzco* (1991), and *Las Crónicas y los Andes* (1995).

Contributors

José A. Rodríguez Garrido, Professor of Spanish and Colonial Literature at the Pontificia Universidad Católica del Perú, has written a number of articles, including "Las citas de los cronistas españoles como recurso argumentativo en la Segunda parte de los *Comentarios reales*" (1993), "Espinosa Medrano, la recepción del sermón barroco y la defensa de los americanos" (1994), "La identidad del enunciador en los *Comentarios reales*" (1995), and "Retórica y tomismo en Espinosa y Medrano" (1995). He is currently completing his doctoral dissertation on Colonial Spanish American theater at Princeton University.

Carmela Zanelli, Professor of Latin American Literature at the Pontificia Universidad Católica del Perú, is completing her doctoral dissertation at the University of California at Los Angeles on Garcilaso's concept of tragedy in the *General History of Perú*. Among her publications are "La loa del *Divino Narciso* de Sor Juana Inés de la Cruz y la doble recuperación de la cultura indígena mexicana" (1994) and "La doble dimensión trágica de la historia: el caso de Gonzalo Pizarro en la *Historia General del Perú* del Inca Garcilaso de la Vega" (1996).

INDEX OF NAMES

Index

Index

Index